Tom Hutchinson

hotline

starter

teacher's book

OXFORD UNIVERSITY PRESS

Oxford University Press
Walton Street, Oxford OX2 6DP

Oxford New York Toronto
Delhi Bombay Calcutta Madras Krachi
Petaling Jaya Singapore Hong Kong Tokyo
Nairobi Dar es Salaam Cape Town
Melbourne Auckland

and associated companies in
Berlin Ibadan

Oxford and Oxford English are trade marks of Oxford
University Press

First published 1991

ISBN 0 19 435483 0

© Oxford University Press, 1991
Second impression 1992

Printed in Hong Kong

**The tests at the back of this book
may be photocopied freely for
classroom use.**

Acknowledgements

The author would especially like to record his gratitude to his wife Pamela and his children, without whose support and patience *Hotline* would not have been possible.

The publishers would like to thank all of the ELT teachers and advisors around the world who have given generously of their time to talk about their needs and to comment on the manuscript and sample units of *Hotline*. Our thanks are especially due to:

Silvia Ronchetti (Instituto Superior del Profesorado en Lenguas Vivas, Buenos Aires) in Argentina. Freddy Désir (Inspection de l'Enseignement Secondaire de l'Etat, Brussels), Norbert Jacquinet (Institut Notre-Dame, Brussels) in Belgium. Edit Nagy (National Institute of Education, Budapest), Lyane Szentirmay (Madách Imre Gimnázium, Budapest), Judit Sióréti (Városmajori Gimnázium, Budapest), Ilona Jobbágy (Könyves Kálmán Gimnázium, Budapest) in Hungary. Orazio Marchi (Progetto Speciale Lingue Straniere, Forlì) in Italy. Diana England and Monica Green (International House, Lisbon) in Portugal. Patsy Fuller (Freelance Teacher), Luis Fernandez (I.B. Alexandre Satorras, Mataro), Vincenc Haro and Merce Fosch (I.B. Ferran Casablanca, Sabadell), Eleanor Tompkins (La Salle Congres, Barcelona), Ana Coll (I.B. Narcis Monturiol, Barcelona), Victoria Alcalde (I.B. San Isidro, Madrid), Joaquin Rojo (I.B. Francisco de Goya, Madrid), Pedro Horillo and Margarita Hernandez (I.B. Verdaguer Parc de la Ciutadella, Barcelona), Pilar Gomez (Instituto Cid Campeador, Valencia) in Spain. Carroll Klein (Koç Özel Lisesi, Istanbul) in Turkey.

Special thanks are due to a panel of British teenagers, Juliet Kinsman, Zuleika Melluish, Pema Radha, Alex Huskinson and Mark Killingley, who advised on the Victoria Road storyline and on the Reading and Listening topics and to whom we are indebted for the natural, colloquial teenage language of the Victoria Road characters.

'Be-bop-a-lula', words and music by Gene Vincent and T. Davis, used by kind permission of Carlin Music Corporation, Iron Bridge House, 3 Bridge Approach, Chalk Farm, London, NW1 8BD.
'Save me', words by John Raby.
The publishers and the author would like to thank the following for their kind permission to use extracts from copyright materials:
Guinness Publishing Ltd.: two facts from the Guinness Book of Records. Copyright ©1983 Guinness Superlatives Ltd. Octopus Publishing Group: extract from *It can't be true* by Jane Read.

Illustrations by:

Kevin Baverstock, Terry Beard, Roger Fereday/Linda Rogers, Robina Green, Nick Harris, Leo Hartas, Nick Hawken, Jonathon Heap, Ian Heard, Stephen Holmes, Conny Jude, Michael Kumon, Dave Murray, Savicis Neocleous, Denis Ryan/Artists Partners, Tech Graphics.

The publishers would like to thank the following for their permission to reproduce photographs:
Ace/Mauritius Bildagentur; Action Plus/Chris Barry, Mike Hewitt; Allsport/David Cannon; Aquarius Picture Library; Capital Radio; J.A. Cash; Colorific/Frank Herman, Duncan Raban/All Action, Anthony Suan Black; Star 1987; Colorsport; Greg Evans; Mary Evans Picture Library; Feature Pix; Fortean Picture Library; Sally and Richard Greenhill; Robert Harding; Hulton Deutsch Collection; Image Bank/Inone, Elaine Sulle, P. Tesman; Looks Magazine/Steve Cartwright; Niall McInerney; Mizz Holiday Special/Mike Prior; Palace/Aquarius; Retna/Jenny Acheson, Tammy Arroyd, E.J. Camp, Sam Emerson/Onyx, Gary Gershoff, Adrian Green, Trevor Leighton, C.L. Kirsch, Greg Noakes, Steve Rapport, Paul Rider, Paul Slattery, Chris VD Vooren; Rex Features/Brendan Beirne, D. Graves, Nils Jorgensen, Levenson; D.C. Thomson and Co. Ltd; Universal/Aquarius; Elizabeth Whiting Associates.

Design by Holdsworth Associates.
Victoria Road photography by John Walmsley.
Victoria Road design by Keith Shaw
Stills photography by Rob Judges.

Studio photography by Martyn Chillmaid, Paul Freestone, Mark Mason, Garry and Marilyn O'Brien.

The characters in Victoria Road were played by:
Sarah Buckley, Matthew Christmas, Joseph Derrett, Natalie Kowlessur, Tito Menezes, Robert Page, Graham and Sue Page, Simon Richards, Paul and Pat Rose, Sarah Rose, Patrick Short, Matthew Starling.

The publishers would like to thank the following for their help with the Victoria Road photo story:
Ardmore Adventure Holidays; Banstead Sports Centre; Cannon cinema, Ewell; Epsom and Ewell High School; London and Country Buses; McDonalds; Met Police Public Relations; Mrs Moretta; Frances Myers; NESCOT drama department; One Stop Shop, Burgh Health; Pickfords; St Andrews School, Leatherhead; St David's School, Ashford; Therfield School, Leatherhead; Thorndike Youth Theatre; Rose and Brian Walsh; Whitgift Centre, Croydon; Worcester Park Football Club.

Who is *Hotline* for?

Hotline is a four-year course for teenagers. The whole course takes learners from beginner to intermediate level. Each year provides approximately ninety hours of teaching. *Hotline Starter* is the first year of the *Hotline* course. It is for beginners.

What are the special features of *Hotline*?

Hotline brings together the best of modern and traditional aspects of language teaching. It incorporates modern ideas, such as skills development, learner training and project work. At the same time, *Hotline* has a sound grammar-based syllabus and a clear, practical methodology. *Hotline* is, therefore, both learner-centred and teacher-friendly. Each of the features is explained in greater detail below.

What kind of language syllabus does *Hotline* use?

The syllabus in *Hotline* is structurally graded and develops on a loopback principle. This means that constant revision is built into the syllabus progression. This loopback principle operates in a number of ways:

- At the end of each unit there is a Learning diary. The learners are asked to look back through the unit and consider how well they have learnt the new items in the unit. A simple self-check is provided in the Workbook (see below).

- Units 6, 10 and 14 are revision units. Here learners revise the work of the previous units.

- Each subsequent year of *Hotline* begins with a substantial revision cycle, which recycles the structures taught in the previous year(s). In *Hotline Elementary*, the second book in the course, the first three units thoroughly revise the present tenses and the past simple tense taught here in *Hotline Starter*, before introducing new grammatical forms.

In these ways, learners are given every opportunity to refresh and reinforce their knowledge of basic grammar, so that they have a firm foundation on which to build.

What does *Hotline Starter* consist of?

Student's Book. This contains:

- ten main units plus an introduction and three revision units;
- pronunciation practice activities;
- a vocabulary list.

Cassette. This contains:

- Victoria Road dialogues;
- texts for listening activities;
- pronunciation practice activities;
- songs.

Workbook. This provides further practice and reinforcement of the items in the Student's Book. It contains:

- grammar consolidation;
- write-in grammar activities;
- vocabulary activities;
- self-checks for students to assess how well they have learnt the work of the unit;
- culture spots. These describe aspects of life in Britain and invite the learners to compare them with those in their own country. Teacher's notes for these are included in the Teacher's Book.

The Workbook is tied closely to the Student's Book. Each section in the Student's Book has further practice activities in the Workbook.

Teacher's Book. This contains:

- a description of the course;
- an introduction to project work;
- lesson notes, which provide explanations of language and cultural points that arise in each unit, and detailed guidance for handling each activity;
- tapescripts;
- answer keys for the Student's Book activities;
- answer keys for the Workbook activities;
- three tests (in the revision units).

What does the Student's Book unit contain?

The first unit is an Introduction unit. It provides the students with some basic language and some basic learning tools (See page T3.)

Each of the ten main units (2, 3, 4, 5, 7, 8, 9, 11, 12, 13) provides approximately seven or eight hours of teaching. Each unit contains the following elements:

- Introduction page
- Victoria Road
- Language work (In Units 2, 3, 5, 7, 8 this is integrated into other sections and is not a separate section.)
- Reading
- Listening
- Interaction
- Project
- Learning diary.

A unit works like this:

The **Introduction page** presents and illustrates the contents and main grammar points of the unit.

Victoria Road introduces the main language items for the unit.

In **Language work** the students analyse and practise the new grammar points in detail.

The **Reading** section develops the students' reading skills and extends the main grammar points or introduces a new point.

The **Listening** section develops the students' listening skills and extends the main grammar point or introduces a new point.

The **Interaction** section develops the students' speaking skills and extends the main grammar point or introduces a new point.

The **Project** provides the opportunity for students to relate the language of the unit to their own lives. It also provides practice in writing.

Finally, in the **Learning diary**, the students review the unit and consider how well they know the new language.

Each section ends with a **Follow-up** activity. These activities reinforce the work of the section. They are optional activities. They can be used either for additional classwork or for homework.

Let's look at the sections in more detail.

1 INTRODUCTION PAGE

The first page of each unit provides a list of what is in the unit. The list shows the contents and the new grammar. The main grammar point of the unit is illustrated with examples.

This Introduction page can be used in a number of ways:

a for pre-teaching. You can use the examples provided to introduce the main grammar point.

b for revision. At the end of each unit students look back to assess how well they have learnt what they should have learnt.

c for learner training. Students can see what each unit is about and what they will be learning. They are, therefore, more involved in the learning process. In this way students can develop both a better understanding of what is involved in learning a language and a more responsible attitude towards the process.

2 VICTORIA ROAD

Each unit has an episode in a continuing story about the young people who live in Victoria Road.

The characters in *Victoria Road* are:

Terry Moore.
Sue and Vince Scott. They are twins and they live next door to Terry.
Kamala Wijeratne, Sue's best friend. Kamala's parents own the local newsagent's shop.
Casey Royston, Terry and Vince's friend.
Jane Fox, a friend of Sue's.
Darren Tooley, Jane's boyfriend.

The characters are first introduced in Unit 2. Terry has just moved into the neighbourhood next door to Sue and Vince. Sue overhears Terry saying that she is bossy. She decides to get her revenge and she arranges a date for Terry with Jane Fox. Sue knows that Jane has got a boyfriend – a big boy called Darren . . . .
Each unit develops the story further.

The Victoria Road story plays a number of roles:

a It continues the story. *Victoria Road* is an amusing, but realistic 'soap opera'.

b It introduces the main language item for the unit.

c It provides 'Useful expressions'. The language in *Hotline* is natural, modern English. In the 'Useful expressions' component, students work out the meaning of idiomatic expressions that occur in the story. They give the equivalent in their own language. This activity has a number of aims:

   • It encourages students to work out meaning from context.
   • It provides useful everyday expressions.
   • It develops a sense of linguistic comparison, so that students learn that they cannot translate word for word.

d It provides comprehension practice and oral practice.

e It illustrates aspects of daily life in Britain. Some of these are followed up in the Workbook.

3 LANGUAGE WORK

The focus in *Hotline* is on enabling learners to *use* language, but an important element in this is helping learners to understand and feel comfortable with the basic structures of English. They will then feel more confident in language use.

Each section of the unit has a Language work element and in the later units there is a separate Language work section.

In Language work students study the new language structures in detail. The most important aspect of this section is the cognitive approach to grammar. This works in a number of ways:

First, the students find and complete examples of the structure in the Victoria Road story or some other section of the unit.

Secondly, in the 'Build up' activities, the students work out the grammar rules for themselves. They complete substitution tables and grammar rules.

Thirdly, the students are encouraged to compare the English structure to that in their own language.

Finally, when the students have thoroughly analysed the structure, they do controlled practice activities.

4 READING

A principal feature in *Hotline* is the development of skills as well as language knowledge.

The Reading section provides interesting texts on a variety of themes. Activities encourage students to develop good reading strategies, such as skimming, scanning, looking for information, matching texts to pictures, etc. Students do not have to understand everything in the texts.

The activities provide a step-by-step approach to each text, as well as pre-reading and post-reading tasks. It is important to follow the instructions for dealing with the texts carefully.

The Reading sections also consolidate and develop the students' vocabulary.

5 LISTENING

The Listening section provides a range of spoken texts which develop the students' ability to listen effectively. The texts include conversations, set-piece dialogues (e.g. buying something in a shop), stories, factual texts, interviews, etc. The activities are intended to make the students think about what they are going to hear, so that they listen in a context. As with the Reading section, there are pre-listening, while-listening and post-listening tasks. It is important to follow the instructions for the activities carefully.

6 INTERACTION

The Interaction section provides opportunities for developing speaking skills. Three types of activity are used:

   • role play in structured situations, e.g. at the shops;
   • drama role play, where students make their own plays;
   • interviews, e.g. with pop stars.

7 PROJECT

The Project section provides opportunities for students to use the language of the unit to write about their own lives. Project tasks are related to the theme of each unit. Detailed guidance for doing project work is provided below on pages viii–xi.

8 THE LEARNING DIARY

This completes the loop. The students look back to the Introduction page and say how they feel about the language items of the unit. A self-check is provided in the Workbook for students to check their knowledge.

The Learning diary is part of the process of learner involvement. It encourages the students to become more active as learners and to take on more responsibility for their own learning. It also provides evidence for you, as teacher, of things that have not been learnt very well and which may need further practice. If you find that some things have not been learnt very well, there are a number of ways of proceeding. First, however, you must decide whether an error merits further attention. There are some errors that are best seen as developmental errors. An example of this is omitting the -s on the third person of the present simple. There is a lot of evidence to suggest that this is an inevitable stage of learning, just like a baby crawling before it can walk. It is therefore not worth spending a lot of time on it in the early stages of learning. However, there may be some things that do require attention. Here are some possible strategies:

a Revise the section of the unit in which the item occurs.

b Get students to say what they find confusing about the item and why.

c Find the item in a grammar book and prepare a supplementary lesson on it. There are many good grammar reference books available with exercises.

d Get the students to find the item in a grammar book and work out for themselves what the problem is.

e (More ambitious) Get students to prepare a mini-lesson on the item. They must give their mini-lesson to another group.

For any of these strategies to work, it is essential to cultivate an open and healthy attitude towards errors in your class. Help students to realize that making errors is a necessary part of learning a language. The important thing is to use them positively as a means of guiding the learning process.

Learning strategies

One of the main features of *Hotline* is developing good learning strategies. When a useful learning strategy is first introduced, it is shown in a grey box (see, for example, page 7, Exercise 4). Encourage students to use these strategies as much as possible.

PRONUNCIATION PRACTICE

This section is at the end of the book on pages 111–14. It contains:

- an introduction to the phonemic alphabet, showing the basic sounds of English;
- activities focusing on specific points of pronunciation. There are activities for each unit.

The Pronunciation practice activities can be done at any time in the unit, as time allows.

Lesson notes

The lesson notes provide:

- detailed guidance for teaching each activity;
- notes on language use;
- notes on content and cultural points.

The remainder of this Introduction is concerned with general guidance for handling project work.

Workbook key

The Workbook key at the back of the book (pages T121–30) provides answers to all the Workbook activities, including the self-checks.

Tests

There are revision tests for each of the units 6, 10 and 14 at the back of the book, together with an answer key. The tests may be photocopied for classroom use.

An introduction to project work

Project work is a major feature of *Hotline*. Project work is not a new methodology. Its benefits have been widely recognized for many years in the teaching of subjects like Science, Geography and History. In language teaching, however, it is a relative newcomer.

The aim of this section is to provide a simple introduction to project work, to enable you to introduce it smoothly into your classroom.

1 Why do project work?

What benefits does project work bring to the language class? This teacher from Spain expresses it very well:

'Pupils don't feel that English is a chore, but is a means of communication and enjoyment. They can experiment with the language as something real not as something that only appears in books.'
(*Marisa Cuesta, Spain*)

As this teacher indicates, project work captures better than any other activity the two principal elements of a communicative approach. These are:

a a concern for motivation, that is, how the learners relate to the task;

b a concern for relevance, that is, how the learners relate to the language.

We could add to these a third element:

c a concern for educational values, that is, how the language curriculum relates to the general educational development of the learner.

Let's look at these elements in a bit more detail.

a Motivation

Positive motivation is the key to successful language learning and project work is particularly useful as a means of generating this positive motivation. If you talk to teachers who do project work in their classes, you will find that this is the feature that is always mentioned – the students really enjoy it. But why is project work so motivating? There are three reasons.

Firstly, project work is very personal. The students are writing about their own lives – their house, their family, their town, their dreams and fantasies, their own research into topics that interest them. Students, in other words, are being given the opportunity to tell the world about themselves.

Secondly, project work is a very active medium. Students aren't just receiving and producing words. They are:

- collecting information;
- drawing pictures, maps, diagrams and charts;
- cutting out pictures;
- arranging texts and visuals;
- colouring;
- carrying out interviews and surveys;
- possibly making recordings, too.

Project work is learning through doing.

Lastly, project work gives a clear sense of achievement. It enables all students to produce a worthwhile product. As another teacher comments:

'There is feedback from the students as they realize what they can do with the English they have learned.'
(*Jesus-Angel Vallejo Carrasco, Spain*)

This feature of project work makes it particularly well suited to the mixed ability class, because students can work at their own pace and level. The brighter students can show what they know, unconstrained by the syllabus, while at the same time the slower learners can achieve something that they can take pride in, perhaps compensating for their lower language level by using more visuals.

b Relevance

A foreign language can often seem a remote and unreal thing. This inevitably has a negative effect on motivation, because the students don't see the language as relevant to their own lives. If learners are going to become real language users, they must learn that English can be used to talk about their own world.

Project work helps to bridge this relevance gap in three ways.

Firstly, project work helps to integrate the foreign language into the network of the learners' own communicative competence. It encourages the use of a wide range of communicative skills, enables learners to exploit other spheres of knowledge and provides opportunities for them to write about the things that are important in their own lives.

Secondly, project work helps to make the language more relevant to learners' actual needs, because they are learning how to communicate about their own world – about their house, their family, their town, etc. Project work thus enables students to rehearse the language and factual knowledge that will be of most value to them as language users.

Thirdly, project work establishes a sounder relationship between language and culture. The purpose of learning a foreign language is to make communication between *two* cultures possible. English is not just for talking about the ways of the English-speaking world. It should also be a means for learners to tell the world about their own culture. Project work helps to create this approach. With project work the language thus acts as a bridge, enabling two cultures to communicate with each other.

c Education

There is a growing awareness among language teachers that the process and content of the language class should contribute towards the general educational development of the learner. Project work is very much in tune with modern views about the purpose and nature of education.

Firstly, there is the question of educational values. Most modern school curricula require all subjects to encourage initiative, independence, imagination, self-discipline, co-operation and the development of useful research skills. Project work is a way of turning such general aims into practical classroom activity.

Secondly, cross-curricular approaches are encouraged. For language teaching, this means that students should have the opportunity to use the knowledge they gain in other subjects in the English class. Project work clearly encourages this.

2 Yes, but . . .

Project work brings considerable benefits to the language classroom, but it is important to be aware of the implications of the way of working.

a Noise

Teachers are often afraid that the project classroom will be noisier than the traditional classroom and that this will disturb other classes in the school. But project work does not *have* to be noisier than any other activity. Students will often need to discuss things and they may be moving around to get a pair of scissors or to consult a reference book. And some activities do require a lot of talking. If the students are doing a survey in their class, for example, there will be a lot of moving around and talking. However, this kind of noise is a natural part of productive activity.

Remember that the traditional classroom has quite a lot of noise in it, too. There is usually at least one person talking (and teachers usually talk rather loudly!) and there may be a tape recorder playing, possibly with the whole class doing a drill. There is no reason why project work should be any noisier than thirty or forty students giving a choral response – quite the opposite, in fact.

Project work is a different way of working and one that requires a different form of control. In project work, students are working independently. They must, therefore, take on some of the responsibility for managing their learning environment. Part of this responsibility is learning what kind of, and what level of, noise is acceptable. When you introduce project work, you also need to encourage and guide the learners towards working quietly and sensibly. Remember that they will enjoy project work and will not want to stop doing it because it is causing too much noise, so it should not be too difficult to get your students to behave sensibly.

b Time

It takes longer to prepare, make and present a project than it does to do more traditional activities. But bear in mind two points.

Firstly, not all project work needs to be done in class time. Obviously, if the project is a group task, most of it must be done in class, but a lot of projects are individual tasks. Projects about My family, My home, etc. can be done at home. You will be surprised how much of their own time students will gladly devote to doing projects.

Secondly, when choosing to do project work, you need to recognize that you are making a philosophical choice in favour of the quality of the learning experience over the quantity. Project work provides rich learning experiences – rich in colour, movement, interaction and, most of all, involvement. In this respect, projects are doubly valuable. They are not just rich learning experiences in themselves. The positive motivation that they generate colours the students' attitude to all the other aspects of the language programme. Learning grammar and vocabulary will appear more relevant, because the students know they will need these things for their project work.

c Use of L1

It is likely that most students will speak in their mother tongue while they are working on their projects. However, rather than seeing this as a problem, we should consider its merits.

Firstly, it is a natural way of working. It is a mistake to think of L1 and L2 as two completely separate domains. Learners in fact operate in both domains, constantly switching from one to the other, so it is perfectly natural for learners to use L1 while working on an L2 product. As long as the final product is in English, it doesn't matter if the work is done in L1.

Secondly, project work can provide some good opportunities for realistic translation work. A lot of the source material for projects – leaflets, maps, interviews, texts from reference books, etc. – will be in the mother tongue. Using this material in a project provides useful translation activities.

Thirdly, there will be plenty of opportunities in other parts of the language course for learners to practise oral skills. Project work should be seen as a chance to practise that most difficult of skills – writing. There is no need to worry if the students use L1 to do it.

d Different levels

Some teachers are concerned that, without the teacher's firm control, the weaker students will be lost and will not be able to cope. Again, the answer to this worry is to see the positive side of it. Not all students want or need the teacher's constant supervision. By encouraging the more able students to work independently, you are free to devote your time to those students who need it most.

Paradoxically, it is often in the traditional classroom that the weaker students can be neglected, because the brighter students take more than their share of the teacher's attention.

It would be wrong to pretend that project work does not have its drawbacks. It certainly demands a lot of the teacher in terms of preparation and classroom management skills. It also requires a change of attitude about what is really valuable in language teaching and you need to work with your students to develop a responsible working environment. But, in practice, most teachers find that their worst fears about project work do not materialize. The work is so motivating for the students that it produces its own momentum. The noise of the well-managed project classroom is the sound of creativity. And that's what we want to encourage, not suppress.

3 Getting started

The key to successful project work is good preparation.

a You'll need some basic materials and equipment:

- scissors;
- rulers;
- glue;
- large sheets of paper or card.

b It's a good idea to have some reference books available:

- a dictionary;
- a grammar book;
- an atlas.

Students will want to know new words or constructions for expressing their ideas, and if you haven't got reference books available, the students will ask you! This will not only become tiresome for you, but it also destroys an opportunity for learners to become more independent and to develop some useful research skills.

c Try to keep a stock of magazines, maps and leaflets in the class. You need to develop squirrel habits! Collect any material you can find. It's amazing how much printed material is available free from shops, travel agents, banks, etc. Remember two important points.

Firstly, the material does not have to be in English. Indeed, as already noted, material in L1 can provide opportunities for some creative translation work.

Secondly, you do not have to provide all the material yourself. Encourage the students to provide material as well. They will often have a stock of old comics and magazines at home.

d Teach your learners how to do project work. Before starting any project, discuss with the students how they will tackle it. What materials will they need? Where will they get them? etc. If the project requires a particular kind of activity, such as an interview, a graph or a chart, make sure the students know how to do it.

Use each project not only to learn and practise language but also to help your students to learn a bit more about project work.

e In *Hotline*, project work comes at the end of a unit, so it practises the language students have learnt in the unit. But do bear in mind that you can't anticipate all the language the learners will need. A lot of language learning goes on during the actual project work itself, as students look for new words or expressions. In project work, learners not only learn new vocabulary, they also develop the skills of looking for words they do not know or alternative ways of expressing what they want to say.

Preparation, then, is the key to making project work a success. Prepare your classroom by providing some basic materials. Prepare your students by practising the skills and techniques they will need. Most important of all, prepare yourself for a new way of working that is challenging but very satisfying.

4 Evaluation

Assessment of project work is a difficult issue to tackle. This is not because project work is difficult to assess, but because the best way to assess project work may conflict with official procedures for assessing a student's work. There are some guidelines for assessing projects, but, of course, you know best what is necessary and possible in your own system.

There are two basic principles for assessing project work:

a The most obvious point to note about project work is that language is only a part of the total project. Consequently, it is not very appropriate to assess a project only on the basis of linguistic accuracy. Credit must be given for the overall impact of the project, the level of creativity it displays, the neatness and clarity of presentation and, most of all, the effort that has gone into its production. There is nothing particularly unusual in this. It is normal practice in assessing creative writing to give marks for style and content. Many education systems also require similar factors to be taken into account in the assessment of students' oral performance in class.

So a wide-ranging 'profile' kind of assessment that evaluates the whole project is needed.

b The second principle is that, if at all possible, don't correct mistakes on the final project itself – or at least not in ink. It goes against the whole spirit of project work. A project usually represents a lot of effort and is something that the students will probably want to keep. It is thus a shame to put red marks all over it. This draws attention to things that are wrong about the project over the things that are good. On the other hand, students are more likely to take note of errors pointed out to them in project work, because the project means much more to them than just any piece of class work.

So what do you do about errors? There are two useful techniques:

a Encourage the students to do a rough draft of their project first. Correct this in your normal way. The students can then incorporate corrections in the final product.

b If errors occur in the final product, correct it in pencil or on a separate sheet of paper. It is then up to the students whether they wish to correct the finished piece of work.

But fundamentally, the most important thing to do about errors is to stop worrying about them. Projects are real communication. When we communicate, all we can do is the best we can with what we know. And because we usually concentrate on getting the meaning right, errors in form will naturally occur. It's a normal part of using and learning a language.

Students invest a lot of themselves in a project and so they will usually make every effort to do their best work. And remember that any project will only form part of the total amount of work that the students produce in the language course. There will be plenty of opportunities to evaluate accuracy in other parts of the language programme. Project work provides an opportunity to develop creativity, imagination, enquiry and self-expression, and the assessment of the project should reflect this.

5 Conclusion

Project work is one of the most exciting developments in language teaching. It combines in practical form both the fundamental principles of a communicative approach and the values of good education. It has the added virtue of being a long-established and well-tried method of teaching in other subject areas.

	LANGUAGE WORK	READING	LISTENING	WORD WORK
1 Introduction p.3	Short and long forms of *to be* The alphabet Numbers 1–100 *his/her* *a/an*		Radio 581	
2 You p.10 VICTORIA ROAD Victoria Road rap	*to be* – positive – negative – questions Plurals *this/these* Adjective and noun	Are you a Bros fan?	The leisure centre	
3 People p.19 VICTORIA ROAD Terry's date	*have/has got* – positive – negative – questions Genitives *a/an* + job	A family	Blind Date	Family relationships
4 Time p.27 VICTORIA ROAD At the dance	*can/can't* Questions with *can/can't* *on/at*	Terry's timetable	Telling the time	
5 Places p.35 VICTORIA ROAD At the cafe	Imperatives *must/mustn't* there is/there are – positive – negative – questions	A computer	House for sale	International words
6 Revision p.44		The School of Music and Dance	What's the time?	Revision
7 Sport p.47 VICTORIA ROAD Do you know Terry Moore?	The present simple – positive – negative – questions	A footballer's week	Karen's day	
8 Time out p.55 VICTORIA ROAD Kamala misses the bus	Object pronouns *to/at* *some/any*	Paradise Island	Paradise Island (2)	

INTERACTION	PROJECT	PRONUNCIATION	LEARNING OBJECTIVES
		Vowels Consonants	Greetings Introducing yourself Identifying other people Spelling Counting to 100 Ordering a meal Asking for help
At the shops	You	Spelling /h/	Asking for and giving personal information Introducing other people Expressing likes and dislikes Identifying and describing things Buying things in a shop
Your radio show	My family	/ɒ/, /ɔː/	Asking about and describing people Expressing family relationships Describing someone's job Talking about possessions Describing personality
Kamala's appointment	My ideal school	/æ/, /ɑː/	Expressing ability Describing a school timetable Telling the time Making an appointment Using time expressions
Polite requests	My home	/æ/, /ʌ/	Giving commands Giving instructions and warnings Using international words Asking about and describing a house Making polite requests
An interview	Star square Pop chain	Revision	
A day in your life	A sports survey	/ɒ/, /əʊ/	Asking about and describing regular activities Talking about sport
Making suggestions	Holiday	/uː/, /juː/	Asking someone to do something Describing a place Describing facilities Expressing advantages and disadvantages Making suggestions Describing a holiday

	LANGUAGE WORK	READING	LISTENING	WORD WORK

9 Clothes p.63
VICTORIA ROAD
A strange girl
	The present continuous
	– positive
	– negative
	– questions
	
	The present continuous
	  and the present simple
	Words with no singular
		Fashion parade	A new pair of
			  jeans
				Clothes

10 Revision p.73		Selina and Kelly	Different worlds or one world?	
11 Mystery p.77 VICTORIA ROAD In the park	The past simple of *to be* – positive – negative – questions Years The past simple – regular verbs	Was it Nessie?	The Grey Lady	
12 The news p.87 VICTORIA ROAD Sue's coat	The past simple – irregular verbs – negative – questions	Amazing escapes	Band Aid	Irregular past tenses
13 The movies p.97 VICTORIA ROAD Terry's story	Adverbs Adverbs and adjectives Ordinal numbers Dates	James Dean	The death of James Dean	Actors and films
14 Revision p.107		Who killed Ruth Less?	Ruth Less (2)	

Wordlist p.115

Irregular verbs p.120

INTERACTION	PROJECT	PRONUNCIATION	LEARNING OBJECTIVES
At the clothes shop	Fashion page	Unstressed /ə/	Asking and answering about current activities Describing clothes Buying clothes in a shop
How do you help?	Grammar game	Revision	
Your play	Mysteries	/ɪ/, /iː/	Asking about and describing past events Narrating a story Writing a play
Interview role play	A class newspaper	/v/	Asking about and describing past events Narrating a story Interviewing someone
At the movies	The movies	/ɜː/	Describing actions Expressing sequential order Giving a biography Giving dates Making arrangements Talking about the cinema
Your own Top Twenty	Your final episode	Revision	

INTRODUCTORY LESSON

The main aim of the first lesson is to get the students to use English. So start using English yourself straightaway. Introduce yourself in English and give your instructions in English. If you start off giving simple instructions in English, you will very quickly be able to conduct the whole lesson in English. In this way you will:

- show that English is used for real communication;
- encourage students by your own example to use English freely;
- get students used to working out meaning from context.

These are very important lessons for students to learn.

Don't worry if students have a few problems at first. Use gestures and mime as much as possible. For example, when you say *Open your books*, open your book to demonstrate. Repeat the words and the demonstration, if necessary.

There will, of course, be some activities where you need to use the mother tongue, for example, if you want to discuss a topic of interest in more detail. But these activities should be relatively few. The best general rule for the English classroom is: Speak English.

- Start Unit 1.

UNIT 1   Introduction

Unit 1 provides some basic tools and knowledge to get the students started. It provides:

- some basic structures: *I'm*, *He/She's*, numbers, *his/her*, *a/an*;
- some basic functions: introducing yourself and other people, buying a meal;
- some basic learning tools: the alphabet, useful classroom vocabulary, expressions for asking for help;
- some basic learning strategies: making rules, working out meaning from context;
- an introduction to the phonetic alphabet (see page 111).

What's your name?

- Introduce yourself. Say *Hello. I'm ... .*
- Get a few students to introduce themselves to you.
- Say and demonstrate *Open your books.*

- Students look at the pictures of Sonia, and Jason Donovan.
- Point to each and ask *Who's this?* Students may know the people. Both are international pop stars. Or they can find the names in the speech bubbles.
- Students give their answers.
- Say *Listen*.
- Play the tape. Students follow in their books.
- Play the tape again.

- Play the tape again. Stop after each line. Students repeat.
- Say *Close your books*. Students listen and repeat again.
- Choose one student. Play the first line again. The student repeats. Correct and repeat as necessary.
- Choose another student for the next line and so on.

- Divide the class into pairs.
- Choose one pair. Demonstrate the activity.
- Repeat with another pair.
- All pairs do the activity.
- They reverse roles and repeat.
- Students turn to face a new partner. Repeat the activity.

FOLLOW UP

- Students look at the picture at the bottom of the page.
- Students stick a photograph of themselves in their exercise book. They write a speech bubble about themselves for the picture.

EXTRA ACTIVITY

If you have some spare time at the end of the lesson, get students to look through *Hotline*. Ask them to find a page that they like. Discuss students' choices. This activity can be carried out in the mother tongue.

What's your name?

1 ▭ **Listen.**

Hello. My name's Sonia. I'm from Britain.

Hi. I'm Jason Donovan. I'm from Australia. What's your name?

2 **Listen again and repeat.**

3 **Work with your classmates. Ask and answer.**

Example
A '*Hello, I'm Maria. What's your name?*'
B '*My name's Carlo.*'

FOLLOW UP

4 **Introduce yourself.**

Hi. My name's Julia. I'm from Italy.

Who's this?

- Divide the class into pairs.
- Students look at the pictures and the list of names.
- Ask *Who are these people?*
- Students look for the names in the list.
- Point to the picture of Cory Aquino. Ask: *Who's this?* When a student replies, say *Yes, she's Cory Aquino.*
- Point to Mikhail Gorbachev. Ask *Who's this?* When a student replies, say *Yes, he's Mikhail Gorbachev.*
- Continue with other pictures. Students give their answers. They use the structure: *He's . . ./She's . . .*

Answer key
1 *Boris Becker*	5 *Mikhail Gorbachev*
2 *Arancha Sanchez*	6 *Diego Maradona*
3 *Kylie Minogue*	7 *Princess Diana*
4 *Nelson Piquet*	9 *Tina Turner*

- Ask *Where are the people from?*
- Students look at the list of countries. They draw lines to match the names of the people to the countries.
- Students give their answers.

Answer key
(See Exercise 2.)

- Students look at the example. Read it out.
- Get one student to give the next sentence.
- Students write the remaining sentences.
- Students read out their answers.

Answer key
5 *This is Mikhail Gorbachev. He's from the USSR.*
2 *This is Arancha Sanchez. She's from Spain.*
4 *This is Nelson Piquet. He's from Brazil.*
9 *This is Tina Turner. She's from the USA.*
1 *This is Boris Becker. He's from Germany.*
7 *This is Princess Diana. She's from Britain.*
6 *This is Diego Maradona. He's from Argentina.*
3 *This is Kylie Minogue. She's from Australia.*

An important feature of *Hotline* is the cognitive approach to grammar. Students are encouraged to identify and formalize rules for themselves. In this activity students are introduced to the idea of a grammar rule.

- Divide the class into pairs.
- Students look at the examples.
- Explain the difference between short and long forms.

Answer key
The long form is the full grammatical form but, when speaking, people usually use the short form.

- Students complete the gapped sentences.
- Write the short and long (gapped) sentences on the board.
- Choose students to complete the sentences on the board. Other students compare their own answers.

Answer key
is   am   is   is

A GAME

- Each student chooses one of the famous people.
- Students move around the class and introduce themselves.

FOLLOW UP

- Students look at the examples.
- Ask *Who is your favourite pop star/sports star?*
- Students give their answers. They use *My favourite pop star is . . . .*
- Find the most popular pop and sports star in the class.
- Students find or draw pictures of their favourite pop and sports stars. They stick them in their exercise books and write about them as in the examples.

Some useful words

This activity introduces some useful classroom vocabulary. It also encourages the students to work out the meaning of unknown words. Use it as a filler at the end of this or a later lesson.

- Students look at the picture and the list of words.
- Students try to work out what the missing words are. These are possible clues, but it will depend a lot on the students' own mother tongue.
pencil: similar to pen
cassette recorder: a similar word in a lot of languages.
book: on the cover of *Hotline*. You have told them to open their books.
teacher: If you haven't used the word already, show them the cover of this book.
window: This should be the only word left.
- Students give their answers.
- Call out the words. Students must point to or show the thing you call out.
- Point to the things in the classroom. Students say the name.

Who's this?

▼1 **Match the names of the people to the places.**

⑧ Cory Aquino	☐ the USSR
☐ Mikhail Gorbachev	Ⓗ the Philippines
☐ Arancha Sanchez	☐ the USA
☐ Nelson Piquet	☐ Britain
☐ Tina Turner	☐ Argentina
☐ Boris Becker	☐ Brazil
☐ Princess Diana	☐ Australia
☐ Diego Maradona	☐ Spain
☐ Kylie Minogue	☐ Germany

▼2 **Write about the people.**
Example
This is Cory Aquino. She's from the Philippines.
This is Mikhail Gorbachev. He's from . . . .

5

6

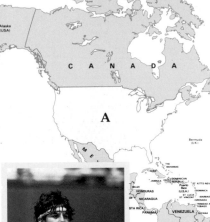

3

4

2

8

9

7

1

4

A grammar rule

3 Short and long forms

Look.

short form	long form
I'm Jason Donovan.	= **I am** Jason Donovan.
She's from Spain.	= **She is** from Spain.

Complete these with the long form.

He's Boris Becker. = He .... Boris Becker.

I'm from Greece. = I .... from Greece.

My name's Sonia. = My name .... Sonia.

What's your name? = What .... your name?

A GAME

4 Choose one of the famous people. Introduce yourself to the class.

Example
Hello, I'm Princess Di. I'm from Britain.

FOLLOW UP

5 Introduce your favourite pop star and your favourite sports star.

Example

My favourite pop star.

My favourite sports star.

Some useful words

Look at the picture. Find the missing words in this list.

desk   pen   blackboard   bag   door
window   teacher   pencil   book
cassette recorder

Check your answers with your teacher or a dictionary.

Fast Cars

The alphabet

 • Play the tape. Students follow in their books and repeat.

• Books closed. Play the tape again. Students listen and repeat.

• Write letters on the board. Students call out the name.

 a • Students look at the cars. Ask *Do you know their names?*

• Students give their ideas.

b • Students look at the letters.

• Choose students to read out the letters.

c • Play the tape. Stop after each one. Students write the missing letters in the correct place.

• Play the tape again. Students check their answers.

• Students give their answers.

Number 1 is an MGB GT.
Number 2 is a Toyota MR2 T-Bar.
Number 3 is a TVR S Convertible.
Number 4 is a VW Golf GTI.
Number 5 is a Jaguar XJS.
Number 6 is a Ford Escort XR3i Cabriolet.

 • Divide the class into pairs.

• Choose one pair. Demonstrate the activity. One student points to a car and asks *What's this?* The other student gives the name of the car.

• Repeat with another pair.

• All pairs do the activity.

• They reverse roles and repeat.

 • Ask *Which is your favourite car here?*

• Call out each name in turn. Students put up their hands. Find the most popular car.

Numbers 0–10

 • Play the tape. Students follow in their books and repeat.

• Books closed. Play the tape again. Students listen and repeat.

• Write numbers on the board. Students call out the name.

> **Note**
> For '0' we can say *zero* or *oh*. 'Oh' is more common in British English; in American English 'zero' is more common.

A GAME

• Students look at the number plates of the cars for one minute.

• Divide the class into pairs.

• Choose one pair. Demonstrate the activity. One student reads the number plate of one of the cars. The other student gives the name of the car.

• Repeat with another car.

• All pairs do the activity.

• They reverse roles and repeat.

> **Note**
> **Number plates**
> The first letter in a British number plate shows the year when the car was first registered.
> **A** was 1983. The letter changes each year. Cars are registered nationally in Britain, so the letters do not show which town the car is from. Before 1983, the letter was at the end, after the numbers.

FOLLOW UP

• Students write the numbers in words.

> **Answer key**
> *zero* (or *oh*) *one*   *seven*   *five*   *nine*
> *eight*   *three*   *two*   *four*

Radio 581

a • Students look at the picture. Ask *Who is in the picture?*

• Students look at the dialogue for the answer.

> **Answer key**
> *a DJ (disc jockey)*

• Students look at the dialogue. Ask *What do you think is happening?*

> **Answer key**
> *It's a radio phone-in programme. Steve wants a record for his girlfriend.*

b • Make sure everyone understands the task.

• Play the tape twice. Students listen.

• Students fill in the missing words. Write the gapped dialogue on the board.

• Play the tape again. Students check their dialogues.

- Choose students to complete the dialogue on the board. Other students compare their answers.

DJ This is the Hotline programme on Radio 581. I'm Candy Jones and Steve Turner is on the line. Hello, Steve.

Steve Hi.

DJ Who is your record for, Steve?

Steve It's for my girlfriend, Kate. It's her birthday today.

DJ Happy birthday, Kate. How old is she?

Steve Oh, I don't know. She's sixteen, I think.

DJ Thank you, Steve. Now for Steve and his girlfriend, Kate, here's Donna Summer.

2
- Divide the class into pairs.
- Demonstrate the activity with one pair.
- Students read the dialogue in pairs.
- They reverse roles and repeat.

Numbers 11–20

3
- Students look at the list of numbers and the words.
- Make sure students understand the task.
- Play the tape. Stop after each word. Students draw lines to connect the numbers and words.
- Write the numbers on the board. Get students to write the correct word for each number.
- Play the tape again. Students listen and repeat.

Make a rule: his/her

4
In this activity students formalize a rule for themselves using the information in the dialogue.
- Students look at the pictures and the gapped sentences. They complete the sentences.
- Write the sentences on the board. Get students to complete them.

> **Answer key**
> *Her name's Kate. It's her birthday today.*
> *His name's Steve. Kate is his girlfriend.*

- Say *Look at the dialogue in Exercise 1. Find examples to support your answer.*
- Students translate the sentences. Write the translations on the board.
- Students note any differences.
- Ask *What is the rule for 'his' and 'her' in English?* Students give their ideas in the mother tongue.

> **Answer key**
> *We use 'his' with a male possessor. We use 'her' with a female possessor.*

5 a
- Students complete the answers.
- Students give their answers.

> **Answer key**
> 1 *Her*   3 *his*   5 *her*
> 2 *his*   4 *her*

b This is a role-play activity.
- Divide the class into pairs.
- Students choose their roles.
- Explain the activity.
- Pairs make their dialogues. Go round and help with any problems.
- Students reverse roles and repeat.
- Get two pairs to demonstrate their dialogues in front of the class.

FOLLOW UP

6
- Students write one of the dialogues they role played in Exercise 5b.

≡Fast Cars

The alphabet

1 Listen and repeat.

A B C D E F G H I
J K L M N O P Q R
S T U V W X Y Z

2
a Look at these cars. Do you know their names?

b Here are their names. They are all mixed up.

S	XJS	T-Bar	MR2
VW	MG	TVR	GTI
XR3i	BGT		

c  Listen and write the names below the cars.

3 Ask and answer.

Example
A *'What's this?'*
B *'It's a TVR S Convertible.'*

4 Which car do you like best? What is the most popular car in the class?

Numbers 0–10

5  Listen and repeat.

0	1	2	3	4	5
zero (oh)	one	two	three	four	five

6	7	8	9	10
six	seven	eight	nine	ten

A GAME

6 How good is your memory? Work with a partner. Look at the cars for one minute.

A Read one of the number plates.
B (book closed) Write the number. Say which car it is.

Example
A *'A four two nine B T H.'*
B *'It's the VW Golf.'*

FOLLOW UP

7 Write these numbers in full.

Example
    0 1 7 5 9 8 3 2 4
zero

....

Toyota ....

.... Convertible

.... Golf ....

Jaguar ....

Ford Escort .... Cabriolet

6

Radio 581

1
a Look at the dialogue.

b 📼 Listen and complete it.

DJ This .... the Hotline programme on Radio 581. .... Candy Jones and Steve Turner is on the line. ...., Steve.

Steve Hi.

DJ Who is .... record for, Steve?

Steve It's for .... girlfriend, Kate. .... her birthday today.

DJ Happy ...., Kate. How old is .... ?

Steve Oh, I don't know. .... sixteen, I think.

DJ Thank you, Steve. Now for Steve .... his girlfriend, Kate, here's Donna Summer.

2
Work with a partner. Read the dialogue.

Numbers 11–20

3
📼 Listen and match the numbers to the correct words.

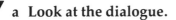

11	thirteen
12	sixteen
13	fourteen
14	eighteen
15	eleven
16	nineteen
17	twenty
18	twelve
19	seventeen
20	fifteen

Make a rule: his / her

4
Complete these sentences. Write 'his' or 'her'.

...... name's Kate.   ...... name's Steve.

It's ...... birthday today.   Kate is ...... girlfriend.

Translate these sentences. Is the rule the same in your language?

When do we use 'his'? When do we use 'her'?

5
a Here are some sentences. Write 'his' or 'her'.

1 My record is for my girlfriend. .... name's Kate.

2 This record is for Michael and .... girlfriend.

3 My record is for my boyfriend. It's .... birthday today.

4 This record is for my girlfriend. It's .... birthday.

5 This record is for Kate and .... boyfriend.

b You are the DJ. Your partner is on the line. He/She wants a record for someone. Make the dialogue.

FOLLOW UP

6
Write the dialogue from Exercise 5b.

Fast food

Numbers 20–100

 a • Play the tape. Students follow in their books and repeat.

• Books closed. Play the tape again. Students listen and repeat.

b • Go round the class. Students count from 30 to 60. Choose students at random so that they do not know when it is their turn.

c • Write the numbers on the board. Students call out the name.

 a • Students look at the menu. Ask *What is in the menu?*

• Students give their answers and practise saying the words.

b • Students look at the dialogues.

• Make sure everyone understands the task.

• Play the tape twice. Students listen.

• Students fill in the missing words. Write the gapped dialogue on the board.

• Play the tape again. Students check their dialogues.

• Get students to complete the dialogue on the board. Other students compare their answers.

Can I help you?
A hamburger and an apple juice, please.
Anything else?
No, thank you.
That's £1.19, please.
Thank you.

Can I help you?
An eggburger and french fries.
Anything else?
Yes, a cola, please.
That's £1.95, please.
Thank you.

 • Divide the class into pairs.

• Demonstrate the activity with one pair.

• Students read the first dialogue in pairs.

• They reverse roles and repeat for the second dialogue.

a/an

BUILD UP

 a • Students look at the chart. Choose students to read the words.

b • Ask *What is the rule for 'a' and 'an'?* Students give their ideas in the mother tongue.

Answer key

We use 'a' when the word begins with a consonant.
We use 'an' when the word begins with a vowel.

---

c • Students write the words in the correct list.

• Copy the list onto the board. Students complete it.

Answer key

a: *pen   desk   bag   girlfriend   record*
an: *orange   apple   egg   umbrella*

 This is a role-play activity.

• Divide the class into pairs.

• Students choose their roles, the customer or waiter/waitress.

• Explain the activity. Students can use the dialogues in Exercise 2 to help them.

• Pairs make their dialogues. Go round and help with any problems.

• Students reverse roles and repeat.

• Get two pairs to demonstrate their dialogues in front of the class.

FOLLOW UP

 Students write one of the dialogues they role played in Exercise 5.

Asking for help

These are useful expressions to help you conduct your class in English as much as possible. You can practise them all now, or practise one or two in each of the next few lessons.

- Demonstrate the expressions. Translate, if necessary.
- Choose the first expression. Say *Think of an example to ask me.*
- Choose students. They point to or show an object and ask their question, for example: (pointing to a chair) *What's this called?* Give the answer. Don't be afraid to say *I don't know. Look it up in your dictionary.*
- Continue with the other expressions now or in a later lesson.
- Make sure students use the expressions when they ask for help.

▶ **Pronunciation: page T111**

CULTURE SPOT
Workbook page 8

- Students look quickly at the pictures.
- Ask *What do you already know about British money?*
- Students discuss any experiences they have had with British money.
- Students work in pairs.
- Read each question in turn.
- Discuss each question. Encourage students to compare their money with the British system.

Answer key

£10.08

Fast food

Numbers 20–100

1 a **Listen and repeat.**

21	twenty-one	30	thirty
22	twenty-two	40	forty
23	twenty-three	50	fifty
24	twenty-four	60	sixty
25	twenty-five	70	seventy
26	twenty-six	80	eighty
27	twenty-seven	90	ninety
28	twenty-eight	100	a hundred
29	twenty-nine		

b **Count from thirty to sixty.**

c **Say these numbers in full.**

   65 97 56 83 71 44 32

2 a **Look at the menu. Say the words.**

b **Listen and complete the dialogues.**

Can .... help you?

A .... and an .... ,
please.

Anything else?

No, thank you.

That's £1.19, ...

....

Can I help you?

An .... and ....

Anything else?

Yes, a .... , please.

That's £........ , please.

Thank you.

3 **Work with a partner. Read the dialogues.**

Fat Cat Cafe

Apple juice **54p**

Cola **40p**

Orange juice **56p**

Hamburger **65p**

Eggburger **80p**

Cheeseburger **75p**

French fries **50p**

▶ Pronunciation: page 111

a/an

 4 a Look.

a	an
a hamburger	**an** apple juice
a cola	**an** orange juice
	an eggburger

b When do we use 'a'? When do we use 'an'? Explain the rule in your own language.

c Add these words to the correct list.

pen   apple   girlfriend
desk   bag   record
orange   egg   umbrella

 5 Look at the menu. Make new dialogues.

FOLLOW UP

 6 Write one of your dialogues from Exercise 5.

Asking for help

Practise these expressions.

What's this called?

What does .... mean?

How do you say .... in English?

How do you pronounce .... ?

How do you spell .... ?

Four new elements are introduced in this unit:

- The contents of the unit are displayed, so that learners can see what they will be learning in the unit.

- We meet the young people from *Victoria Road*.

- Students do their first project.

- At the end of the unit students review their progress in the first Learning diary.

Contents

At this stage it is not necessary to discuss the contents in detail. Draw the students' attention to the list. Tell them that they will come back to the list at the end of the unit.

The Victoria Road characters

- Students look at the picture of the Victoria Road characters.

- Ask *Which character do you like best?*

- Students give their ideas and say why.

Victoria Road Rap

Note
A rap is a kind of musical rhyme. It comes from the West Indies. It is performed to music, but the words are spoken, not sung.

 • Say *We're going to find out the names of the characters.*

a • Students look at the pictures of the characters and the list of names.

- Students look at the song.

- Make sure everyone understands the task.

- 📼 Play the tape. Students listen.

- Students fill in the missing names.

- Play the tape again. Students check their songs.

- Students give the missing names. Don't say whether they are correct or not.

b • Students look at the story on page 12 and check their answers.

Answer key
*Terry   Terry   Sue   Sue   Vince
Casey   Kamala   Kam* (Kam is a short nickname for Kamala.)

c • Students complete the names.

Answer key
*Terry Moore
Casey Royston
Kamala Wijeratne
Sue Scott
Vince Scott*

- Point to the characters in the pictures on pages 10 and 11. Students give the names.

- Ask general questions about the characters:
  *Where are they from?
  What is the name of the street?
  What are Sue and Vince?
  Who is Kam?*

- Play the song again. Students sing the song.

FOLLOW UP

 • Students write a verse for their name to fit the song. They can use the verses in the 'Victoria Road Rap' as a model. Casey's verse will probably be the easiest.

- 📼 Play the tape again. There is a blank piece of music for the students' own verse.

2 you

to be

VICTORIA
ROAD

Contents

		Grammar points
12	**Victoria Road:** Welcome to Hartfield	**the verb 'to be': statements**
14	**Reading:** Are you a Bros fan?	**the verb 'to be': negative**
15	**Listening:** The leisure centre	**the verb 'to be': questions**
16	**Interaction:** At the shops	**plurals; this / these**
18	**Project:** You	

1 a 🔊 **Listen and write the names in the correct places.**

Vince   Kamala   Sue   Casey   Terry   Kam

Victoria Road Rap

My name's .... , ... Moore.

And this is .... , the girl next door.

Hi there, kids. My name's ....

Pleased to meet you. How do you do?

> *Chorus*
> Victoria Road, Victoria Road, Victoria Road,
> rap, rap, rap.
> Victoria Road, Victoria Road, Victoria Road,
> rap, rap, rap.

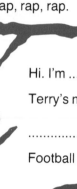

Hi. I'm .... I'm her brother.

Terry's my friend. And here's another.

.... Royston is my name.

Football is my favourite game.

> *Chorus*
> Victoria Road, Victoria Road, Victoria Road,
> rap, rap, rap.
> Victoria Road, Victoria Road, Victoria Road,
> rap, rap, rap.

.... is who I am.

But you're my friend. So call me ....

We're from Hartfield. Where are you from?

Add your name and sing our song.

> *Chorus*
> Victoria Road, Victoria Road, Victoria Road,
> rap, rap, rap.
> Victoria Road, Victoria Road, Victoria Road,
> rap, rap, rap.

b Look at the story on page 12. Check your answers.

c Now complete the names.

.... Moore   .... Scott

.... Royston   .... Scott

.... Wijeratne

FOLLOW UP

2 Write a rhyme for your name and add it to the song.

11

VICTORIA ROAD

Welcome to Hartfield

Work out the meaning

In this activity students look through the story to work out the meaning of some new words. They should be able to work them out from the context. This is an important strategy for students to develop.

- Divide the class into pairs.
- Students open their books and read the words.
- Explain the activity.
- Students look through the picture story to find the words and work out the meaning. They can refer to the full text, too.
- Students give their answers.

Answer key
(possible clues)

brother, *girl*, *friend*: these are in the 'Victoria Road Rap'.

boy: Mrs Moore says, 'How old are the boy and girl next door?' Students know Sue is the girl, so Vince must be the boy.

neighbour: Terry is moving in next door to Sue. She says, 'Are you our new neighbour?' What do you call someone who lives next door?

twins: Terry says, 'They're fifteen. They're twins.' Brother and sister of the same age must be twins.

sister: Terry says, 'Vince is all right, but his sister's bossy.' Sue must be Vince's sister.

- Say *Now look at the full dialogue.*
- Play the tape. Students listen and follow in their books.
- Play the tape again, if necessary.
- Ask *What happens in this episode?* Using the pictures students give a summary of the story in the mother tongue.

Answer key

In this episode Terry and his family are moving into Victoria Road. He meets the next door neighbours, Sue and Vince. Sue introduces herself, Vince, Casey and Kamala. Later Sue overhears a conversation between Terry and his mother. She hears Terry say that she is bossy. Sue decides to get her revenge.

Notes
See you is an informal way of saying goodbye.
bossy means 'always telling people what to do'.

- Books closed. Play the tape again. Stop after each utterance. Students repeat.
- Repeat any utterances that students find difficult.

Useful expressions

- Divide the class into pairs.
- Students look at the list of expressions. They write a translation in the boxes. They use the story and context to work out an appropriate mother-tongue expression. If students find this difficult, say *What would you say in that situation?*

Note
A lot of these expressions are idioms and cannot be translated word for word. Make sure students understand this.

- Students give their answers. Discuss as necessary.

- Divide the class into groups of 3.
- Students choose their roles.
- Students read the dialogue.
- If time, change roles and do the dialogue again.
- Choose one group to act the dialogue in front of the class.

A grammar table: 'to be'

As part of the cognitive approach to grammar, *Hotline* has a number of tasks where students must complete a substitution table. This is the first example. When it is complete, make sure students understand how these tables work.

- Divide the class into pairs.
- Students complete the table. They use the dialogue to help them.
- Copy the table onto the board.
- Choose students to come out and complete the table.
- Students quote examples from the dialogue to justify the rule in the table.
- Students make ten sentences using the table.

Answer key

I	am '*m*	
He She It	*is* '*s*	*from England.* 15.
We You They	*are* '*re*	*in the garden.*

FOLLOW UP

- Students complete the dialogue.
- Choose one pair to read the dialogue.

Answer key

Hi	*neighbour*	*it*	*his*	*Moore*	*old*
He's	*like*	*but*	*right*		

Welcome to Hartfield

Work out the meaning

1 What do you think these words mean? Look through the story. Make a guess.

brother   sister   friend   neighbour
boy   girl   twins

Check your ideas with your teacher or a dictionary.

2 🔊 Listen and follow in your books.

Sue Hi, are you our new neighbour? What's your name?

Terry Terry Moore. I . . .

Sue I'm Sue. This is my brother, Vince. We're twins.

Terry Oh, hel . . .

Sue Say hello, Vince. And this is his friend, Casey.

Kamala Hi, Sue.

Sue That's my best friend. Her name's Kamala.

Sue See you. Bye.

Terry Goodbye.

Later

Mrs Moore How old are the boy and girl next door?

Terry They're fifteen. They're twins.

Mrs Moore Oh, what are their names?

Terry Vince and Sue.

Mrs Moore What are they like?

Terry Vince is all right, but his sister's bossy.

Sue Huh. I'm not bossy. You just wait, Terry Moore!

3 Listen again and repeat.

> Hi. Are you our new neighbour? What's your name?

> Terry Moore. I...

1

> This is my brother, Vince. We're twins.

> Oh, hel....

2

> Hi, Sue.

> That's my best friend. Her name's Kamala.

3

VICTORIA ROAD   12

> How old are the boy and girl next door?

> They're fifteen.

4

> What are they like?

> Vince is all right, but his sister's bossy.

5

A grammar table: 'to be'

6 We can use a table to show a grammar rule. This is a table. Complete it with these words.

She 's are 'm 're It is We

I	am	
	....	from England.
He	....	15.
......	....	
......	....	in the garden.
......	....	
You	....	
They		

> Huh. I'm not bossy. You just wait, Terry Moore.

6

Useful expressions

4 How do you say these expressions in your language?

See you.	
How old are . . .?	
What are they like?	
He's all right.	
She's bossy.	
You just wait!	

5 Work in a group of 3. One person is Terry, one is Sue, one is all the other people. Read the story.

FOLLOW UP

7 Kamala is talking to Sue. Complete their conversation.

Kamala Hi, Sue.

Sue ...., Kam.

Kamala Is that boy your new

.... ?

Sue Yes, ... is.

Kamala What's .... name?

Sue Terry ....

Kamala How .... is he?

Sue .... fifteen.

Kamala What's he .... ?

Sue He's a bit quiet, ... he's all

....

13

READING

Are you a Bros fan?

a • Students look at the pictures.

• Ask *Do you know these people?* Students give their answers.

b • Students read the statements. They underline any unknown words.

The aim of this activity is to get students to match what they hear to what they read.

• Explain the activity.

• Play the tape. Students listen.

• Play the tape again. Stop after each utterance. Students give the name of the pop star.

• Play the tape again. Stop after each utterance. Ask *Do you agree with this comment?* Students give their ideas.

• Students give their ideas.

The verb 'to be': negative

BUILD UP

a • Divide the class into pairs.

• Students complete the sentences. They use the statements in Exercise 1 to help them.

Answer key
'm not   isn't   aren't

b • Students complete the table.

• Copy the table onto the board.

• Choose students to come out and complete the table.

• Students quote examples from the statements to justify the rule in the table.

• Students make six sentences using the table.

Answer key

I	am not / 'm not	bad.
He She It	is not / isn't	very good.
We You They	are not / aren't	rubbish.

• Students look at the sentences.

• Get one student to do the first sentence.

Note
Students must complete these sentences to give a statement that is factually correct for themselves. Different students may, therefore, give different answers.

• Students complete the remaining sentences.

• Students give their answers.

Answer key
Answers will depend on students' own situation and opinions.

• Students move round the class. They ask *Who is your favourite pop star?*

• Students continue asking till they have found three people with the same favourite.

FOLLOW UP

Students choose three pop stars or groups that they like and three that they don't like. They stick pictures of the stars into their exercise books and write their opinions in speech bubbles for each one, as in Exercise 1.

LISTENING

- Students look at the picture. Ask *Who is in the picture?*

Answer key
Terry

- Students look at the card.
- Make sure everyone understands the task.
- Play the tape twice. Students listen.
- Students fill in the information. While they are doing this, copy the card onto the board.
- Play the tape again. Students check their dialogues.
- Rewind the tape.
- Get students to complete the card on the board. Other students compare their answers.

Woman What's your name?
Terry Terry Moore.
Woman How do you spell Moore?
Terry M double O R E.
Woman How old are you? Are you 16?
Terry No, I'm not. I'm 15.
Woman What's your address?
Terry 20 Victoria Road, Hartfield.
Woman What's your telephone number?
Terry 732983.
Woman Welcome to the Leisure Centre, Terry. That's £5.50, please.

The verb 'to be': questions

BUILD UP

2 **a**
- Students look at the example.
- Get one student to read the example aloud.
- Get another student to give the next sentence.
- Students make the remaining sentences.
- Students give their answers.

Answer key
Is Sue
Are you
Is he

b
- Choose one student to explain the rule.

Answer key
To make questions with 'to be' we put the verb in front of the subject.

3
- Students look at the example.
- Get one student to read the example aloud.
- Get another student to give the next sentence.
- Students make the remaining sentences.
- Students give their answers.

Answer key
Is Sue his sister?
Are they twins?
Are they all right?
Are they sixteen?
Is Casey their friend?
Is he fifteen, too?
Are Kamala and Casey our neighbours, too?
Is Kamala your friend?

4 **a**
- Students look at the dialogue.
- Make sure everyone understands the task.
- Play the tape. Students listen.
- Students fill in the questions. While they are doing this, write the gapped dialogue on the board.
- Play the tape again. Students check their dialogues.
- Get students to complete the dialogue on the board. Other students compare their answers.

b
- Divide the class into pairs.
- Demonstrate the activity with one pair.
- Students read the dialogue in pairs.
- They reverse roles and repeat.

5
- Divide the class into pairs.
- Explain the activity.
- Students choose their roles.
- Pairs make their dialogues.
- The 'interviewer' completes the card in his/her book with information from his/her partner.
- Go round and help with any problems.
- Students reverse roles and repeat.
- Get two pairs to demonstrate their dialogues in front of the class.

FOLLOW UP

6
Students make and complete a membership card for themselves. They write their dialogue for Exercise 5.

READING

Are you a Bros fan?....

1 a Look at these pop stars. Do you know them?

b Read what people say about them.

> They're my favourite pop group.

> They're rubbish.

> They're all right.

> They aren't very good.

> She's great!

> She's OK.

> She's awful.

> She isn't my favourite singer.

> He's wonderful.

> He isn't bad.

> I'm not a Michael Jackson fan.

> He's terrible.

2 ☞ Now listen. Which pop star are they talking about?

> Example
> He isn't bad.
> *It's Michael Jackson.*

3 What do you think of these people? Use the expressions above.

The verb 'to be': negative

BUILD UP

4 a Look. Complete the sentences.

I .... a Michael Jackson fan.

She .... my favourite singer.

They .... very good.

b Complete the table.

I	am not 'm not	
He She It	....	bad. very good. rubbish.
We You They	....	

5 Make true sentences by completing these.

a I .... from America.

b Michael Jackson .... my favourite pop star.

c My parents .... millionaires.

d Our English teacher .... bossy.

e I .... a girl.

f I .... a boy.

g The Beatles .... terrible.

h English .... my favourite subject.

i My partner and I .... the best students in the class.

6 Who are your favourite pop stars? Do other people like them? Ask them.

FOLLOW UP

7 Choose six pop stars or pop groups. Write your opinion of each one.

LISTENING

 1 Terry is joining the Hartfield leisure centre.

📼 Listen and complete his form.

> ## Hartfield Leisure Centre
>
> Membership Card No: **694/M**
>
> Name: ....
>
> Age: ....
>
> Address: ....
>
> Telephone number: ....

The verb 'to be': questions

BUILD UP

2 **a** Complete the questions.

> Example
> Vince and Sue 　are　 twins.
>
> *Are　Vince and Sue　twins?*
>
> Sue is in the kitchen.
>
> .... in the kitchen?
>
> You are fifteen.
>
> .... fifteen?
>
> He's from Spain.
>
> .... from Spain?

> **b How do we make questions with 'to be'?**
> **Explain in your own language.**

 3 Mr Moore is asking Terry some questions. Use these cues. Make the questions.

> Example
> Vince / our neighbour
> *Is Vince our neighbour?*
>
> Sue / his sister
> they / twins
> they / all right
> they / sixteen
> Casey / their friend
> he / fifteen, too
> Kamala and Casey / our neighbours, too
> Kamala / your friend

 4 **a Listen again and complete the dialogue.**

Woman ....?

Terry Terry Moore.

Woman ....?

Terry M double O R E.

Woman .... Are you 16?

Terry No, I'm not. I'm 15.

Woman .... address?

Terry 20 Victoria Road, Hartfield.

Woman .... telephone

............................?

Terry 732983.

Woman Welcome to the leisure centre, Terry. That's £5.50, please.

b Work with a partner. Read the dialogue.

5 Interview your partner. Complete his/her card.

> ## Hartfield Leisure Centre
>
> Membership Card No: ....
>
> Name: ....
>
> Age: ....
>
> Address: ....
>
> Telephone number: ....

FOLLOW UP

6 Make a membership card for yourself. Write your dialogue for Exercise 5.

INTERACTION

At the shops

 a • Divide the class into pairs.

 • Students look at the pictures. Ask *Who are the people? Where are they?*

 • Students look at the dialogue. Ask *What is the woman buying?*

 • Students look through the dialogue to find the names of the items.

 • Make sure everyone understands the task.

 • Students make the dialogue by putting the correct sentence in each speech bubble.

 b • Play the tape. Students listen and check their dialogues.

 • Students amend their dialogues, if necessary.

 • Play the tape again. Students check their dialogues.

At the shops
How much are these postcards?
The small postcards are 10p each and the large postcards are 20p each.
Can I have these four, please?
That's 40p, please.
And how much is this yellow T-shirt?
It's £5.
I'll take it, please.
That's £5.40 altogether, please.
Here you are.
Thank you. That's 60p change.
Thank you.

 c • Demonstrate the activity with one pair.

 • Students read the dialogue in pairs.

 • They reverse roles and repeat.

Plurals

BUILD UP

 a • Students look at the examples.

 • Ask *What difference can you see?*

 b • Students explain the rule for making the plural.

> **Answer key**
> *We add -s.*

 • Call out some more words. Students give the plural.
 Use these words: *book, bag, girl, boy, friend, apple, pen.*

this/these

BUILD UP

 a • Students complete the sentences.

 • Ask *When do we use 'this' and when do we use 'these'?*

> **Answer key**
> *We use 'this' with singular nouns and 'these' with plural nouns.*

 b • Students look at the example.

 • Get one student to read the example aloud.

 • Get another student to give the next sentence.

 • Students make the remaining sentences.

 • Students give their answers.

> **Answer key**
> *are these*
> *is this*
> *are these*
> *are these*
> *is this*
> *is this*
> *is this*
> *are these*

> **Note**
> Make sure students pronounce *watches* /wɒtʃɪz/ and *badges* /bædʒɪz/ correctly.

Adjective and noun

BUILD UP

a • Students look at the examples.

 • Ask *Which word is the adjective?*

> **Answer key**
> *small   large   green   red*

 b • Ask *Where is the adjective?*

> **Answer key**
> *in front of the noun*

 c • Students translate the expressions.

 • Write the English expressions and the translations on the board.

 • Ask *What differences can you see?*

• Get one student to give the first example.
• Students describe the remaining things.
• Students give their answers.

Answer key
a red tracksuit
a black tracksuit
a white T-shirt
a yellow T-shirt
green pens
blue pens
a small badge
a large badge

 • Divide the class into pairs.
• Explain the activity.
• Students choose their roles.
• Pairs make their dialogues. Go round and help with any problems.
• Students reverse roles and repeat.
• Get two pairs to demonstrate their dialogues in front of the class.

FOLLOW UP

 Students write a dialogue from Exercise 6.

INTERACTION

At the shops

1 a Make the dialogue. Put each sentence in the correct speech bubble.

That's 40p, please.
That's £5.40 altogether, please.
Thank you.
It's £5.
Here you are.
How much are these postcards?
And how much is this yellow T-shirt?
Thank you.
I'll take it, please.
Can I have these four, please?
The small postcards are 10p each and the large postcards are 15p each.
That's 60p change.

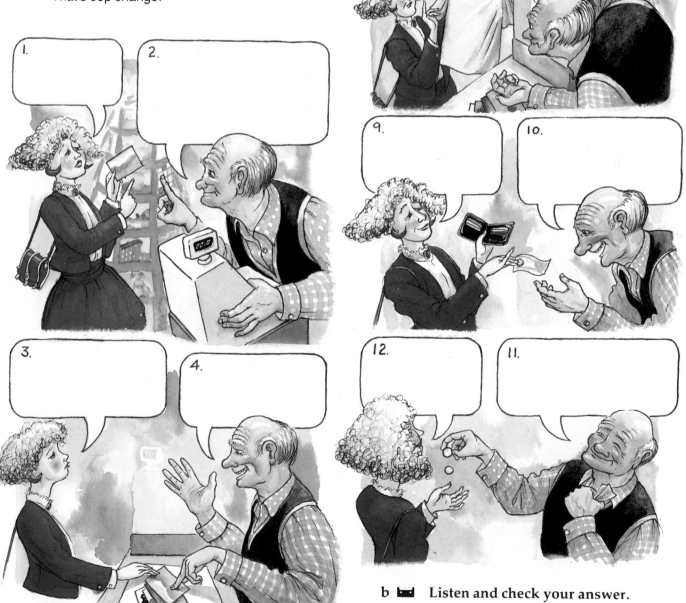

b 🔊 Listen and check your answer.

c Practise the dialogue in pairs.

Plurals

 a Look.

a postcard   four postcards

a T-shirt   two T-shirts

b How do we make the plural?
Explain in your own language.

this / these

a Complete these with 'this' or 'these'.

....
green T-shirt   postcards

b Complete these sentences.

> Example
> *How much are these red apples?*

How much .... red apples?

How much .... radio?

How much .... watches?

How much .... badges?

How much .... green umbrella?

How much .... cassette recorder?

How much .... pens?

Adjective and noun

 a Look.

the **small** postcards   this **green** T-shirt
the **large** postcards   these **red** apples

b Where is the adjective?

c Translate them. Is it the same in your language?

---

5 Describe these things. Use these words.

red   yellow   **blue**   **green**

white   **black**   small   **large**

6 Look at the pictures above. Make dialogues. Use the dialogue in Exercise 1 as a model.

A You are a customer. Buy two things from the shop.

B You are the sales assistant.

FOLLOW UP

7 Write one of your dialogues from Exercise 6.

17

PROJECT

You

This is the students' first project. It is important to give students guidance on how to do the project, but don't be too prescriptive. Students should be encouraged to be creative. This should not be a problem in this case, as it is a very personal project. This project can be done as an individual project or as a group project. It will work best as an individual project.

- Students look at Vince's project
- Ask *What parts of his life has Vince put in his project? What illustrations has he used?*
- Students give their ideas.
- Students collect similar information about their own lives.
- Students plan their project.
- Students produce a rough draft of their project.
- Discuss the rough drafts and suggest corrections.
- Students produce a finished project. Students can do their project either on a large poster or in a book. This project will work best as a poster.
- Students display their projects.
- Discuss the projects. Ask *What did you find easy or difficult in doing the project? What did you like or dislike about doing the project?*

▶ **Pronunciation: page T112**

LEARNING DIARY

> **Note**
> Discuss in the mother tongue.

A Students look at the contents list on page 10. They draw a face next to each item to show how well they think they know it.

B Students do the self-check in the Workbook on page 16.

C Divide the class into pairs or groups of three or four.

Students compare their answers. Go round the class and check for any common problems.

Students compare their self-check results with the faces they drew.

- In the whole class ask *What problems did you find with the self-check?*
- Students suggest problem areas.
- Take remedial action, as necessary. (See Introduction page vii for possible strategies.)
- Ask *What did you like best in this unit? What didn't you like?* Students give their responses. Ask *Why?* Take note of student responses. They can help you to adjust your teaching towards the things that motivate the students most.

CULTURE SPOT
Workbook page 15

- Students look quickly at the Culture spot.
- Ask *What do you already know about writing addresses?*
- Students give their ideas. Discuss these ideas.
- Ask *Did you find anything interesting or unusual?*
- Students give their ideas.
- Read the comparison question.
- Encourage students to compare their way of writing addresses with the British way.

You can start immediately with the Victoria Road story on page 20, or you can pre-teach the language of describing people, using the material on page 19. If you wish to pre-teach the language, use the following procedure.

> **Note**
> At this stage you only need to introduce the grammar items, so that students can understand the story more easily. There are exercises later for more concentrated practice. Spend no more than 8 minutes on the pre-teaching.

1 Introduce hair colours.

- Use yourself and pupils or the pictures on page 19. (You can use the picture of Tom Hutchinson on the back cover for blond hair, too.)

- Point to Sue and say *fair hair*. Students repeat.

- Repeat for *dark* and *blond*.

- Point to people or pictures. Students give the correct hair colour.

2 Introduce *have got*.

- Say *I have got … hair*.

- Ask a student *What colour hair have you got?*

- Elicit reply *I have got … hair*.

- Repeat with three or four more students.

3 Introduce *has got*.

- Point to Sue. Say *She has got fair hair*.

- Point to other students or characters in the book. Ask *What colour hair has he/she got?*

- Elicit response *He/She's got … hair*.

4 • Ask random questions, using students or characters:
   What colour hair/eyes have you got?
   What colour hair/eyes has he/she got?

5 • Students look at the text on page 19.

- Choose students to read the texts about Sue and Kamala aloud.

6 • Start the Victoria Road story on page 20.

PROJECT

You

Here's your first project. Make a project about YOU.

- Give some information about yourself.
- Show some of your favourite things.

Use Vince's project as a model.

3 people

Contents

Grammar points

20	**Victoria Road:** Terry's date	**have / has got**
23	**Reading:** A family	**genitives**
24	**Listening:** Blind Date	**a / an + job**
25	**Interaction:** Your radio show	**have / has got: questions**
26	**Project:** My family	

The main grammar point in this unit is:

have / has got

> I have got fair hair.
> I have got blue eyes.
> I haven't got dark hair.
> What colour hair have you got?

Kamala has got black hair.
She has got brown eyes.
She hasn't got blond hair.
Has she got blue eyes?

have/has got

VICTORIA ROAD

Terry's date

- Books closed. Ask *What happened in the last episode of 'Victoria Road'?*
- Students give their responses. Ask follow-up questions. They can use the mother tongue at this stage.

Answer key
Terry moved in next door to Vince and Sue. Sue introduced herself, Vince, Kamala and Casey. Later Sue overheard Terry talking to his mother. He said that Sue was bossy. Sue decided to get her revenge.

- Students open their books and read the questions.
- Choose students to read the questions aloud. Make sure everyone understands the questions.
- Students look through the picture story to find the answers to the questions. They can refer to the full text, too.
- Students give their answers to the questions.

Answer key
Sue, Terry and Kamala
They are at the leisure centre.
They are talking about the dance on Saturday. Sue has got a date for Terry.
Jane Fox is Terry's date.
Darren Tooley is Jane's boyfriend.

- Ask *What happens in this episode?* Using the pictures students give a summary of the story. (Students use the mother tongue, if necessary at this stage.)
- Explain any new vocabulary that students need to understand the dialogue.

Answer key
Sue has arranged a date for Terry for the dance. She describes the girl to Terry. However, Kamala suspects that Sue is playing a trick on Terry, because Sue is exaggerating Jane's attractiveness ('long blond hair') and because Jane Fox has already got a boyfriend. His name is Darren and he is very big.

- Say *Now look at the full dialogue.*
- Play the tape. Students listen and follow in their books.
- Play the tape again, if necessary.
- Ask *What is Sue up to?* Students give their ideas.

Notes
blind date When someone arranges a date with an unknown person, we call this a 'blind date'.

Well, she has *not* got blond hair. Kamala uses the full form for emphasis.

the big guy 'guy' is an informal word for men or teenage boys.

from West Street School Darren Tooley goes to a different school from the Victoria Road characters, because he lives in a different part of the town.

What are you up to? We use this expression when we suspect someone's motives. Kamala suspects that Sue is playing a trick on Terry.

- Students read the statements and tick the boxes.
- Choose students to read each statement and give the answer.
- Ask *How do you know?* Students use the dialogue to justify their answers.

Note
This is a very important stage, because it shows whether students have understood the dialogue.

Answer key
a *R*   b *R*   c *W*   d *W*
e *D*   f *R*   g *D*

- Books closed.
- Play the tape again. Stop after each utterance. Students repeat.
- Repeat any utterances that students find difficult.

Terry's date

1 Look at the story.

- Who are the people?
- Where are they?
- What are they talking about?
- Who are:
  Jane Fox
  Darren Tooley?

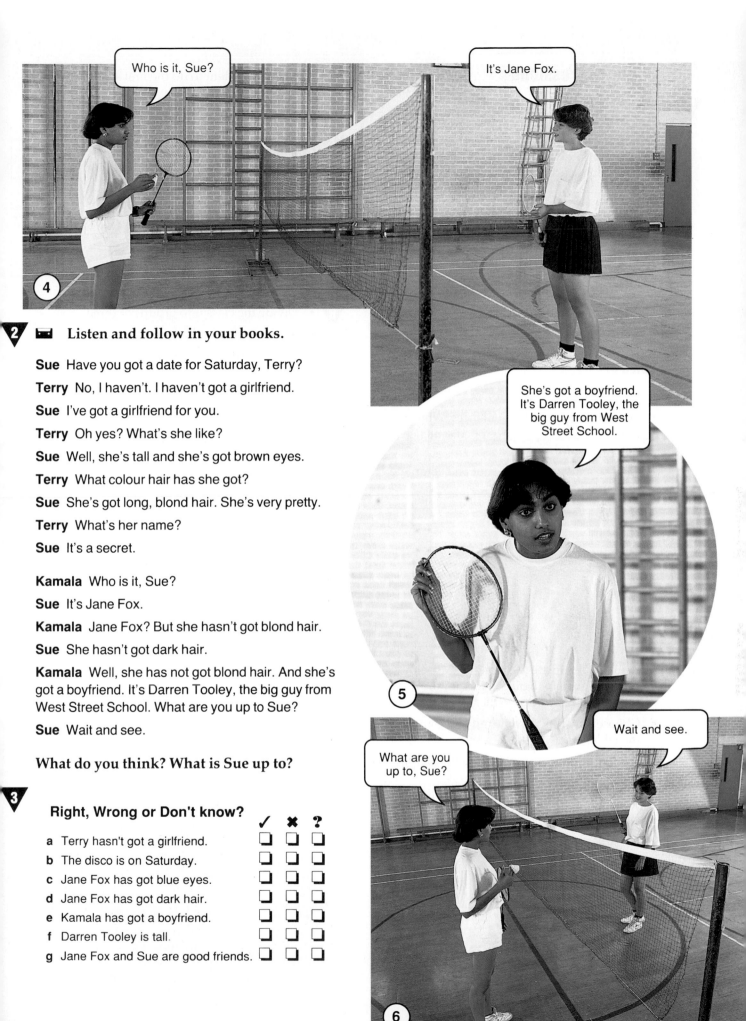

Who is it, Sue?

It's Jane Fox.

(4)

2 📼 **Listen and follow in your books.**

Sue Have you got a date for Saturday, Terry?

Terry No, I haven't. I haven't got a girlfriend.

Sue I've got a girlfriend for you.

Terry Oh yes? What's she like?

Sue Well, she's tall and she's got brown eyes.

Terry What colour hair has she got?

Sue She's got long, blond hair. She's very pretty.

Terry What's her name?

Sue It's a secret.

Kamala Who is it, Sue?

Sue It's Jane Fox.

Kamala Jane Fox? But she hasn't got blond hair.

Sue She hasn't got dark hair.

Kamala Well, she has not got blond hair. And she's got a boyfriend. It's Darren Tooley, the big guy from West Street School. What are you up to Sue?

Sue Wait and see.

What do you think? What is Sue up to?

She's got a boyfriend. It's Darren Tooley, the big guy from West Street School.

(5)

What are you up to, Sue?

Wait and see.

3

Right, Wrong or Don't know?

		✓	✗	?
a	Terry hasn't got a girlfriend.	❏	❏	❏
b	The disco is on Saturday.	❏	❏	❏
c	Jane Fox has got blue eyes.	❏	❏	❏
d	Jane Fox has got dark hair.	❏	❏	❏
e	Kamala has got a boyfriend.	❏	❏	❏
f	Darren Tooley is tall.	❏	❏	❏
g	Jane Fox and Sue are good friends.	❏	❏	❏

(6)

4 **Listen again and repeat.**

21

Useful expressions

 • Divide the class into pairs.
- Students look at the list of expressions. They write a translation in the boxes. They use the story and context to work out an appropriate mother-tongue expression.

Note
A lot of these expressions are idioms and cannot be translated word for word. Make sure students understand this.

- Students give their answers. Discuss as necessary.

have/has got

BUILD UP

 a • Divide the class into pairs.
- Students complete the sentences. While they are doing this, copy the gapped sentences onto the board.
- Choose students to come out and complete the sentences.

Answer key
have got
've got
haven't got
has
's got
has not got (*hasn't got* also possible)
hasn't got

b • Students complete the table. They use the dialogue to help them. While they are doing this, copy the table onto the board.
- Choose students to come out and complete the table.
- Students quote examples from the dialogue to justify the rule in the table.
- Students make ten sentences using the table.

Answer key

I	have		
We	've		
You	have not		
They	haven't		long hair.
		got	
He	has		brown eyes.
She	's		
It	has not		
	hasn't		

 • Get one student to do the first sentence.
- Students make the remaining sentences.
- Students give their answers.

Answer key
(**g–j** will depend on the student's individual situation.)

a	*has*	**f**	*has*
b	*has*	**g**	*have/haven't*
c	*hasn't*	**h**	*has/hasn't*
d	*have*	**i**	*have/haven't*
e	*hasn't*	**j**	*have/haven't*

 • Divide the class into groups of three.
- Students choose their roles.
- Students read the dialogue.
- If time, change roles and do the dialogue again.
- Choose one group to act the dialogue in front of the class.

FOLLOW UP

 • Students do Exercise 9 in class or for homework.

Answer key

| *Have* | *date* | *haven't* | *have* | *like* |
| *'s got* | *hair* | *tall* | *colour* | *has* | *her* |

READING

Genitives

BUILD UP

- Students look at the examples.
- Choose one student to read them aloud.
- Call out other names. Students give the relationship.
  Example: You say: *Kamala and Sue*. Student says: *Kamala is Sue's best friend*. Use these examples: Terry and Sue; Vince and Casey; Jane Fox and Darren Tooley.

- Students look at the pictures of the British royal family at the bottom of the page.
- Ask *Who are the people? What do you know about them?*
- Students give their ideas.

- In this activity students use the information in the text to work out the meaning of the words. **Don't** give the meanings of the words. Students must work them out.
- Divide the class into pairs.
- Students read the list of words. Read them aloud.
- Explain the activity.
- Students use the clues and the family tree to work out the meanings of the words. Allow time for all pairs to work out all of the words before eliciting answers.
- Students give their answers.
- Ask *How do you know?* Students justify their ideas from the text and the tree.

Using a pattern

In this activity students use a semantic pattern to predict unknown vocabulary. This is an important strategy. It encourages students to take risks when they do not know a particular word.

- Students look at the list of words.
- Make sure students understand the two examples.
- Students complete the list.
- Students give their answers.

> **Answer key**
> *granddaughter   grandfather   grandparents*

- Ask *How did you work out the answer?* Students give their ideas.

- Explain the activity.
- Students use the family tree to complete the sentences.
- Write the gapped sentences on the board.
- Choose students to complete the sentences on the board. Pay attention to the apostrophe.

> **Answer key**
> a *Prince Andrew's*
> b *Prince Charles' and Princess Diana's*
> c *grandfather*
> d *mother*
> e *Prince William's*
> f *Princess Diana's*

FOLLOW UP

Students can do this activity in groups or as individuals.

- Students choose a famous family, for example another royal family or a family from a TV show.
- Students draw a family tree and write ten sentences about the members of the family. They use the sentences in Exercise 3 as a model.

Useful expressions

5 How do you say these in your language?

Have you got a date?

I haven't got a girlfriend.

What is she like?

What colour hair has she got?

It's a secret.

She's got a boyfriend.

a big guy

What are you up to?

Wait and see.

have / has got

BUILD UP

6 a Look at the story, and the examples on page 19 again. Find these incomplete sentences and complete them.

I .... fair hair.

I............................. a girlfriend for you.

I have not got blue eyes.

I .... a girlfriend.

She .... got dark hair.

She............................. long, blond hair.

Well, she .... blond hair.

She .... dark hair.

b Now complete this table.

I We You They	have .... have not		
		got	long hair.
He She It	.... 's .... hasn't		brown eyes.

7 Write true sentences. Use 'have', 'has', 'haven't' or 'hasn't'.

a Jane Fox .... got brown eyes.

b Sue .... got a secret.

c Terry .... got a girlfriend.

d Kamala and Casey .... got black hair.

e Sue .... got a sister.

f Jane Fox .... got a boyfriend.

g I .... got short hair.

h My best friend .... got fair hair.

i I .... got three brothers.

j We .... got a fast car.

8 Work in a group of three. Each person takes one part. Read the story.

FOLLOW UP

9 Complete this conversation.

Terry .... you got a .... for the dance, Casey?

Casey No, I .... Have you?

Terry Yes, I ....

Casey What's she .... ?

Terry She .... long, blond .... and she's ....

Casey What .... eyes .... she got?

Terry Brown.

Casey What's .... name?

Terry I don't know.

READING

Genitives

BUILD UP

1 Look.

Sue is **Vince's** sister.
Vince is **Sue's** brother.   sister   brother

2 Look at the family below. Who are the people?

3 What do these words mean?

husband	son	daughter
wife	grandson	parents
mother	grandmother	father

Read the clues. Use the diagram to find the meanings of these words.

Princess Bea's mother is called Fergie.
Prince Philip is the Queen's husband.
Princess Diana and Prince Charles have got two sons.
Princess Anne and Captain Mark Philips have got a
    son and a daughter.
Princess Diana is Prince Charles' wife.
The Queen is Prince William's grandmother.
The Queen and Prince Philip have got three
    grandsons.
Peter and Zara Philips' parents are Princess Anne
    and Captain Mark Philips.

Using a pattern

W O R D   W O R K

4 Complete the list.

son	grandson
daughter	....
mother	grandmother
father	....
parents	....

5 Complete these sentences.

a Fergie is .... wife.

b Prince William is .... son.

c Prince Philip is Princess Bea's ....

d The Queen is Prince Edward's ....

e Prince Harry is .... brother.

f Prince Charles is .... husband.

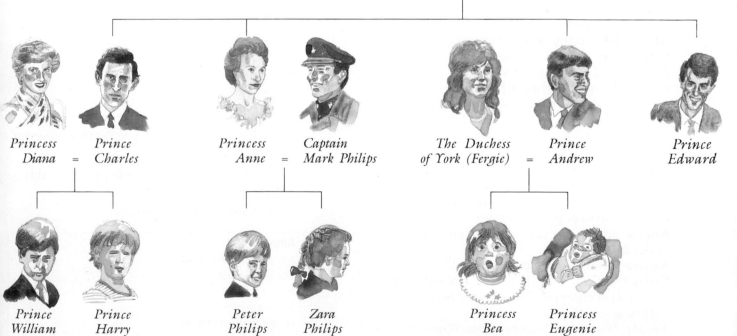

The Queen   =   Prince Philip

Princess Diana = *Prince Charles*   *Princess Anne* = *Captain Mark Philips*   *The Duchess of York (Fergie)* = *Prince Andrew*   *Prince Edward*

Prince William   *Prince Harry*   *Peter Philips*   *Zara Philips*   *Princess Bea*   *Princess Eugenie*

FOLLOW UP

6 Describe a famous family from your country.

23

LISTENING

Blind Date

- Divide the class into groups of three or four.
- Students look at the picture. Ask: *Who is in the picture? What is happening?*
- Students give their ideas. Don't say at this stage whether they are right or wrong.
- ▣ Play the first part of the tape. Students listen and check their predictions.

Answer key

It's a radio show in which a person chooses one of three possible blind dates.

- Students look at the chart.
- Make sure everyone understands the task.
- ▣ Play the tape again. Students listen.
- Students complete the chart. While they are doing this, write the gapped chart on the board.
- Play the tape again. Students check their charts.
- Get students to complete the chart on the board. Other students compare their answers.

▣ Blind Date: part 1

DJ And now it's time for Blind Date. On the line is Angela Thompson. She's from Leeds. Hello, Angela.

Angela Hi. Call me Angie.

DJ OK, Angie. Your three possible dates are on the line. Are you ready?

Angela Yes. Number 1. Where are you from?

Caller 1 I'm from London.

Angela What colour hair have you got?

Caller 1 I've got dark hair and I've got brown eyes.

Angela And what's your job?

Caller 1 I haven't got a job. I'm a student.

Angela Who's your favourite pop group?

Caller 1 Dire Straits.

Angela Thank you. Number 2. Where are you from?

Caller 2 I'm from Liverpool. I've got fair hair and blue eyes.

Angela Oh, er ... right. Well, um, what's your job?

Caller 2 I'm a shop assistant.

Angela Who's your favourite pop group?

Caller 2 Deacon Blue.

Angela Who? How do you spell that?

Caller 2 Deacon, that's D-E-A-C-O-N and then Blue, as in blue eyes. They're from Scotland. They're great.

Angela Thank you. Number three. Where are you from?

Caller 3 I'm from Birmingham.

Angela What colour hair have you got?

Caller 3 I've got blond hair.

Angela And what colour eyes have you got?

Caller 3 I've got green eyes.

Angela What's your job?

Caller 3 I'm an engineer.

Angela Who's your favourite pop group?

Caller 3 Um, I haven't got a favourite.

Angela Thank you.

- In their groups students decide which date Angie will choose.
- Collect students' ideas. Write on the board how many choose each date.
- ▣ Play the tape. Students listen and check their ideas.

▣ Blind Date: part 2

DJ Well, Angie. They're your three dates. Choose one.

Angela Oh, I don't know. Number 1 has got a nice voice, but well, I mean, his favourite group is Dire Straits. They're terrible. Number 3 is blond with green eyes. Mmmmm. But he's an engineer and he hasn't got a favourite pop star. Boring. Number 2 is fun. But who are Deacon Blue?!

DJ Well. Who is your blind date, Angie?

Angela It's number ... 2.

DJ Number 2 is Jason Reed from Liverpool. And here's your prize – a day trip to Paris for you and Jason. Have a good time!

a/an + job

a
- Students look at the examples.
- Choose one student to read them aloud.

b
- Write the sentences on the board.
- Choose students to write a translation underneath.
- Ask *Is there any difference?*

a
- Divide the class into pairs.
- Students use a dictionary to find the names of the jobs in the pictures.
- Students write down the jobs. They use this structure: *He/She is a/an ... .*
- Students give their answers.

Answer key

She's a shop assistant.
She's a teacher.
He's a farmer.
She's a doctor.
He's a football player.
He's a policeman.

b This activity can be given for homework, if preferred.

- Students write five sentences. They use a dictionary to find unknown words.
- Choose two students to read out their sentences.

- Divide the class into pairs.
- Explain the activity.
- Students choose their roles. One student plays Angie; the other student takes all the other parts.
- Pairs make their dialogues. Go round and help with any problems.
- If time, students reverse roles and repeat.
- Get one pair to demonstrate their dialogues in front of the class.

FOLLOW UP

- Students use the information from the chart they completed in Exercise 2 to write a description for each of the three boys in the 'Blind Date' radio programme.

> **Answer key**
> *Number 1 is from London. He's got dark hair and brown eyes. He's a student and his favourite pop group is Dire Straits.*
> *Number 2 is from Liverpool. He's got fair hair and blue eyes. He's a shop assistant and his favourite pop group is Deacon Blue.*
> *Number 3 is from Birmingham. He's got blond hair and green eyes. He's an engineer. He hasn't got a favourite pop group.*

INTERACTION

have/has got: questions

BUILD UP

 a
- Divide the class into pairs.
- Students complete the sentences. While they are doing this, copy the gapped sentences onto the board.
- Choose students to come out and complete the sentences.

> **Answer key**
> *Have you got*
> *Has she got*

b
- Students complete the table. They use the dialogue from *Victoria Road* and from **a** to help them. While they are doing this copy the gapped table onto the board.
- Choose students to come out and complete the table.
- Students make ten sentences using the table.

> **Answer key**
>
> | | | | |
> |---|---|---|---|
> | Have | I / you / we / they | | brown eyes? |
> | | | got | blond hair? |
> | Has | he / she / it | | a sister? |

c
- Students explain the rule.

> **Answer key**
> *To make questions with 'have/has got' we put 'have' or 'has' in front of the subject.*

- Students look at the example.
- Get one pair to read the example aloud.
- Get another pair to give the next dialogue.
- Students make the remaining dialogues.
- Choose pairs to do each dialogue in front of the class.

YOUR RADIO SHOW

 a
- Divide the class into groups of five.
- Students look at page 24 again. Ask *What happened on the show? What questions did Angie ask?*

b
- Make sure students understand the activity.
- Students choose their roles.
- Each student decides what he/she will say. Go round and help where necessary.

c
- Students act their shows in groups.
- Choose two or three groups to act their shows in front of the class.

FOLLOW UP

Students write the dialogue between the person and one of the dates.

continued on T26

LISTENING

Blind Date

 1 Listen to the radio programme. What is it about?

2 Listen again and complete this chart.

	1	2	3
from			
hair			
eyes			
job			
favourite pop star			

3 Who does Angie choose?
- What do you think?
- Listen to the second part and find out.

a/an + job

 4 a Look.

I'm **a** student.
He's **an** engineer.

b Compare this to your own language.

 5 Use a dictionary.

a Say what these people are.

b What about your family? What are their jobs?

> Example
> *My mother is a bank manager.*

6 Work with a partner. Use your chart. Role play the radio show.

FOLLOW UP

7 Use your chart. Describe the three boys.

INTERACTION

have / has got: questions

BUILD UP

1 a Complete these sentences.

You have got a girlfriend.

.... a girlfriend?

She has got fair hair.

.... fair hair?

b Complete this table.

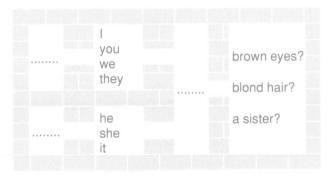

....	I you we they	....	brown eyes? blond hair?
....	he she it		a sister?

c How do we make questions with 'have / has got'? Explain in your own language.

2 Work with a partner. Ask and answer these.

Example
Have you got a brother?
Yes, I've got two brothers.

a brother	a boyfriend / girlfriend
a walkman	a best friend
a computer	a dictionary
a sister	a house or flat
a watch	a favourite record

YOUR RADIO SHOW

3 a Look at the Blind Date show on page 24. Work in a group of five.

b Make your own programme. Each person takes a part.

c Act your radio show.

FOLLOW UP

4 Write one of the dialogues from your show.

Your Blind Date File

You want to go on the Blind Date show. First we need some information about you.

We need a photograph.

And we need some basic information. Please answer these questions.

PUT YOUR PHOTOGRAPH HERE

What's your full name?
What do your friends call you?
Are you male or female?
How old are you?
Where are you from?
What colour eyes have you got?
What colour hair have you got?
How tall are you?

Your likes and dislikes

Now we'd like some information about your likes and dislikes.

Who's your favourite pop star?
Who's your least favourite pop star?
What's your favourite food?
What's your favourite colour?
What's your favourite TV programme?
What are your favourite things?
What's the worst thing in the world?

The opposite sex

Give us your ideas about the opposite sex.

Describe your ideal date.
Describe your least ideal date.

Yourself

Lastly, can we have your ideas about yourself?

Which of these do you think you are? Tick them.

good-looking ☐	fun ☐	happy ☐
interesting ☐	boring ☐	bossy ☐
intelligent ☐	friendly ☐	shy ☐
quiet ☐	nice ☐	honest ☐

continued from T25

Your Blind Date File

- Say *Look at 'Your Blind Date File'*. Ask *What is it about?*
- Students give their ideas (in the mother tongue if necessary).

> **Answer key**
> *It's a form for people who want to go on the Blind Date Show. It asks for information about the person.*

- Ask *What kind of information does the form ask for?* Say *Look through the form. Find any questions (or words) you do not understand.*
- Students look through the form and note the questions.
- Students give their ideas. Explain where necessary. (Alternatively, get students to look for the unknown words in a dictionary and guess what the questions mean.)

From here, students can do the task individually, or you can use the file for a pair work activity. For pair work, proceed as follows:

- Divide the class into pairs.
- One student in each pair closes his/her book. The other student asks the questions in turn and notes the answers on a separate sheet of paper.
- Students reverse roles and repeat.
- Choose some students to say what they found out about their partner.
- At home, students complete their Blind Date File and stick a photograph in it.

PROJECT

My family

This project is an individual project.
It can be done in class or at home.

- Introduce the project topic.
- Revise family members and ways of describing people.
- Discuss what students can put in a project about their family.
- Students look at the picture on page 26. Read the instructions in **a** and **b** aloud.
- Students look at the family tree on page 23. Make sure students understand the conventions for drawing a family tree.
- Students plan their project.
- Students produce a rough draft of their project.
- Discuss the rough drafts and suggest corrections.
- Students produce a finished project. Students can do their project either on a large poster or in a book.
- Students display their projects.
- Discuss the projects. Ask:
  What did you find easy or difficult in doing the project?
  What did you like or dislike about doing the project?
  How did you illustrate your project?

▶ **Pronunciation: page T112**

LEARNING DIARY

> **Note**
> Discuss in the mother tongue.

A Students look at the contents list on page 19.

   They draw a face next to each item to show how well they think they know it.

B Students do the self-check in the Workbook on page 23.

C Divide the class into pairs or groups of three or four.

   Students compare their answers. Go round the class and check for any common problems.

   Students compare their self-check results with the faces they drew.

   In the whole class ask *What problems did you find with the self-check?* Students suggest problem areas.

   Take remedial action, as necessary. (See Introduction page vii for possible strategies.)

Ask What did you like best in this unit? What didn't you like? Students give their responses. Ask Why? Take note of student responses. They can help you to adjust your teaching towards the things that motivate the students most.

CULTURE SPOT
Workbook page 23

• Students look quickly at the Culture spot.

• Ask *What do you already know about this topic?*

• Students give their ideas. Discuss these ideas.

• Students read the notes.

• Encourage students to compare their culture's custom with the British use of titles.

UNIT 4 Time

You can start immediately with the Victoria Road story on page 28, or you can pre-teach *can/can't*, using the material on page 27. If you wish to pre-teach the language, use the following procedure.

> **Note**
> At this stage you only need to introduce the grammar items, so that students can understand the story more easily. There are exercises later for more concentrated practice. Spend no more than 5 minutes on the pre-teaching.

1 Introduce *can*.

   • Mime dancing (or use the picture on page 27). Say *I can dance.*

   • Choose a student. Ask *Can you dance?*

   • Elicit response *Yes, I can.*

   • Choose another student. Ask *What can he/she do?*

   • Elicit response *He/she can dance.*

   • Repeat with three more students.

   • Repeat whole procedure for two other verbs, for example: *sing, play tennis, swim,* or *speak English.*

2 Introduce *can't*.

   • Students look at the picture on page 27.

   • Point to the girl. Say *She can dance.* Students repeat.

   • Point to the boy. Say *He can't dance.* Students repeat.

   • Mime flying. Say *I can't fly.*

   • Choose a student. Ask *Can you fly?*

   • Elicit response *No, I can't.*

   • Choose another student. Ask *What can't he/she do?*

   • Elicit response *He/she can't fly.*

   • Repeat with three more students.

   • Repeat whole procedure for other verbs, for example *ski, play the guitar.*

3 • Start the Victoria Road story on page 28.

PROJECT

My family

This is my Mom. Her name's Marion.

This is my Dad. His name's John.

This is my little sister Claire. She's ten.

This is my big brother, Simon. He's an architect.

This is Simon's girlfriend. Her name's Julia.

This is my little brother, Bobby. He's seven.

```
Albert    =  Bertha      Raymond   =  Ena
Clark        Clark       Wilson       Wilson
              |                        |
              └───────────┬───────────┘
                          |
                 John  =  Marion
                          |
        ┌────────┬────────┴────────┬────────┐
      Simon      Me             Claire     Bobby
```

a Write about your family.

- Find a photograph of your family.
- Write some information about the people in your photograph.

  their names
  their relationships to you
  their jobs

b Draw a family tree for your family.

- Describe the people in your family tree.

  Example
  My grandmother has got dark hair and brown eyes. She's tall.

- Who do you look like in your family?

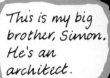

Learning diary

A Look at the first page of this unit. How well do you know these things now? Look at each point in the contents list.

If you know it well, draw a happy face.

If you know it fairly well, draw a face like this.

If you don't know it well, draw a sad face.

B Try the self-check in the Workbook.

C Compare your answers with a partner. Discuss any problems with your teacher.

3

▶ Pronunciation: page 112

4 time

Contents

Grammar points

28   **Victoria Road:** At the dance

30   **Language work**   **can / can't**

31   **Reading:** Terry's timetable   **days of the week**

32   **Listening:** Telling the time   **times of day**

33   **Interaction:** Kamala's appointment   **on / at + time**

34   **Project:** My ideal school timetable

can / can't; times

The main grammar point in this unit is:

can / can't

VICTORIA ROAD

At the dance

- Books closed. Ask *What happened in the last episode of 'Victoria Road'?*
- Students give their responses. Ask follow-up questions. They can use the mother tongue at this stage.

Answer key
Sue told Terry that she has arranged a date for him for the dance on Saturday. The girl's name is Jane Fox. However, Jane has already got a boyfriend, who is very big. Kamala wondered what Sue was up to.

- Students open their books and read the questions.
- Choose students to read the questions aloud. Make sure everyone understands the questions.
- Students look through the picture story to find the answers to the questions. They can refer to the full text, too.
- Students give their answers to the questions. (Students use the mother tongue, if necessary at this stage.)

Answer key
Sue, Kamala, Terry, Jane Fox and Darren Tooley
They are at the dance at the leisure centre.
Terry asks Jane Fox to dance, but her boyfriend is there. He tells Terry to go away. Sue is very amused. She has got her revenge.

- Explain any new vocabulary that students need to understand the dialogue.

- Say *Now look at the full dialogue.*
- Play the tape. Students listen and follow in their books.
- Play the tape again, if necessary.
- Ask *Why is Sue pleased?*

Answer key
She heard Terry say that she was bossy. Now she has got her revenge.

- Students read the statements and tick the boxes.
- Choose students to read each statement and give the answer.
- Ask *How do you know?* Students use the dialogue to justify their answers.

Note
This is a very important stage, because it shows whether students have understood the dialogue

Answer key
a R	b D	c W
d W	e W	f D
g W	h D	i R

- Books closed. Play the tape again. Stop after each utterance. Students repeat.
- Repeat any utterances that students find difficult.

Useful expressions

- Divide the class into pairs.
- Students look at the list of expressions. They write a translation in the boxes. They use the story and context to work out an appropriate mother-tongue expression.

Note
A lot of these expressions are idioms and cannot be translated word for word. Make sure students understand this.

- Students give their answers. Discuss as necessary.

Note
All right? This expression has a lot of different meanings depending on the context. Here it means: 'Do you understand?' or 'Is that clear?' It can be used in normal conversation, but here Darren Tooley uses it in a threatening way.

- Divide the class into groups of four.
- Explain the activity.
- Students choose their roles.
- Students read the dialogue.
- If time, change roles and do the dialogue again.
- Choose one group to act the dialogue in front of the class.

FOLLOW UP

- Students can do Exercise 7 in class or for homework.

Answer key
your	girl	hair	can't	over	near
got	aren't	Can	the (or *that*)	can	
boyfriend					

At the dance

1 Look at the story.

- Who are the people?
- Where are they?
- What happens?

> Terry, can you see that girl over there? She's your date.

2 🔊 Listen and follow in your books.

Sue Terry, can you see that girl over there? She's your date.

Terry Where? I can't see a girl with blond hair.

Sue Well, her hair's fair really. She's over there near the door.

Terry Oh yes, I can see her.

Sue Well, go on, Terry.

Terry Er, excuse me. Would you like to dance?

Jane I . . . er . . . I'm sorry. I can't.

Terry What? Can't you dance? Everybody can dance.

Jane No, I mean, I . . . .

Darren Can't you hear, stupid? The answer is 'No'. All right?

Jane This is my boyfriend, Darren.

Terry Oh, er, sorry.

Sue Ha, ha, ha! Oh, Terry, your face. It's so funny.

> Excuse me. Would you like to dance?

> I... er... I'm sorry. I can't.

> What? Can't you dance? Everybody can dance.

VICTORIA ROAD   28

Can't you hear, stupid? The answer is 'No'.

This is my boyfriend, Darren.

Oh, er, sorry.

Ha, ha, ha. Oh, Terry, your face. It's so funny.

Right, Wrong or Don't know?

		✓	✗	?
a	Sue, Kamala and Terry are at the dance.	❑	❑	❑
b	Kamala has got a date.	❑	❑	❑
c	Sue can't see Jane Fox.	❑	❑	❑
d	Jane Fox is near the window.	❑	❑	❑
e	Jane has got blond hair.	❑	❑	❑
f	Casey is at the dance.	❑	❑	❑
g	Jane's boyfriend isn't at the dance.	❑	❑	❑
h	Darren Tooley can't dance.	❑	❑	❑
i	Sue is pleased.	❑	❑	❑

 Listen again and repeat.

Useful expressions

5 How do you say these in your language?

over there

Her hair's fair.

really

near the door

Go on.

Excuse me.

Would you like to dance?

Stupid!

The answer is 'No'.

All right?

It's very funny.

6 Work in a group of four. Each person takes a part. Read the story.

FOLLOW UP

7 Complete this conversation.

Vince Where's .... girlfriend, Terry?

Terry What girlfriend?

Vince Your date — the .... with

blond .... I .... see her.

Terry She's .... there .... the door.

Vince She hasn't .... blond hair. But

why .... you with her?

Terry .... you see .... big guy with her?

Vince Yes, I ....

Terry That's her ....

Vince Oh.

29

LANGUAGE WORK

can/can't

BUILD UP

- Divide the class into pairs.
- Students complete the table. They use the Victoria Road dialogue to help them.
- Copy the table onto the board.
- Choose students to come out and complete the table.
- Students quote examples from the dialogue to justify the rule in the table.
- Students make ten sentences using the table.

> **Answer key**
>
> | I He She It We You They | can can't | see. dance. hear. |
> | --- | --- | --- |

Questions with 'can/can't'

a
- Students complete the sentences. While they are doing this, copy the gapped sentences onto the board.
  - Choose students to come out and complete the sentences.

> **Answer key**
> *Can you see*
> *Can't you*

b
- Students complete the table. They use the words from the table in Exercise 1.
  - Copy the table onto the board.
  - Choose students to come out and complete the table.
  - Students make six sentences using the table.

> **Answer key**
>
> | Can Can't | I he she it we you they | see? dance? hear? |
> | --- | --- | --- |

a
- Divide the class into pairs.
  - Students look at the pictures. They read the cue for each one.
  - Choose one pair. Demonstrate the activity using the example.
  - Repeat with another pair.
  - Remind students that they must make a note of the answers for **b**.
  - All pairs do the activity.
  - They reverse roles and repeat.

> **Note**
> Students may want to ask about activities that are not illustrated here. They may use their dictionaries to find words they need. For example: *Can you play tennis/the violin?*

b
- Choose students to tell the class what they have found out. They give answers like the example.

FOLLOW UP

- Students say what they can and can't do.
- Get one student to make a sentence with *I can/can't . . .* about a picture in Exercise 3.
- Get another student to make another sentence.
- Students make the remaining sentences.
- Students give their answers.

> **Answer key**
> (Choice of *can* or *can't* depends on student.)
> *I can/can't speak English.*
> *I can/can't play the guitar.*
> *I can/can't swim.*
> *I can/can't play badminton.*
> *I can/can't sing.*
> *I can/can't ski.*
> *I can/can't read music.*
> *I can/can't dance.*
> *I can/can't drive a car.*

READING

 • Play the tape. Students follow in their books and repeat.

• Books closed. Play the tape again. Students listen and repeat.

• Go round the class and say *Sunday, Monday, Tuesday*, etc. Point to students at random. The student must give the next day of the week.

2 Students have to understand abbreviations to do this activity.

• Divide the class into pairs or groups of three or four.

• Students look at the timetable. Ask *What is it? Whose is it?*

• Say *Can you guess what the subjects on the timetable are?*

• In their groups, students work out the names of the subjects. (Many will probably be similar in their own language.)

• Students give their ideas.

• Students look at Terry's homework diary. They work out the missing subjects in Terry's timetable.

• Groups give their answers.

> **Answer key**
> Monday: *Science*
> Tuesday: *French, Music*
> Wednesday: *English*
> Thursday: *Maths*
> Friday: *Technology*

3 a • Students continue working in pairs or groups.

• Students make a large chart like the one in the book.

b • Students read Terry's timetable in detail. They complete the first column of the chart. Students can add other information that is different from their own school, for example, the times or lengths of lessons.

• Students complete the second column with information about their own school.

• Copy the chart onto the board.

• Choose students to come out and complete the chart.

c • Students look at the chart on the board. They identify differences and similarities.

Notes
Terry and his friends go to a secondary school. The students here are aged 11 to 18. This timetable shows the National Curriculum, which was introduced into British schools in 1989. All students study these subjects to the age of 16.

RE is Religious Education.

PE is Physical Education.

French is the commonest foreign language in schools. Some schools also offer German and a few teach Spanish.

Registration At the start of the morning and the afternoon, the class teacher checks who is absent (not at school). Students must stay at school for the whole of the school day, unless they go home for lunch.

Assembly All schools must start the day with a period of collective worship. The whole school (teachers and students) come together, usually in the school hall. There is a religious service and any important notices are read out. The assembly is usually conducted by the headmaster or headmistress.

Break Some schools also have a break in the middle of the afternoon. Students would then go home a quarter of an hour later. Students are not allowed to leave the school during break.

Lunch Most students stay at school for their lunch. They may bring sandwiches or have a cooked school lunch. Some students go home for lunch or they buy a lunch at a local cafe.

homework diary Students get homework every day. They keep a diary to show what they must do. In a lot of schools parents are expected to sign the diary when the work has been done.

4 • Students go round the class. They ask *What are your two favourite subjects?*

• They continue till they find someone else with the same two favourites.

A GAME

5 • Divide the class into pairs.

• Students study Terry's timetable for one minute.

• Choose one pair. Demonstrate the activity.

• Repeat with another pair.

• All pairs do the activity.

• They reverse roles and repeat.

FOLLOW UP

6 Students write their own timetable in English.

LANGUAGE WORK

can / can't

BUILD UP

1 Put these words in the table.

can't   dance   hear   We   can   They

I		
He		
She	....	see.
It	....	....
....	....	....
You		
....		

Note: 'can't' is the short form of 'cannot'.

Questions with can/can't

2 **a** Look at the Victoria Road story. Complete these sentences:

.... that girl over there?

.... hear?

b Use the words in the table in Exercise 1. Put them in this table.

	....		
	....		
	....		
....	....		...............?
....	....		...............?
	....		...............?
	....		
	....		

3 **a** Ask people in your class what they can do.

Example
A 'Can you speak English?'
B 'Yes, I can.'

Use these cues.

speak English

swim

play the guitar

read music

dance

play badminton

sing

ski

drive a car

b Tell the class what you find out.

Example
He can play tennis. He can swim. He can't play the guitar. He can't read music.

FOLLOW UP

4 Look at the pictures in Exercise 3. Can you do these things? Write your answers.

READING

1 📻 **Listen and repeat.**

Sunday   Monday   Tuesday   Wednesday   Thursday   Friday   Saturday

2 **Here's Terry's school timetable. Read Terry's homework diary and complete the timetable.**

	MONDAY	TUESDAY	WEDNESDAY	THURSDAY	FRIDAY
9.00 / 9.10			REGISTRATION		
9.30			ASSEMBLY		
	English	Technology	Technology	Geography	Science
10.25 / 10.40			BREAK		
	R.E. *Snoozing*	*boring*	History	....	English
11.35					
	French	Maths	....	Technology	Maths
12.30 / 1.25			LUNCH		
1.30			REGISTRATION		
	....	🎵	Science	French	....
2.25					
	Maths	English	Science	*physical exhaustion* P.E.	Art
3.20					

Monday
English: pp 16-17 ex 6 and 7 for Wed. ✓
French: learn new words p 62 for ✓
    test on Tues.

Tuesday
Tech: computers p 17 ex 9 for Fri.
Maths: p 18 for Thurs.
Music: practise song p 23 for next Tues.

Wednesday
Science: write report on experiment
    for Mon.

3 **Compare Terry's school timetable to yours.**

a **Make a chart like this.**

Terry's school	our school

b **Complete the chart with this information.**

How many subjects has Terry got? What are they?
How many subjects have you got? What are they?
How many periods has Terry got of each subject?
How many periods have you got of each subject?

c **What differences are there? What things are the same?**

4 **Ask people in your class: 'What are your two favourite subjects?'**

A GAME

5 **Look at Terry's timetable for one minute.**

A Close your book.
B Ask questions.

Example
B *'Has Terry got French on Monday?'*
A *'Yes, he has.'*
B *'You're right.'* (or *'You're wrong.'*)

FOLLOW UP

6 **Write your timetable in English.**

LISTENING

Telling the time

 In this activity students use the information they have to predict what the pattern is.

a • Divide the class into pairs.

• Students look at the clocks and the times.

• Students work out what the missing times are. They can use these two clues:
  - All the times before the half hour have *past* and all those after the half hour have *to*.
  - The same numbers are used each side of the half hour: *twenty past, twenty to*, etc.

b • Copy the gapped times onto the board.

• Choose students to come out and complete them. Don't say at this stage whether they are right or wrong.

• Play the tape. Students listen and check their predictions.

• Complete the sentences on the board correctly.

c • Play the tape again. Students listen and repeat.

Five past two
Twenty-five to five
Eight o'clock
Half past four
Quarter to ten
Ten past eleven
Twenty to three
Quarter past one
Twenty past nine
Ten to twelve
Twenty-five past seven
Five to six

 • Students look at the clocks.

• Play the first example on the tape. Students complete the clock face.

• Check that everyone understands the task.

• Play the remaining examples.

• Draw blank clock faces on the board.

• Choose students to come out and complete them.

1 What's the time?
  It's twenty-five to one.
2 What's the time?
  It's ten past twelve.
3 What's the time?
  It's five to nine.
4 What's the time?
  It's four o'clock.
5 What's the time?
  It's twenty-five past three.
6 What's the time?
  It's half past eight.
7 What's the time?
  It's twenty to six.
8 What's the time?
  It's quarter to ten.

 • Divide the class into pairs.

• Choose one pair. Demonstrate the activity.

• Repeat with another pair.

• All pairs do the activity.

• They reverse roles and repeat.

FOLLOW UP

• Students write the time for each of the clocks in Exercise 2. They can do this exercise in class or at home.

Answer key
(See tapescript for Exercise 2.)

INTERACTION

Kamala's appointment

 a • Divide the class into pairs.

• Students look at the picture. Ask *Who is in the picture?* Elicit *Kamala*.

• Students look at the dialogue.

• Make sure everyone understands the task.

• Students write numbers in the boxes to put the conversation in the right order.

b • Play the tape. Students listen and check their order.

• Discuss any problems.

 Making an appointment

Kamala Can I have an appointment for next Wednesday, please?

Receptionist Yes, can you come at 10.30?

Kamala No, I can't come in the morning. Have you got an appointment in the afternoon after 4 o'clock?

Receptionist No, I'm sorry, not on Wednesday. Can you come on Thursday at 5.15?

Kamala Quarter past five? Yes, that's OK.

Receptionist Fine. So that's 5.15 next Thursday. And what is your name?

Kamala It's Kamala Wijeratne.

Receptionist Thank you, Kamala.

Kamala Thank you. Bye.

Receptionist Goodbye.

on/at

BUILD UP

 This is the first activity where the students complete the grammar rule in English. Try to get the learners to discuss grammar in English as much as possible. You may need to confirm it in the mother tongue in the early stages.

a • Students complete the sentence.

• Copy the gapped sentence onto the board.

• Choose one student to complete it.

• Students justify their answer from the dialogue in Exercise 1.

Answer key	
on	*at*

b • Students complete the rule.

• Copy the rule onto the board.

• Choose one student to complete it.

Answer key	
on	*at*

 • Students complete the phrases.

• Call out the times or days. Students give the correct preposition.

Answer key	
on	*at*
at	*at*
on	*at*
on	*on*
on	*at*

 • Divide the class into pairs.

• Demonstrate the activity with one pair.

• Students read the dialogue in pairs.

• They reverse roles and repeat.

 a • Divide the class into pairs.

• Explain the activity.

• Students choose their roles.

• Pairs make their dialogues. Go round and help with any problems.

b • Students reverse roles and repeat.

• Get two pairs to demonstrate their dialogues in front of the class.

FOLLOW UP

 • Students write their dialogue.

T33

LISTENING

Telling the time

1 Look at the photos of the clocks.

a What do you think the missing times are?

b Listen and complete the times.

c Listen again and repeat.

five past two   .... to five

eight o'clock   half past four   .... to ten   ten .... eleven   twenty to three

quarter past one   twenty .... nine   ten to twelve   twenty-five past seven ....

2 Listen and put the hands on the clocks.

....

....

....

3 Work with a partner. Look at the clocks in Exercise 2. Ask and answer.

A Point to a clock face and ask, 'What's the time?'.
B Give the answer.

FOLLOW UP

4 Write the times under the clocks in Exercise 2.

32

INTERACTION

Kamala's appointment

 on / at

BUILD UP

2 a **Complete this sentence.**

Can you come .... Thursday .... 5.15?

b **Complete this rule.**

> We use .... with days and .... with times.

3 **Write the correct preposition.**

.... Saturday	.... quarter past ten
.... five o'clock	.... 7.42
.... Wednesday	.... five to three
.... Tuesday	.... Friday
.... Sunday	.... 9.15

4 **Work with a partner. Act the dialogue from Exercise 1.**

5 a **Work with a partner. Make new dialogues.**

A Ask for an appointment.
B Give a day and time.
A You can't go at that time (or on that day). Ask for another time (or day).
B Give a new time (or day).
A Accept.
B Ask for the person's name.

b **Exchange roles and make a new dialogue.**

FOLLOW UP

6 **Write one of your dialogues from Exercise 5.**

1 **Kamala is making an appointment at the dentist.**

a **Put the conversation in the correct order.**

- [ ] Yes, can you come at 10.30?
- [ ] Thank you, Kamala.
- [ ] No, I'm sorry, not on Wednesday. Can you come on Thursday at 5.15?
- [ ] Thank you. Bye.
- [ ] Can I have an appointment for next Wednesday, please?
- [ ] Goodbye.
- [ ] It's Kamala Wijeratne.
- [ ] Quarter past five? Yes, that's OK.
- [ ] No, I can't come in the morning. Have you got an appointment in the afternoon after 4 o'clock?
- [ ] Fine. So that's 5.15 next Thursday. And what is your name?

b **Listen and check your answer.**

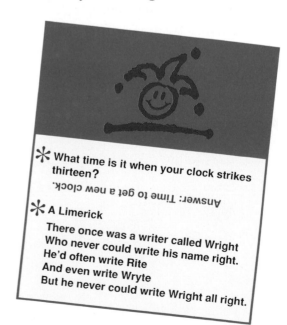

✳ What time is it when your clock strikes thirteen?

Answer: Time to get a new clock.

✳ A Limerick

There once was a writer called Wright
Who never could write his name right.
He'd often write Rite
And even write Wryte
But he never could write Wright all right.

PROJECT

My ideal school timetable

This project does not require a lot of writing. It has two purposes:

- to stimulate thinking about what students want from education;
- to develop students' ability to use dictionaries. Students will probably not know the names of some of the things they want to put in their timetables. Encourage them to use dictionaries and include some dictionary practice. This project can be done as an individual project or as a group project. It will probably work best as a group project, because it will provide some interesting discussion.
It can be done in class or at home.

- Books closed. Ask *What do you think of your school timetable?*
- Students give their ideas.
- Students open their books. They read the questions. Make sure they understand the questions.
- Students discuss the questions.
- Ask *How will you find the names of things to put in your timetable?* Students should use you only as a last resort.
- Give some practice in using dictionaries at this point, if you wish.
- Students plan their timetable.
- Students produce a rough draft of their timetable.
- Discuss the rough drafts and suggest corrections. Refer them back to the dictionary, if necessary.
- Students produce a finished timetable. Students can do their project either as a large poster or in a book.
- Students illustrate their timetable.
- Students display their projects.
- Discuss the projects. Ask *How did you find the words you needed for the project? What have you learnt about finding words that you need?*

▶ **Pronunciation: page T113**

LEARNING DIARY

> **Note**
> Discuss in the mother tongue.

A Students look at the contents list on page 27. They draw a face next to each item to show how well they think they know it.

B Students do the self-check in the Workbook on page 31.

C Divide the class into pairs or groups of three or four.

Students compare their answers. Go round the class and check for any common problems.

Students compare their self-check results with the faces they drew.

In the whole class ask *What problems did you find with the self-check?* Students suggest problem areas.

Take remedial action, as necessary. (See Introduction page vii for possible strategies.)

Ask *What did you like best in this unit? What didn't you like?* Students give their responses. Ask *Why?* Take note of student responses. They can help you to adjust your teaching towards the things that motivate the students most.

CULTURE SPOT
Workbook page 30

- Divide the class into pairs or groups of three or four.
- Students look quickly at the text.
- Ask *What is the text about?*
- Students give their ideas.
- Ask *What do you already know about this topic?*
- Students give their ideas. Discuss these ideas.
- Say *Read the Culture spot text. Note anything that you find interesting or unusual.*
- Ask comprehension questions about the text.
- Students give their answers. Explain any words that students need.
- Ask *Did you find anything interesting or unusual?*
- Students give their ideas.
- Read each comparison question in turn.
- Discuss each question. Encourage students to compare their situation with the one in the text.

UNIT 5 Places

You can start immediately with the Victoria Road story on page 36, or you can pre-teach imperatives, using the material on page 35. If you wish to pre-teach the language, use the following procedure.

> **Note**
> At this stage you only need to introduce the grammar items, so that students can understand the story more easily. There are exercises later for more concentrated practice. Spend no more than 5 minutes on the pre-teaching.

1   Introduce positive imperatives.

- Books closed. Choose a student. Say *Stand up.* Use gesture to show what you want.

- Repeat with other students.

- Repeat procedure with *Sit down.*

- Choose more students and give more instructions, for example: *Come here./Pick up your book/pen*, etc.

2   Introduce negative imperatives.

- Choose a student. Say *Stand up.*

- Choose another student. Say *Don't stand up.* Show what you mean.

- Choose other students. Say *Stand up* to some and *Don't stand up* to others.

- Repeat procedure with *Sit down* and *Don't sit down.*

3   Students look at the examples on page 35.

- Choose one student to read the imperatives.

4   • Start the Victoria Road story on page 36.

PROJECT

My ideal school timetable

What do you think of your school timetable?

- Do you like your lessons?
- What lessons would you really like to have at school?

    Example
    pop music, sport, karate, driving

- When would you really like to be at school?
- Would you like to start earlier or later?
- Would you like to have a shorter day?
- Would you like to go to school on Sundays, too?

Write your ideal school timetable. Show the subjects and the times of your lessons.

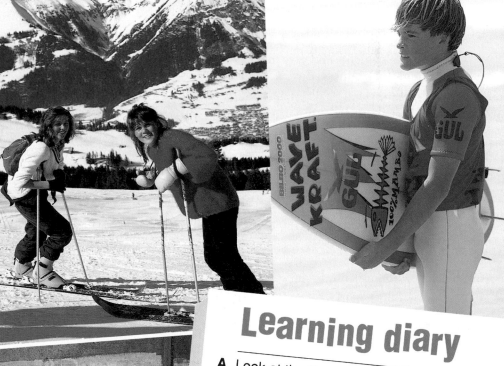

Learning diary

A Look at the first page of this unit. How well do you know these things now? Look at each point in the contents list.

If you know it well, draw a happy face.

If you know it fairly well, draw a face like this.

If you don't know it well, draw a sad face.

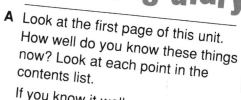

B Try the self-check in the Workbook.

C Compare your answers with a partner. Discuss any problems with your teacher.

4

▶ Pronunciation: page 112

5 places

Contents   Grammar points

36	**Victoria Road:** At the cafe	imperatives
38	**Reading:** A computer	must / mustn't
40	**Listening:** House for sale	there is / are
42	**Interaction:** Polite requests	Would you like to ...?
43	**Project:** My home	

The main grammar points in this unit are:

imperatives

there is / are

There is a computer on the table.
There are two books on the table.
There isn't a bag on the table.
Is there a pen on the table?

VICTORIA ROAD

At the cafe

- Books closed. Ask *What happened in the last episode of 'Victoria Road'?*
- Students give their responses. Ask follow-up questions. They can use the mother tongue at this stage.

Answer key
Sue had overheard Terry saying that she was bossy. She arranged a blind date for Terry with a girl called Jane Fox, who has a very big boyfriend called Darren. At the dance Terry asked Jane to dance. Jane's boyfriend appeared and told Terry to go away. Terry was very annoyed, but Sue was pleased.

- Students open their books and read the questions.
- Choose students to read the questions aloud. Make sure everyone understands the questions.
- Students look through the picture story to find the answers to the questions. They can refer to the full text, too.
- Students give their answers to the questions.

Answer key
Sue, Kamala, Terry and *Darren Tooley*
(See the summary of the last episode, above.)
They are in a cafe.
(See the summary of the last episode, above.)

- Ask *What happens in this episode?* Using the pictures, students give a summary of the story. (Students use the mother tongue, if necessary at this stage.)
- Explain any new vocabulary that students need to understand the dialogue.

Answer key
Sue and Kamala are in a cafe. Kamala has to leave. Terry comes in. He buys a cheeseburger and a drink. Terry is still annoyed with Sue, because of the date with Jane Fox, so he doesn't want to sit with her. Sue insists and takes hold of Terry's tray. Terry pulls away. His drink spills down the neck of someone sitting at the next table. It is Darren Tooley! Terry drops his tray and runs.

- Say *Now look at the full dialogue.*
- Play the tape. Students listen and follow in their books.
- Play the tape again, if necessary.

Notes
at the dentist You can say 'at the dentist's', as with 'at the doctor's' but you can't hear the 's' after 'st', so most people nowadays say 'at the dentist'.

I'm not friends with you means 'I'm annoyed with you and I don't want to be your friend'.

- Students read the statements and tick the boxes.
- Choose students to read each statement and give the answer.
- Ask *How do you know?* Students use the dialogue to justify their answers.

Note
This is a very important stage, because it shows whether students have understood the dialogue.

Answer key
a *R*
b *W*
c *W* (We don't know from this story, but from the dialogue on page 33, we know that it is at 5.15.)
d *W* (Kamala needs 45 minutes to get there.)
e *R*
f *D*
g *R*
h *R*

- Books closed.
- Play the tape again. Stop after each utterance. Students repeat.
- Repeat any utterances that students find difficult.

Useful expressions

5
- Divide the class into pairs.
- Students look at the list of expressions. They write a translation in the boxes. They use the story and context to work out an appropriate mother-tongue expression.

> **Note**
> A lot of these expressions are idioms and cannot be translated word for word. Make sure students understand this.

- Students give their answers. Discuss as necessary.

Imperatives

BUILD UP

6
a
- Divide the class into pairs.
- Students read the examples.
- Students draw two columns in their exercise books and write the examples from **a**.

b
- Students look for more examples of imperatives in the story and add them to their columns.
- Draw two columns on the board.
- Students give examples. Write them in the columns.

> **Answer key**
> *Put your tray here.*   *don't go*
> *Get out of the way!*   *Don't touch it!*

c
- Explain the activity.
- Play the tape. Pause after each instruction. Students follow the instructions.

Stand up.
Don't sit down.
Pick up your exercise book.
Open your book.
Pick up your pen.
Close your eyes.
Don't open your eyes.
Sit down.
Write your name in your book.
Draw a face.
Open your eyes.
Look at your picture.

7
- Divide the class into groups of three.
- Students choose their roles.
- Students read the dialogue.
- If time, change roles and do the dialogue again.
- Choose one group of three to act the dialogue in front of the class.

FOLLOW UP

8
- Students can do Exercise 8 in class or at home.

> **Answer key**
> a *Kamala and Sue are at a cafe.*
> b *It's half past four.*
> c *Kamala must go because she has got an appointment at the dentist.*
> d *Terry's drink is a chocolate milk shake.*
> e *Terry's cheeseburger and drink are £1.75.*
> f *The boy at the next table is Darren Tooley.*

At the cafe

1 Look at the story.
- Who are the people?
- What do you know about them?
- Where are they?
- Why is Terry angry with Sue?

2 📼 Listen and follow in your book.

Kamala It's half past four. I must go, Sue.

Sue Oh, don't go, Kam. Here's Terry. He's still angry with me.

Kamala I'm sorry, Sue. I've got an appointment at the dentist and I mustn't be late.

Sue Oh, OK. See you tomorrow.

Kamala Hi, Terry.

Sue Hi, Terry.

Terry Hello, Kamala.

Terry A cheeseburger and a chocolate milk shake, please.

Assistant That's £1.75, please.

Sue Sit here, Terry.

Terry Don't talk to me, Sue. I'm not friends with you.

Sue Don't be silly, Terry. Put your tray here.

Terry Don't touch it!

Sue Be careful, Terry!

Terry Oh, my drink!

Boy Aargh.

Darren You again!

Terry Get out of the way!

Darren Come here!

Aargh.

Don't touch it!

Oh, my drink!

Don't be silly, Terry. Put your tray here.

You again!

5

Get out of the way!

Come here!

6

Right, Wrong or Don't know?

		✓	✗	?
a	Sue and Kamala are at the cafe.	❏	❏	❏
b	Sue has got an appointment at the dentist.	❏	❏	❏
c	Kamala's appointment is at five o'clock.	❏	❏	❏
d	The dentist is near the cafe.	❏	❏	❏
e	Terry isn't friends with Sue.	❏	❏	❏
f	Sue's drink is a chocolate milkshake.	❏	❏	❏
g	Terry can't find a seat.	❏	❏	❏
h	The boy is Jane Fox's boyfriend.	❏	❏	❏

4 Listen again and repeat.

Useful expressions

5 How do you say these in your own language?

I must go.

I mustn't be late.

He's angry with me.

I'm not friends with you.

Don't be silly.

Be careful!

Get out of the way!

Come here!

Imperatives

BUILD UP

6 a **Look.**

Be careful!	Don't be silly!
Sit here!	Don't talk to me!

b **Find more examples of imperatives in the Victoria Road story. Put them in the correct column.**

c 🔊 **Listen and follow the instructions.**

7 Work in a group of three. One person is Terry, one person is Sue, one person is all the other parts. Read the story.

FOLLOW UP

8 Answer these questions in full sentences.

a Where are Kamala and Sue?
b What's the time?
c Why must Kamala go?
d What is Terry's drink?
e How much are Terry's cheeseburger and drink?
f Who is the boy at the next table?

READING

A computer

- Students look at the pictures.
- Choose one student to read out the instructions.
- Students give their answers.

Answer key
They are about computers.
The object is called a disk.

In this activity students must work out which instruction goes with which picture. They can use a range of different clues (see **3** below). Don't give the answers. The aim of the exercise is that students should use what they already know to work out the meaning.

a
- Divide the class into pairs.
- Students read the instructions on the screen. They match the correct picture.
- Students give their answers.

Answer key
d *Keep the disk in its envelope.*
f *Keep the disk between 18° and 50°C.*
Put the disk on the tray.
a *Put the disk into the drive carefully.*
c *Don't touch this part.*
g *Don't put the disk near a magnet.*
b *Don't bend the disk.*
e *Don't write on the disk with a ballpoint pen or a pencil.*

b
- Students find the instruction that is not real by identifying the one which does not fit any of the pictures.

Answer key
Put the disks on a tray.

- Ask *Why must you do these things with disks?*
- Students give their ideas.

Answer key
(possible answers)
If you don't put it in the disk drive carefully, you can bend the disk.
If you bend it, it will not spin smoothly in the disk drive and the computer will not be able to read it.
If you touch the disk itself you can erase data.
Keeping the disk in its envelope keeps dust off the disk.
A ballpoint pen can make a groove in the disk.
When you use a pencil, small bits of graphite dust can fall onto the disk.
The plastic of the disk is affected by extreme temperatures.
Data is recorded on disks by magnets in the disk drive. Another magnet can corrupt the data.

- Ask *Do you know any other rules for looking after disks or computers?*
- Students give their ideas.

This activity encourages the students to think consciously about how they can work out meaning from context. This will help the students to become more confident in dealing with unknown words or passages where they do not know every word.

- Divide the class into groups of four.
- Students discuss how they did the task.
- Groups give their ideas. Get students to give examples.

Answer key
(possible clues)
international word
similarity to mother tongue
pictures
existing knowledge about computers and disks
general knowledge about science
logic

All these words, except *keyboard*, are in the exercise instructions or the text on the screen. Students should be able to work out the meanings.

must/mustn't

BUILD UP

a
- Students complete the sentences.
- Copy the gapped sentences onto the board.
- Choose one student to complete them.

b

Note
This section will only be relevant if the mother tongue uses 'must', and 'mustn't' differently.

- Choose another student to write a translation under each sentence on the board.
- Ask *What differences can you see?*

- Students look at the example.
- Get one student to read the example aloud.
- Students look at the instructions on the computer screen. Get another student to give the next sentence.
- Students make the remaining sentences.
- Students give their answers.

Answer key
You mustn't bend the disk.
You mustn't touch this part.
You must keep the disk in its envelope.
You mustn't write on the disk with a ballpoint pen or a pencil.
You must keep the disk between 18°C and 50°C.
You mustn't put the disk near a magnet.

FOLLOW UP

Students write their rules about what they must and must not do in the classroom.

International words

This activity introduces students to the concept of language borrowing. It is important for students to appreciate that many words are similar in several languages, as they can then use their mother-tongue knowledge to work out or guess words that they may not know in English. Many English words are now used internationally. English is also a great borrower of words from other languages. In this activity, students first consider computer vocabulary, where many languages use the English terms. They then look at more general words which may be similar in the mother tongue. Some of these are English words, some are words that English has borrowed from other languages and some are words that derive from a common origin.

- Divide the class into pairs or small groups.
- Introduce the topic. Read the instructions aloud to 'Do you know what they are?'
- Students look at the words. They note down:
  - the ones that they have heard of.
  - the meanings, if they know them.

Note
The words may not be exactly the same in the mother tongue, but may be similar.

- Students give their ideas.

Answer key
a bit the basic unit of a computer's memory. Bit is short for binary digit.

a kilobyte Eight bits make a byte. A kilobyte is a thousand bytes. The size of a computer's memory is usually given in kilobytes (e.g. 64K)

a mouse a device used on a number of computers for moving around the screen and giving instructions to the computer. It is faster than using the keyboard.

a VDU a monitor

a floppy disk/a hard disk Information is stored on disks. A hard disk is built into the computer and cannot be removed. A floppy disk is much smaller and can be put into and removed from the disk drive.

hardware/software Hardware is the computer itself – the keyboard, the VDU, the disk drive. Software is the computer programs. If you compare it with a cassette recorder, the actual recorder is hardware; the cassettes you play on it are the software.

RAM/ROM Most computers have two kinds of memory. Random Access Memory (RAM) contains data that can be changed. You can also use the data in RAM in any order. The second type of memory is Read Only Memory (ROM). Data in ROM cannot be changed and can only be used in the set sequence. ROM is used for the computer's basic functions.

- Students look at the second part of the activity.
- Read the instructions aloud.
- Students look at the list and say whether they are used in the mother tongue.
- Students look through the book and find more words that are similar in English and their mother tongue.
- Students give their ideas.
- Ask *Do you know any words from our (your) language that are used in English?*
- Students give their ideas.

READING

A computer

1 Look at the pictures on the envelope.

- What are they about?
- Look at the monitor.
  Read the instructions
  on the screen.
- Find the name of this:

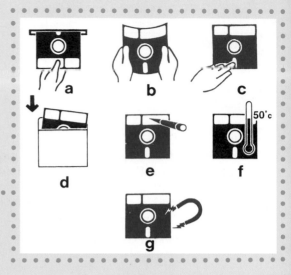

a   b   c

d   e   f

g

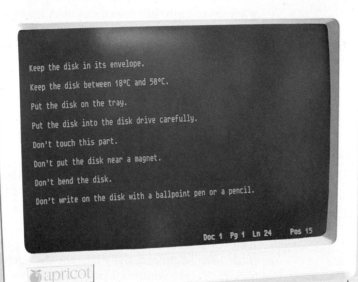

Keep the disk in its envelope.

Keep the disk between 18°C and 50°C.

Put the disk on the tray.

Put the disk into the disk drive carefully.

Don't touch this part.

Don't put the disk near a magnet.

Don't bend the disk.

Don't write on the disk with a ballpoint pen or a pencil.

Doc 1 Pg 1 Ln 24   Pos 15

2 a Match the instructions on the screen to the correct picture. Note there are eight instructions but only seven pictures.

b One of the instructions is not a real instruction. Which one?

3 How did you match the instructions and the pictures? What clues did you use?

4 Label these things in the pictures.

an envelope	a ballpoint pen
a magnet	a disk
a monitor	a keyboard
a disk drive	a screen

38

must / mustn't

a Look at the Victoria Road story. Complete these.

I .... go.

.... be late.

b Translate the sentences.

6 Say what you must and mustn't do with a computer disk.

Example
You must put the disk into the disk drive carefully.

FOLLOW UP

Write five things that you must do and five things that you mustn't do in your classroom.

INTERNATIONAL WORDS

A lot of computer words are international. Look at the computer words on this page. Are they the same in your language?

Here are some more words. Do you know what they are?

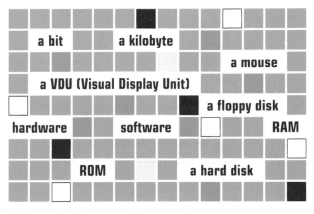

a bit   a kilobyte

a mouse

a VDU (Visual Display Unit)

a floppy disk

hardware   software   RAM

ROM   a hard disk

A lot of other words are the same or very similar in different languages.

Do you recognize any of these words? What are they in your language?

a supermarket	sport
a disco	a hi-fi
a bar	a stereo
a toilet	a video
a shop	jeans
a sandwich	coffee
a jumbo jet	a menu
a pizza	a restaurant
a film	football
pop music	a goal

Find some more words in this book that are the same or similar in your language.

What words has your language given to English?

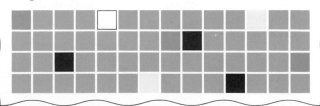

LISTENING

House for sale

Note
The situation in this section is very typical in Britain. Most people in Britain own their own house (usually with a mortgage). People also move house quite frequently, either to get a larger house or because they need to move to another town for a new job. If they want to move they have to sell their existing house and buy a new one. It can be a long, expensive and frustrating process. In this story, a buyer is coming to look at a house that's for sale. The house shown here is a typical British house.

 In this activity students work out the meaning of new words from the context. Explain and discuss the context fully, but don't give the meaning of the words in the list.

a • Divide the class into pairs.

• Students look at the house.

• Explain the situation.

• Students read the words in the list.

• Choose one student to read out the words.

• ▪️▪️ Play the tape once. Students listen.

▪️▪️ **House for sale**
Seller Oh, hello. Are you here about the house?
Buyer Yes.
Seller Come in. Well, this is the hall.
Buyer Hmm, it's big.

Seller Oh, this is our dog. Down, boy. Sit. Good boy.

Seller There are three rooms downstairs. Oh, and there's a toilet, too. This is the living room.

Seller This is the dining room. No, don't sit down!

Buyer Oh!
Seller That's our cat. And this is the kitchen.
Buyer Very nice.
Seller And now we can go upstairs.
Buyer Excuse me, where's the downstairs toilet?
Seller Oh, sorry, the loo is under the stairs.
Buyer Thank you. Er, what's this door? Is it a cellar?
Seller No, don't open it!

Seller No, there isn't a cellar here. That's a cupboard.
Buyer Oh, I see.

Seller Here we are, upstairs. There are three bedrooms. This is our son's bedroom . . . .

Seller This is our bedroom.
Seller That's my husband. This is our daughter's bedroom.
Buyer Mm, this is nice.
Seller This is the bathroom.

Seller And that's my daughter.
Buyer Oh, pleased to meet you.
Seller Would you like to go outside now.
Buyer No, er thank you. I must go. I . . .

Seller There's a garage and there are two gardens. Down, boy!
Buyer No, No. I must go. Thank you. Goodbye.

b • Students label as many parts of the house as they can.

• Play the tape again. Students listen again.

• Students complete the diagram.

• Point to the parts of the house. Students give the names.

• Students correct their diagrams, if necessary.

Answer key
1 *hall*	5 *toilet*	9 *bathroom*
2 *living room*	6 *cupboard*	10 *garage*
3 *dining room*	7 *stairs*	11 *garden*
4 *kitchen*	8 *bedroom*	

The two boxes that are not numbered are for *downstairs* (kitchen, living room etc.) and *upstairs* (bedroom, bathroom etc.).

• Play the tape again.

• Students follow on their labelled diagrams.

• They listen for another word for 'toilet'.

Answer key
loo
Note
This is an informal, but polite word and is the most likely to be used.

there is/there are

BUILD UP

- Students complete the table.
- Copy the gapped table onto the board.
- Choose students to come out and complete the table.
- Students make six sentences using the table.

Answer key

There	is	a cellar.
	isn't	
	are	three bedrooms.

- Get one student to give the first sentence.
- Students make the remaining sentences.
- Students give their answers.

Answer key

a	*are*	e	*are*	h	*are*
b	*is*	f	*isn't*	i	*is*
c	*isn't*	g	*aren't* (There are nine rooms if		
d	*aren't*		you include the hall as a room.)		

there is/there are: questions

BUILD UP

a
- Students complete the sentences. (Play the tape again, if you want to remind students.)
- Copy the sentences onto the board.
- Choose students to complete them.

b
- Students give the rule.

Answer key

We put 'is' or 'are' in front of 'there'.

a
- Divide the class into pairs.
- Choose one pair. Demonstrate the activity.
- Repeat with another pair.
- All pairs do the activity.
- They reverse roles and repeat.

Answer key

Is there a cellar?
No, there isn't.

Are there two gardens?
Yes, there are.

How many bedrooms are there?
There are three bedrooms.

Is there a toilet downstairs?
Yes, there is.

How many rooms are there downstairs?
There are five rooms downstairs.

b
- Students ask and answer. They use the questions in **a**.
- Students reverse roles and repeat.
- Ask *What differences are there between a typical home in our country and the British house here?*
- Students give their ideas.

FOLLOW UP

a
- Students learn the new words for a test.
- Students write the dialogues from Exercise 5a in class or at home.

Answer key

(See Answer key for Exercise 5a.)

LISTENING

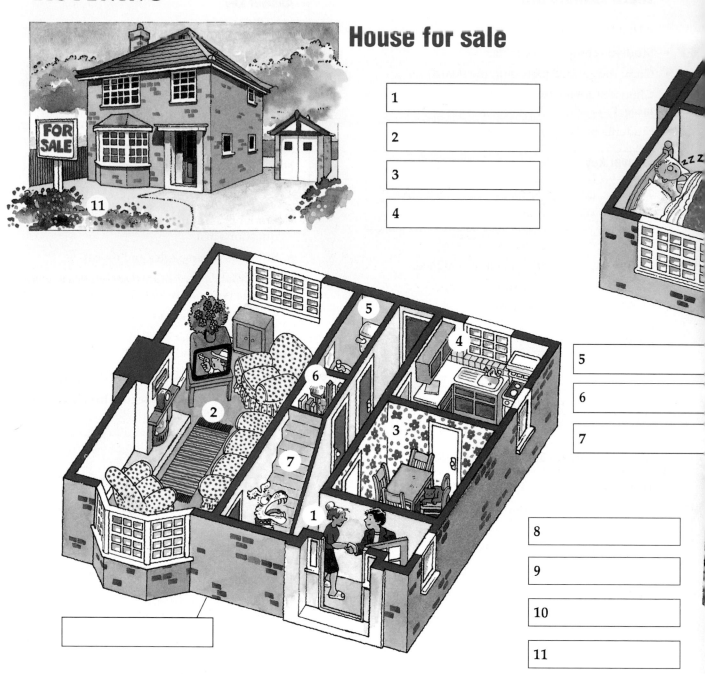

House for sale

1 _____

2 _____

3 _____

4 _____

5 _____

6 _____

7 _____

8 _____

9 _____

10 _____

11 _____

_____

1

a 🔊 Look at this house. Some people want to buy it. Listen and match these words to the correct places.

dining room	hall	toilet
upstairs	stairs	cupboard
living room	garage	kitchen
downstairs	bedroom	
bathroom	garden	

b Label the diagram.

c Listen again. Find another word for 'toilet'.

there is / there are

BUILD UP

2 Complete the table with these words.

isn't   are   is

		....	a cellar.
		....	
There			
		....	three bedrooms.

40

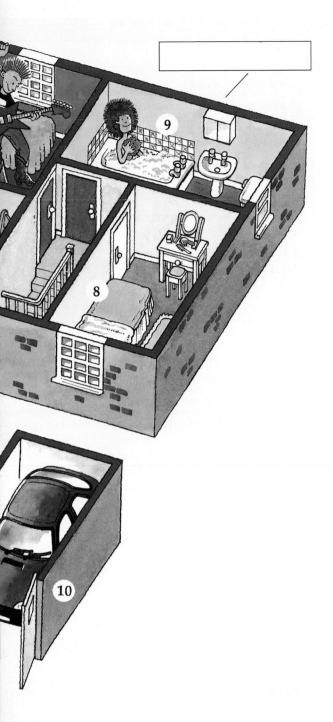

there is / there are : questions

BUILD UP

4
a Complete the questions.

There is a garage.

.... a garage?

There are two toilets.

.... two toilets?

b How do we make questions with 'there is / are'? Explain in your own language.

5
a Work with a partner. One person is the buyer. One is the seller of the house. Ask and answer.

Example
A *How many rooms are there upstairs?*
B *There are four rooms upstairs.*
A *Is there a garage?*
B *Yes, there is.*

Use these cues.

How many rooms / upstairs?
a garage?
a cellar?
two gardens?
How many bedrooms?
a toilet / downstairs?
How many rooms / downstairs?

b Ask your partner about his / her house or flat.

Example
How many rooms are there in your house?

FOLLOW UP

6
a Learn the new words.

b Write your dialogues from Exercise 5a.

3 Look at the house again. Complete these sentences with the correct word.

a There .... two toilets.

b There .... a loo under the stairs.

c There .... a cellar.

d There .... two bathrooms.

e There .... two gardens.

f There .... a bathroom downstairs.

g There .... eight rooms in the house.

h There .... three bedrooms.

i There .... a cupboard downstairs.

✳ How can you tell if an elephant has been in the fridge?
Answer: Because there are footprints in the butter.

41

INTERACTION

Polite requests

 a • Divide the class into pairs.

• Students look at the requests and answers.

• Get one pair to read the example.

• Students match the remaining items.

• Pairs give their answers.

> **Answer key**
> *Excuse me. Where's the loo?*
> *It's upstairs.*
>
> *Excuse me. What's the time?*
> *It's five past nine.*
>
> *Excuse me. Have you got change for a pound?*
> *Yes, here you are.*
>
> *Excuse me. Is there a telephone near here?*
> *Yes, there's one in King Street.*
>
> *Excuse me. Can you speak English?*
> *Yes, I can. Can I help you?*
>
> *Excuse me. What's that called in English?*
> *It's a tree.*

b • Students match their dialogues to the correct picture.

• Point to a picture. Choose a pair. They give the dialogue.

• Repeat for the other pictures.

> **Answer key**
> 1 *Excuse me. Where's the loo?*
> 2 *Excuse me. Is there a telephone near here?*
> 3 *Excuse me. Can you speak English?*
> 4 *Excuse me. Would you like to dance?*
> 5 *Excuse me. What's the time?*
> 6 *Excuse me. Have you got change for a pound?*
> 7 *Excuse me. What's that in English?*

c • Students practise the dialogues in pairs.

• They reverse roles and repeat.

 2 • Divide the class into new pairs.

• Students choose their roles.

• Explain the activity.

• Choose one pair. Demonstrate with the first two dialogues.

• Pairs make their dialogues. Go round and help with any problems.

• Students reverse roles and repeat.

• Choose pairs to demonstrate each dialogue in front of the class.

> **Answer key**
> *Excuse me. Would you like to dance?*
> *No, I'm sorry. I can't.*
>
> *Excuse me. Where's the loo?*
> *I'm sorry. I don't know.*
>
> *Excuse me. What's the time?*
> *I'm sorry. I don't know.*
>
> *Excuse me. Have you got change for a pound?*
> *No, I'm sorry. I haven't.*
>
> *Excuse me. Is there a telephone near here?*
> *I'm sorry. I don't know.*
>
> *Excuse me. Can you speak English?*
> *No, I'm sorry. I can't.*
>
> *Excuse me. What's that called in English?*
> *I'm sorry. I don't know.*

 3 • Students remain in their pairs.

• Explain the activity.

• Students choose their roles.

• Elicit suggestions for possible requests. For example:
Excuse me. Where's the computer room?
Excuse me. Is there a dentist near here?
Excuse me. Have you got my pen?

• Pairs make their dialogues. Go round and help with any problems.

• Students reverse roles and repeat.

• Get pairs to demonstrate their dialogues in front of the class.

FOLLOW UP

 4 • Students write their dialogues for Exercise 1b in class or at home.

> **Answer key**
> (See Exercise 1.)

PROJECT

My home

This is an individual project. It can be done in class or at home.
This project provides an opportunity for two kinds of presentation:

- a labelled plan;
- a connected paragraph.

- Students look at page 43.
- Say *Describe the houses here.*
- Students give their ideas.
- Ask *Would you like to live in any of these places? Why/Why not?*
- Students give their ideas.
- Get one student to read the project instructions.
- Check that students know how to draw a labelled plan of a house. Look at pages 40–41 for a model.
- On the board build up a model paragraph using the questions on page 43. Students give their ideas.

Answer key
(possible model)
My home is a ...
It's in ... near ...
There are ... rooms (downstairs and ... rooms upstairs).
There's a (balcony/garage/cellar), but there isn't a (balcony/garden/cellar).
I like my home because ... , but I don't like ...
I would love to live on a boat because ....

- Pay careful attention to sentence linkers.
- (If you prefer, say *Imagine the house on page 40 was your home. Write a paragraph to describe it. Use this as your model.*)
- Students plan their project.
- Students produce a rough draft of their project.
- Discuss the rough drafts and suggest corrections.
- Students produce a finished project. Students can do their project either on a large poster or in a book.
- Students display their projects.
- Discuss the students' paragraphs about their homes. Use some examples to illustrate paragraph construction.

▶ **Pronunciation: page T113**

LEARNING DIARY

Note
Discuss in the mother tongue.

A Students look at the contents list on page 35.

They draw a face next to each item to show how well they think they know it.

B Students do the self-check in the Workbook on page 40.

C Divide the class into pairs or groups of three or four.

Students compare their answers. Go round the class and check for any common problems.

Students compare their self-check results with the faces they drew.

In the whole class ask *What problems did you find with the self-check?* Students suggest problem areas.

Take remedial action, as necessary. (See Introduction page vii for possible strategies.)

Ask *What did you like best in this unit? What didn't you like?*
Students give their responses. Ask *Why?* Take note of student responses. They can help you to adjust your teaching towards the things that motivate the students most.

CULTURE SPOT
Workbook page 40

- Divide the class into pairs or groups of three or four.
- Students look quickly at the text.
- Ask *What is the text about?*
- Students give their ideas.
- Ask *What do you already know about this topic?*
- Students give their ideas. Discuss these ideas.
- Say *Read the Culture spot text. Note anything that you find interesting or unusual.*
- Ask comprehension questions about the text.
- Students give their answers. Explain any words that students need.
- Ask *Did you find anything interesting or unusual?*
- Students give their ideas.
- Read each comparison question in turn.
- Discuss each question. Encourage students to compare their situation with the one in the text.

INTERACTION

Polite requests

1 Look at these requests and answers.

a Match the requests to the answers.

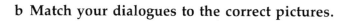

Excuse me. Would you like to dance?
Excuse me. Where's the loo?
Excuse me. What's the time?
Excuse me. Have you got change
   for a pound?
Excuse me. Is there a telephone
   near here?
Excuse me. Can you speak English?
Excuse me. What's that called in English?

It's five past nine.
It's a tree.
Yes, here you are.
Yes, please.
Yes, I can. Can I
   help you?
Yes, there's one in
   King Street.
It's upstairs.

b Match your dialogues to the correct pictures.

c Work with a partner. Practise the dialogues.

2 Here are some different answers to the requests. Make new dialogues with these answers.

No, I'm sorry. I can't.
I'm sorry. I don't know.
No, I'm sorry. I haven't.

3 Work with a partner.

A Make a request.
B Give an answer.

FOLLOW UP

4 Write your dialogues from Exercise 1b.

1

2

3

4

5

6

7

PROJECT

My home

Draw a plan of your home and label the rooms.

Write about your home.

- Is it a house or a flat?
- Where is it?
- How many rooms are there?
- Is there a balcony, a garden or a cellar?

Do you like your home? Say what you like or don't like. Say why.

Look at the places on this page. Would you like to live in any of them? Say why.

Learning diary

A Look at the first page of this unit. How well do you know these things now? Look at each point in the contents list.

If you know it well, draw a happy face.

If you know it fairly well, draw a face like this.

If you don't know it well, draw a sad face.

5

B Try the self-check in the Workbook.

C Compare your answers with a partner. Discuss any problems with your teacher.

UNIT 6   Revision

 • Students look at the picture of the boy and girl.
• Say *Look through this page and find the boy's name.*

Answer key
Justin

• Students write their descriptions of the boy and girl.
• Choose one student to read his/her description of the boy and one student to read his/her description of the girl.

Answer key
(possible answer)
The boy has got short black hair.
He is tall. He is a dancer.
The girl has got long brown hair. She is not very tall. She's a dancer, too.

 • Divide the class into pairs.
• Students read the text.
• Ask questions about the text:
   What is the boy's name?
   How old is he?
   What school does he go to?
   What do you know about his school timetable?
   What are his favourite subjects?
   What can he do?
   How many brothers and sisters has he got?
   What are their jobs?
   What are his parents' jobs?

 • Students remain in their pairs.
• Explain the activity.
• Students complete the dialogue. All the information they need is in the text.
• Choose one pair to read out their dialogue.

Answer key
of Music and Dance
What's your name
How do you spell
How old are you
Are you from
in the afternoon
we have
are your favourite subjects
Can you sing
I can play
an engineer
my sister is a
parents
are both teachers

 • Students read the dialogue in pairs.
• They reverse roles and repeat.

 • Divide the class into new pairs, if you wish.
• Students choose their roles.
• Explain the activity.
• Pairs make their dialogues. They use the questions in Exercise 3. Go round and help with any problems.
• Students reverse roles and repeat.
• Get two pairs to demonstrate their dialogues in front of the class.

FOLLOW UP

 • Students write one of their own dialogues.

LANGUAGE WORK

1 **a** • Students look at the clock faces.

   • Explain the activity.

   • Play the tape. Stop after each time. Students draw the hands.

   • Draw clock faces on the board.

   • Students come out and complete the faces on the board.

   • Play the tape again.

1 What's the time?
   It's quarter past ten.
2 Can I have an appointment for tomorrow, please?
   Yes, can you come at ten past eleven?
3 I must go. The bus is at twenty to four.
4 This is Radio 581. It's a quarter to eight.
5 What's the time?
   It's five to three.
6 When is your appointment?
   It's at five past two.
7 When is the dance?
   It's on Friday at half past nine.
8 When's lunch?
   At one o'clock.

   b • Divide the class into pairs.

   • Choose one pair. Demonstrate the activity.

   • Repeat with another pair.

   • All pairs do the activity.

   • They reverse roles and repeat.

2 • Divide the class into pairs.

   • Students look at the sentences.

   • Demonstrate the activity.

   • Students draw lines to connect the parts of the dialogues.

   • Choose pairs to read out the dialogues.

   • Pairs practise the dialogues.

Answer key

Would you like to dance?
Yes, please.

How much are these pens?
They're 60p each.

Can you swim?
No, I can't.

Would you like a drink?
No, thank you. I've got a milk shake.

How much is this badge?
It's 85p.

What's the time?
It's quarter to nine.

Where's the loo?
It's over there.

WORD WORK

3 • Divide the class into nine groups.

   • Groups write down the words for each category.

   • Draw nine columns on the board. Write the categories at the top of each column.

   • Allocate one of the categories to each group.

   • A member of each group comes out to the blackboard and writes the list for his/her group's category.

   • Other groups check the lists on the board. They can then suggest other words from their own lists.

4 **a** • Students complete the description.

   • Choose one student to read out the description.

Answer key

She has got dark hair and brown eyes.
Her hair is short.

---

   b • Students write descriptions of the other people.

   • Choose students to read out their descriptions.

Answer key

He has got blond hair and grey (or blue) eyes. His
* hair is short.*
She has got ginger hair and green (or blue) eyes.
* Her hair is long.*

FOLLOW UP

5 • Students add words to each of the lists in Exercise 3.

6 revision

READING

1 Look at this picture.
Describe the boy
and the girl.

2 Read this text about the boy.

Justin Gleeson is a dancer. He's 16 and he's a student at the Liverpool School of Music and Dance. He isn't from Liverpool. His home is in London.

The students have dance lessons in the afternoon. But in the morning they must do other school subjects. Justin's favourite subjects are Science, French and Music. He can't sing, but he can play the guitar.

Justin has got a brother and a sister. But he is the only dancer in the family. His brother is an engineer and his sister is a doctor. His parents are both teachers.

3 Complete this interview with Justin.

Interviewer Hello. Today I'm at the Liverpool
School .... Here's one of
the students. .... ?

Justin Justin Gleeson.

Interviewer .... 'Gleeson'?

Justin G – L – double E – S – O – N.

Interviewer ...., Justin?

Justin I'm 16.

Interviewer .... Liverpool?

Justin No, I'm not. I'm from London.

Interviewer Tell me about the school.

Justin We have dance lessons ....

................................., but in the morning

.... other school subjects.

Interviewer What ....

.... ?

Justin Science, French and Music.

Interviewer .... ?

Justin No, I can't, but .... the guitar.

Interviewer Are you the only dancer in your family?

Justin Yes, I am. My brother is ....

and .... doctor.

Interviewer And your .... ?

Justin My mum and dad ....

4 Work with a partner. Role play the dialogue.

5 Your partner is a student at the School of
Music and Dance. He / She can be a dancer, a
singer or a musician. Interview him / her.

FOLLOW UP

6 Write your interview from Exercise 5.

44

LANGUAGE WORK

1 a **Listen and complete the clock faces. Write the times under the clocks.**

1 ....

4 ....

2 ....

5 ....

3 ....

6 ....

b **Work with a partner. Use your completed clocks. Ask and answer.**

A 'What's the time?'

B 'It's ....'

2 **Match these to make dialogues.**

Would you like to dance?
It's quarter to nine.
How much are these pens?
Can you swim?
Would you like a drink?
It's over there.
How much is this badge?
No, thank you. I've got a milk shake.
No, I can't.
What's the time?
They're 60p each.
Yes, please.
It's 85p.
Where's the loo?

W O R D   W O R K

3 **Write down the names of:**

6 rooms
4 sports
3 kinds of clothes
3 drinks
6 members of a family
5 colours
6 school subjects
5 things in a classroom
4 days of the week

4 **Look at these pictures.**

a **Complete this description of the first girl.**

She .... got .... hair and brown ....

Her .... is short.

b **Describe the other people.**

FOLLOW UP

5 **Add one more word to each list in Exercise 3.**

⬛S⬛T⬛A⬛R ⬛S⬛Q⬛U⬛A⬛R⬛E

- Divide the class into pairs.
- Explain the activity.
- Students find and mark the names of the pop stars in the square.
- Students give their answers.
- Ask *Who found them all?*
- Ask *Which of these stars have you heard of? Do you like them?*
- Students give their ideas.

Answer key

```
P O T H E B A L M C L A P T J M C C
T N E W K I D S O N T H E B L O C K
L H M A D O N N A B A W K I D L I
T H E R O L L I N G S T O N E S E D
K I B B N S I M P H Z Z T K S L G
D T L U E N T D I R E S T R A I T S
W H A M A A E P O N R H G P M O T
Z N C O L N T Q W E E O E A E P N O
Z N K L Y J U L E N F X P D R L J N
T E B D O O S U E Y O Y O U I E O E
O S O S U H Q T L S B M L S C M H A
P I X N N P U C R B E U I P C I N T
A C D C G E O M A H U S C N L N H A
V A N I L L A I C E E I E E A D Q C
W E T W E T N U C A W P S U D
K A B B V A P L E U R A B K T P E G
A I T S L E N G W H O M B I O T S M
M S D Y D U R A N D U R A N N L I N
```

POP CHAIN

Students will probably not know most of these titles. Instead they use their knowledge of the language to work out where the breaks must come in the chain. For example, 'to me and' would not make sense, but 'me and my girl' does.

- Divide the class into new pairs.
- Students look at the Pop chain.

Note

If you prefer the students to do the task without being able to look at the key, you can copy the chain onto the board. Students do the task with their books closed.

- Explain the activity. Students draw rings round the first four examples.
- Students find the remaining fourteen. In each case, the last word of one title is the first word of the next.
- When everyone has finished, say *Now turn your books upside down and check your answers in the key.* (If you prefer, get students to exchange books to check with the key.)

Answer key
(See Student's Book.)

▶ **Pronunciation: page T113**

You can start immediately with the Victoria Road story on page 48, or you can pre-teach the present simple tense using the material on page 47. If you wish to pre-teach the language, use the following procedure.

Note
At this stage you only need to introduce the grammar items, so that students can understand the story more easily. There are exercises later for more concentrated practice. Spend no more than 10 minutes on the pre-teaching.

1 Introduce *I live ... .*
   - Say *I live in* (name of your street).
   - Choose a student. Ask *Where do you live?*
   - Elicit the answer *I live in ... .*
   - Repeat with other students.

2 Introduce *He/she lives ... .*
   - Books open. Point to Sue. Say *She lives in Victoria Road.*
   - Choose a student. Ask *Where does Sue live?*
   - Elicit the answer *She lives in Victoria Road.*
   - Repeat with other students. Ask about Sue, Terry and Vince.

3 Contrast *live* and *lives.*
   - Choose one student. Ask *Where do you live?*
   - Student responds.
   - Choose another student. Ask *Where does he/she live?*
   - Student responds.

4 - Don't practise questions intensively at this stage. Students only need to recognize them.

5 - Start the Victoria Road story on page 48.

STAR SQUARE

Don't be a square. Try the Star Square.
Find the names of these singers and groups in the square.

- Duran Duran
- Wham
- Elton John
- the Beatles
- Simple Minds
- Madonna
- New Kids on the Block
- Status Quo
- Depeche Mode
- Genesis
- Black Box
- ZZ Top

```
P O T H E B A L M C L A P T J M C C
T N E W K I D S O N T H E B L O C K
L H J M A D O N N A B A W K I D L I
T H E R O L L I N G S T O N E S E D
K I B B N N S I M P H Z Z T K S L G
D T L U E N T D I R E S T R A I T S
W H A M I A A E P O N R H G P M O T
Z N C O L N T O W E E O E A E P N O
Z N K L Y J U L E N F X P D R L J N
T E B D O O S U E Y O Y O U I E O E
O S O S U H Q T L S B M L S C M H A
P I X N N P U C R B E U I P C I N T
A C D C G E O M A H U S C N L N H A
V A N I L L A I C E E I E E A D Q C
W E T W E T W E T N U C A W P S U D
K A B B V A P L E U R A B K T P E G
A I T S L E N G W H O M B I O T S M
M S D Y D U R A N D U R A N N L I N
```

- Roxy Music
- Wet Wet Wet
- Eric Clapton
- Dire Straits
- Queen
- AC DC
- Neil Young
- Vanilla Ice
- Aha
- Abba
- the Police
- the Rolling Stones

STONE COLD LOVE ME BABY I LOVE YOU BELONG TO ME AND MY GIRL IN MY DREAMS OF YOU CAN DO IT MUST BE LOVE ME OR LEAVE ME AND YOU ARE THE ONE WAY TICKET TO RIDE THE LOVE TRAIN TO YOUR HEART OF

POP CHAIN

Look at the words in the chain. There are eighteen pop song titles.

Here are the first four:

Stone Cold
Cold Love
Love Me, Baby
Baby, I Love You

Find the other fourteen.

Answers

Stone Cold	It Must Be Love
Cold Love	Love Me Or Leave Me
Love Me, Baby	Me And You
Baby I Love You	You Are The One
You Belong To Me	One Way Ticket
Me And My Girl	Ticket To Ride
Girl In My Dreams	Ride The Love Train
Dreams Of You	Train To Your Heart
You Can Do It	Heart Of Stone

► Pronunciation: page 112

7 sport

Contents

Grammar points

48   **Victoria Road:** Do you know Terry Moore?

50   **Reading:** A footballer's week

51   **Listening:** Karen's day

53   **Interaction:** An interview

54   **Project:** A sports survey

the present simple tense: statements

verbs with -es endings

the present simple tense: negative

the present simple tense: questions

The main grammar point in this unit is:

the present simple tense

I live in Victoria Road.

Sue lives in Victoria road too.

I don't live in Victoria Road.

She doesn't live in Victoria road.

They don't live in Victoria Road.

Where do you live?

Does Vince live in Victoria Road?

VICTORIA ROAD

Do you know Terry Moore?

- Books closed. Ask *What happened in the last episode of 'Victoria Road'?*
- Students give their responses. Ask follow-up questions. They can use the mother tongue at this stage.

Answer key
Sue had overheard Terry saying that she was bossy. She arranged a blind date with a girl called Jane Fox, but Jane has got a big boyfriend, called Darren Tooley. He wasn't very pleased when Terry asked Jane to dance. Terry was annoyed with Sue. In the last episode Terry went into a cafe when Sue was there. Sue wanted Terry to sit with her, but he didn't want to. She got hold of his tray. Terry pulled away and his drink spilt down the neck of someone sitting at the next table. It was Darren Tooley. Terry ran out of the cafe.

- Students open their books and read the questions.
- Choose students to read the questions aloud. Make sure everyone understands the questions.
- Students look through the picture story to find the answers to the questions. They can refer to the full text, too.
- Students give their answers to the questions.

Answer key
Darren Tooley, his friends, Casey Royston
In the street, near Victoria Road
They are talking about Terry.
Darren wants to get his revenge for what happened in the cafe.

- Ask *What happens in this episode?* Using the pictures, students give a summary of the story. (Students use the mother tongue, if necessary at this stage.)
- Explain any new vocabulary that students need to understand the dialogue.

Answer key
Darren and his friends are looking for Terry. They ask Casey about him. They find out where Terry lives. They also find out that he goes to school and comes home with his friends, but he comes home alone on Wednesdays, because he plays table tennis at school.

- Say *Now look at the full dialogue.*
- Play the tape. Students listen and follow in their books.
- Play the tape again, if necessary.
- Ask *Why does Darren Tooley want Terry? What is the surprise?* Students give their ideas.

Answer key
Terry annoyed Darren at the dance and then he spilt his drink down Darren's neck. Darren wants his revenge.
The surprise is that they will wait for Terry after school one day and get him.

Notes
Are you his friends? Terry is new to the neighbourhood, so Casey would not know Terry's friends.

He plays table tennis after school. Most schools organize voluntary sports or other activities. These are done at lunchtimes, after school or on Saturday mornings.

- Students answer the questions. They give full answers. Check carefully the use of the *-s* on the 3rd person singular. This activity can be done orally or in writing.

Answer key
a *He wants Terry.*
b *He lives in Victoria Road.*
c *He goes to school at 8.15.*
d *He goes with Casey and some other friends.*
e *They get the bus.*
f *They come home at half past three.*
g *He plays table tennis.*
h *He comes home at quarter past four.*
i *It's a surprise.*

- Books closed.
- Play the tape again. Stop after each utterance. Students repeat.
- Repeat any utterances that students find difficult.

Useful expressions

- Divide the class into pairs.
- Students look at the list of expressions. They write a translation in the boxes. They use the story and context to work out an appropriate mother-tongue expression.

> **Note**
> A lot of these expressions are idioms and cannot be translated word for word. Make sure students understand this.

- Students give their answers. Discuss as necessary.

The present simple tense

BUILD UP

a • Divide the class into pairs.
- Students complete the sentences. While they are doing this, copy the gapped sentences onto the board.
- Choose students to come out and complete the sentences.

> **Answer key**
> *know*
> *knows*
> *come*
> *comes*

- Ask *What do you notice about the verbs?*

b • Students complete the table. They use the dialogue to help them. While they are doing this copy the table onto the board.
- Choose students to come out and complete the table.
- Students make six sentences using the table.

> **Answer key**
>
> | I | | |
> |---|---|---|
> | You | | |
> | We | *live* | |
> | They | | *in Victoria Road.* |
> | | | *at number 20.* |
> | He | | *here.* |
> | She | *lives* | |
> | It | | |

c • Students complete the rule.

> **Answer key**
> *he   she*

- Divide the class into pairs.
- Students choose their roles.
- Students read the dialogue.
- If time, change roles and do the dialogue again.
- Choose one pair to act the dialogue in front of the class.

FOLLOW UP

- Students can do Exercise 8 in class or at home.

> **Answer key**
> (The answers about the student's own life will depend on his/her individual situation.)
> a *lives*
>   *I live in . . .*
> b *goes*
>   *I go to school . . .*
> c *gets*
>   *I get . . .*
> d *comes*
>   *I come home at . . .*
> e *plays*
>   *I play . . .*

Do you know Terry Moore?

Where does he live?

He lives in Victoria Road at number 20.

1 ▼ Look at the story.

- Who are the people?
- Where are they?
- What are they talking about? Why?

Excuse me. Do you know Terry Moore?

Oh yes, I know Terry.

Are you his friend?

Oh, yes. Terry knows m

Casey We come home at half past three.

Darren Does Terry come home at half past three every day?

Casey Er, no. On Wednesday he plays table tennis after school. He comes home late.

Darren On Wednesday? Hmm. What time does he come home?

Casey He gets the quarter past four bus, I think.

Darren Thank you. That's very helpful.

Casey That's OK. I must tell Terry about you.

Darren Oh no, don't do that. It's a surprise.

Casey Oh, I see. OK.

Why does Darren Tooley want Terry? What is the surprise?

2 ▄ Listen and follow in your books.

Darren Excuse me. Do you know Terry Moore?

Casey Oh yes, I know Terry. Are you his friend?

Darren What? . . . Oh, yes. Terry knows me. Where does he live?

Casey He lives in Victoria Road at number 20.

Darren What time does he go to school?

Casey He goes to school with me and some other friends. We get the bus at 8.15.

Darren When do you come home?

3 ▼ Answer these questions.

a Who does Darren Tooley want?
b Where does Terry live?
c When does Terry go to school?
d Who does he go with?
e How do they go to school?
f What time do they come home?
g What does Terry do on Wednesday?
h What time does he come home on Wednesday?
i Why mustn't Casey tell Terry about the boys?

4 ▼ Listen to the story again and repeat.

VICTORIA ROAD

(4)

Does Terry come home at half past three every day?

Er, no. On Wednesday he plays table tennis after school. He comes home late.

(5)

Thank you. That's very helpful.

That's OK. I must tell Terry about you.

Oh no, don't do that. It's a surprise.

(6)

Useful expressions

5 How do you say these in your language?

We get the bus.

He comes home late.

the quarter past four bus

That's very helpful.

Don't do that.

It's a surprise.

Oh, I see.

The present simple tense

BUILD UP

6 a Look at the Victoria Road story. Complete these sentences.

I .... Terry.

Terry .... me.

We .... home at half past three.

He .... home late.

This is the present simple tense. It describes regular activities.

b Complete this table with 'lives' and 'live'.

I			
You			in Victoria Road.
We		....	
They			at number 14.
He			
She		....	here.
It			

c When do we add -s to the verb?

Complete the rule.

> We add 's' with ...., ... and it.

7 Work with a partner. One person is Darren Tooley and one is Casey. Read the dialogue.

FOLLOW UP

8 Complete these sentences about Terry with the correct verb. Then write a sentence about your own life.

a Terry .... in Victoria Road.

I ....

b Terry .... to school with his friends.

I ....

c Terry .... the bus to school.

I ....

d Terry .... home at half past three.

I ....

e Terry .... table tennis.

I ....

READING

A footballer's week

- Divide the class into pairs.
- Students look at the pictures. They say what they are about.

Answer key
a footballer

- Point to people and things in the pictures. Ask *Who/What's this?*
- Students look through the text to find the answers.

- Explain the activity.
- Students read the text and write the day below each picture.
- Point to each picture in turn. Students give their answers.
- Ask *How do you know?* Students justify their answers from the text.

Answer key

1	*Saturday afternoon*	5	*Thursday*
2	*Monday afternoon*	6	*Sunday*
3	*Wednesday*	7	*Tuesday*
4	*Saturday morning*	8	*Thursday afternoon*

- Students read the words.
- Play the tape.
- Ask *What do you notice?*

Answer key
The -es ending is pronounced /ɪz/.

- Explain the rule: *After s, ch and sh we pronounce the -es ending /ɪz/.*
- Play the tape again, if you have time.

Students do this exercise orally at this stage. Pay careful attention to the /ɪz/ endings.
- Students look at the example.
- Get one student to read the example aloud.
- Get another student to give the next sentence.
- Students make the remaining sentences.
- Students give their answers.

Answer key
He goes out with his girlfriend on Sunday.
He plays golf on Monday.
From Tuesday to Friday he goes to the club and practises.
On Tuesday he sees the team doctor.
On Wednesday he watches a video of last week's match.
On Thursday the manager chooses the new team.
On Saturday he gets up at 9.30. He goes to the club at 1 o'clock. He plays a match in the afternoon.

- Students label the pictures.
- Choose students to point to the things in their book.

Students can answer these questions individually or you can organize it as pair work, like this:
- Divide the class into pairs.
- One student asks the questions.
- Students reverse roles and repeat.
- Students report to the class what they have found out.

FOLLOW UP

- Students write a description of Bobby Best's week from Exercise 4. They can do it in class or at home.

Answer key
(See Exercise 4.)

LISTENING

Karen's day

- Students look at the picture.
- Read out the questions.
- Make sure everyone understands the task.
- Play the tape.
- Students give their answers.

> **Answer key**
> a *Karen Spencer*
> b *an ice skater*
> c *in London*
> d *She gets up and goes to bed very early.*

a • Divide the class into pairs.
- Students look at the chart.
- Make sure everyone understands the task. Point out that the first time they will hear is not the first thing in the chart.

b •   Play the tape. Students fill in the times.
- Copy the chart onto the board.
- Choose students to come out and complete the chart.
- Play the tape again, if there are problems.

 Karen's day

Presenter Karen Spencer lives in London. She's fifteen. Every day she goes to school at half past eight. She comes home at half past three. She has her tea at four o'clock and she does her homework from five till seven. What does she do then? She doesn't watch television, she doesn't go to the cinema, she doesn't go to discos. She goes to bed.

Presenter Why do you go to bed at quarter past seven, Karen?

Karen I want to be an ice skater. I practise every day from Monday to Saturday. But I can't practise in the morning or in the afternoon, because I'm at school.

Presenter Can't you practise in the evening?

Karen No, I can't. There are other people at the skating rink in the evening.

Presenter Karen practises early in the morning. Her day starts at four o'clock in the morning. She gets up and has her breakfast. At half past four Mr Spencer takes Karen to the skating rink. She practises for three hours from five o'clock and she finishes at eight o'clock.

Presenter What do you do then, Karen?

Karen I don't go home, because my school is near the skating rink. Between eight o'clock and 8.30 I have a shower and I get dressed. Then it's time for school.

Presenter What do you do on Sundays?
Karen I don't practise on Sundays, but I don't stay in bed. I get up at five o'clock and I do my homework. If I stay in bed, I can't sleep on Sunday night.

The present simple tense: negative

BUILD UP

a • Students read the sentences.
- Explain that this is the negative of the present simple.
- Use the examples on page 47, if you want more examples.

b • Divide the class into pairs.
- Students complete the table.
- Copy the table onto the board.
- Choose students to come out and complete the table.
- Students make ten sentences using the table.

> **Answer key**
>
> | I You We They | don't | go to school. live in Victoria Road. |
> |---|---|---|
> | He She It | doesn't | get up at 4 o'clock. play the guitar. |

c • Ask *Is there an '-s' after 'doesn't'?*
- Students give their answer.
- Explain that the *-s* is on *doesn't*, so it is not needed on the verb.

T51

READING

A ftballer's week

▼ **1** Look at these pictures. What are they about?

1 ————————————— 5 —————————————

2 ————————————— 6 —————————————

3 ————————————— 7 —————————————

4 ————————————— 8 —————————————

▼ **2** Read the text. Write the day below each picture.

Every Saturday afternoon Bobby Best plays football. He is the goalkeeper for Barchester United. What does he do for the rest of the week?

'Sunday and Monday are my weekend. On Sunday I go out with my girlfriend. On Monday my girlfriend goes to work. She works in a bank. I get up late and then I play golf in the afternoon.

From Tuesday to Friday I go to the club at 9 o'clock. The team practises in the morning. On Tuesday the team doctor sees all the players. On Wednesday the manager shows a video of Saturday's match. When we practise on Thursday, the manager watches all the players. In the afternoon he chooses the new team.

On Saturday I get up at 9.30, and I have breakfast. I go to the club at 1 o'clock and the match starts at 2.30.'

▼ **3** 🔊 Listen. You will hear the footballer talking about his week. What do you notice about these words?

practises   watches   chooses

▼ **4** Use the pictures. Describe Bobby Best's week.

Example
He plays football on Saturday afternoon.

▼ **5** Find examples of these things in the pictures. Label them.

team   doctor   player   match
manager   goalkeeper   football club

▼ **6** Answer these questions.

a Do you like football?
b What is your favourite team?
c Who is the manager?
d Who is your favourite player?
e When do football clubs play matches in your country?

FOLLOW UP

▼ **7** Write the answers to Exercise 4.

Karen's day

 1 📼 Look at the picture. Listen and find this information.

a What is the girl's name?
b What does she want to be?
c Where does she live?
d What is unusual about her day?

 2 a Look at the chart.

activity	time
get up	
go to the skating rink	
practise	
have a shower	
get dressed	
go to school	
come home	
have tea	
do her homework	
go to bed	

b Listen again. Write the times in the chart.

The present simple tense: negative

BUILD UP

3 a Look at these sentences about Karen.

She **doesn't go** to the cinema.
She **goes** to bed.

I **don't practise** on Sundays.
I **practise** every day from Monday to Saturday.

b Complete this table with 'don't' and 'doesn't'.

I You We They	....	go to school. live in Victoria Road. get up at 4 o'clock.
He She It	....	play the guitar.

c Is there an -s ending after 'doesn't'?

4 In this activity some of the statements are incorrect. Students complete the sentences so that they are true statements about Karen.

- Students look at the examples.
- Get one student to read one example aloud.
- Get another student to read the next example.
- Students make the remaining sentences.
- Students give their answers.
- Play the tape again to check answers.

Answer key
c *doesn't practise*
d *doesn't take*
e *practises*
f *doesn't go*
g *doesn't want*
h *doesn't finish*
i *doesn't stay*
j *goes*

 5
- Students look at the examples.
- Get one student to read the examples aloud.
- Get another student to give the next sentence.
- Students make the remaining sentences.
- Students give their answers.

Answer key
c *I don't practise in the afternoon.*
d *My mum doesn't take me to the skating rink.*
e *I practise for three hours a day.*
f *I don't go to the cinema in the evening.*
g *I don't want to be a dancer.*
h *I don't finish school at four o'clock.*
i *I don't stay in bed on Sundays.*
j *I go to bed at 7.15.*

 6
- Students discuss Karen's day.
- Ask students about their own sports and hobbies. When do they practise?

FOLLOW UP

- Students use the chart they completed in Exercise 2 to write about Karen's day. The first sentence is given to help them. They can do the exercise in class or at home.

Answer key
She gets up at four o'clock in the morning.
She goes to the skating rink at half past four.
She practises from five o'clock to eight o'clock.
She has a shower at eight o'clock.
She gets dressed between eight o'clock and half past eight.
She goes to school at half past eight.
She comes home at half past three.
She has her tea at four o'clock.
She does her homework from five o'clock to seven o'clock.
She goes to bed at quarter past seven.

INTERACTION

The present simple tense: questions

BUILD UP

 a
- Divide the class into pairs.
- Students complete the sentences. While they are doing this, copy the gapped sentences onto the board.
- Choose students to come out and complete the sentences.

Answer key
Do you
does he

b
- Students give more examples of questions from the Victoria Road story.

c
- Students complete the table. They use the Victoria Road dialogue to help them. While they are doing this copy the table onto the board.
- Choose students to come out and complete the table.
- Students quote examples from the Victoria Road story to justify the rule in the table.
- Students make ten sentences using the table.

Answer key

	I	
Do	*you*	*live in Victoria Road?*
	we	*play tennis?*
	they	*like American football?*
	he	*get the bus to school?*
Does	*she*	
	it	

d • Ask *What happens to the -s?*
Students give their answer.

e • Students complete the sentences. While they are doing this, copy the gapped sentences onto the board.

• Choose students to come out and complete the sentences.

> **Answer key**
> *play   watch*

• Point out that in both cases there is no *-s* ending.

2 **a** • Divide the class into pairs.

• Students read the first two sentences of the dialogue.

• Get one student to read them aloud.

• Get another student to give the next question.

• Students make the remaining questions.

• Choose one pair to give their dialogue.

> **Answer key**
> *do you do*
> *Do you see*
> *does she work*
> *do you do*
> *do you go*
> *does the team practise* (or *do you*)
> *does the doctor see*

b • Pairs make three more questions and answers.

• Choose two pairs to read their questions and answers.

> **Answer key**
> Possible questions:
> *When does the manager choose the team?*
> *What does the manager do on . . . ?*
> *When do you get up on Saturday?*
> *Do you have breakfast on Saturdays?*
> *What time does the match start?*
> *When do you go to the club on Saturdays?*
> *Does your girlfriend watch the match?*

c • Demonstrate the activity with one pair.

• Students read their complete dialogue from **a** and **b** in pairs.

• They reverse roles and repeat.

 a • Divide the class into new pairs.

• Pairs choose a sports star.

b • Students write six possible questions with *How? What? When?*, etc.

• Choose some students to read out their questions.

c • Students choose their roles.

• Pairs make their dialogues. Go round and help with any problems.

• Students reverse roles and repeat.

• Get two pairs to demonstrate their dialogues in front of the class.

FOLLOW UP

 • Students write their interview from Exercise 3 in class or at home.

A Day in Your Life

• Say *Look at 'A Day in Your Life'.* Ask *What is it about?*

• Say *Look through the form. Find any questions you do not understand.* Ask, in particular about questions b, k, q and t. Explain where necessary. (Alternatively, get students to look for the unknown words in a dictionary and guess what the questions mean.)

From here students can do the task individually, or you can use the file for a pair work activity. For pair work, proceed as follows:

• Divide the class into pairs.

• One student in each pair closes his/her book. The other student asks the questions in turn and notes the answers on a separate sheet of paper.

• Students reverse roles and repeat.

• Choose some students to say what they found out about their partner.

• At home, students complete the questionnaire for themselves.

4 Does Karen do these things? Complete the sentences.

Example
She gets up at four o'clock.
She doesn't catch the bus to the skating rink.

a She ....at four o'clock. (get up)

b She .... the bus to the rink. (catch)

c She .... in the afternoon. (practise)

d Mrs Spencer .... Karen to the skating rink. (take)

e Karen .... for three hours a day. (practise)

f Karen .... to the cinema in the evening. (go)

g She .... to be a dancer. (want)

h She .... school at four o'clock. (finish)

i She .... in bed on Sundays. (stay)

j She .... to bed at 7.15. (go)

5 What does Karen say?

Example
I get up at four o'clock.
I don't catch the bus to the rink.

6 What do you think about Karen's life?

FOLLOW UP

7 Use your chart from Exercise 2a. Describe Karen's day. Start like this.

Karen gets up at four o'clock in the morning.

INTERACTION

The present simple tense: questions

BUILD UP

1 a Look at the Victoria Road story on page 48. Complete these questions.

.... know Terry Moore?
What time .... go to school?

b **Find more examples of questions in the story.**

c **Complete this table with these words.**

you   I   she   Do   they   he   we   it   Does

	....		live in Victoria Road?
....	....		play tennis?
	....		like American football?
	....		get the bus to school?
....	....		

d **Look at these sentences. What happens to the -s ending?**

She lives here.
Does she live here?

He gets the bus.
Does he get the bus?

e **Complete these sentences.**

Terry plays table tennis.

Does Terry .... table tennis?

Kamala watches TV.

Does Kamala .... TV?

Look at the text about the footballer's week on page 50.

2 **a** Look at the text about the footballer's week on page 50. Here is part of an interview with him. Complete the questions. Use the verbs in brackets.

Interviewer Do you go to work on Sunday and Monday?

Footballer No, I don't. That's my weekend.

Interviewer What .... on Sunday? (do)

Footballer I go out with my girlfriend.

Interviewer .... your girlfriend on Monday, too? (see)

Footballer No, I don't. She goes to work.

Interviewer Where ....? (work)

Footballer In a bank.

Interviewer What .... on Monday? (do)

Footballer I get up late and then I play golf in the afternoon.

Interviewer When .... to the club? (go)

Footballer I go to the club at 9 o'clock from Tuesday to Friday.

Interviewer When .... ? (practise)

Footballer Every morning.

Interviewer When .... the players? (see)

Footballer On Tuesday.

b Make three more questions and answers for the footballer.

c Work with a partner. Act your interview.

AN INTERVIEW

3 **a** Choose a sports star.

b Make six questions to ask the sports star. Use:

How?   What?   When?   Where?   Do?   Why?

c Act your interview with a partner.

FOLLOW UP

4 Write your interview with the sports star in Exercise 3.

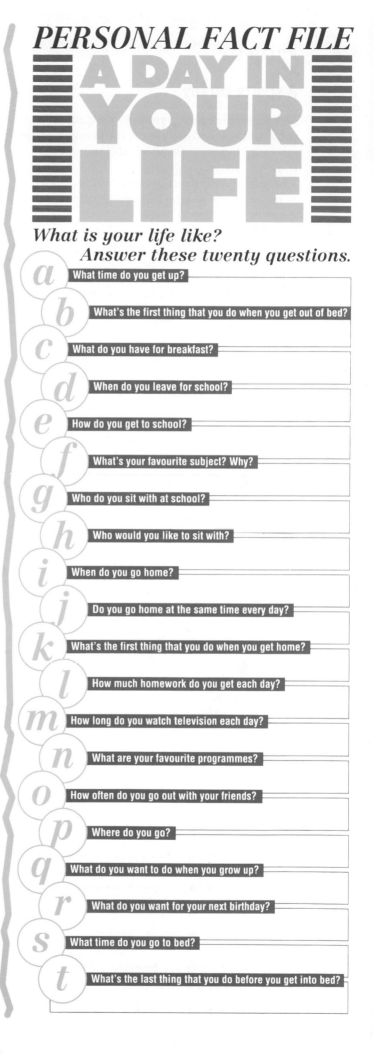

PERSONAL FACT FILE

A DAY IN YOUR LIFE

What is your life like?
Answer these twenty questions.

a What time do you get up?

b What's the first thing that you do when you get out of bed?

c What do you have for breakfast?

d When do you leave for school?

e How do you get to school?

f What's your favourite subject? Why?

g Who do you sit with at school?

h Who would you like to sit with?

i When do you go home?

j Do you go home at the same time every day?

k What's the first thing that you do when you get home?

l How much homework do you get each day?

m How long do you watch television each day?

n What are your favourite programmes?

o How often do you go out with your friends?

p Where do you go?

q What do you want to do when you grow up?

r What do you want for your next birthday?

s What time do you go to bed?

t What's the last thing that you do before you get into bed?

PROJECT

A sports survey

This project is a group project. It is quite a large project. It will require a lot of cooperation in each group to divide up the work and share the results.

The survey itself must be done in class but a lot of the work on making the questionnaire and graph can be done at home.

Students can do their project either on a large poster or in a book. This project will work best as a poster.

You can make the project larger or smaller by varying the number of questions on the questionnaire that each group makes. If you have a lot of time available, each group can ask several questions. If you want to make the task shorter, you can get each group to focus on just one question. For example, if you have six groups, two groups can do a survey on *what sports people play*, two groups can work on *what sports people watch on TV*, two groups can do a survey on *what sports events people go to watch*.

- Divide the class into five or six groups.

- Students look at the questionnaire and the graph.

- Students suggest the names of kinds of sport.

a • Read the questions in the sample questionnaire.

- Students suggest further questions.

- Groups (or you) decide what they will do a survey on. (See above.)

- Groups make a rough draft of their questionnaire.

- Discuss the rough drafts and suggest corrections.

- Students produce a finished questionnaire.

b • Students go round the class. They ask other students the questions on their questionnaire. They write down the answers. If each group member interviews five or six people, they should cover most of the class.

> **Note**
> Students will obviously answer several different questionnaires.

- Students report their results to their group.

c • Students look at the graphs on the page.

- Make sure students know how to draw a graph. If you wish to practise making graphs, ask the students to draw a graph to show this information:
In a class of thirty people, ten people go to school by bus, six go by car, six go by bicycle and the rest walk to school.

- Students produce a rough draft of their graph.

- Discuss the rough drafts and suggest corrections.

- Students produce a finished graph.

- Students write a paragraph about the results of the survey.
There are some example sentences to help them.

- Students collect pictures of sports from magazines. They label each picture with the name of the sport.

- Students make a poster with their questionnaire, graph, paragraph and pictures.

- Students display their projects.

- Discuss the projects. Ask:
Did you find out anything interesting in this project?
What did you find easy or difficult in doing the project?
What did you find out about working together in a group?

▶ **Pronunciation: page T113**

LEARNING DIARY

A Students look at the contents list on page 47.

They draw a face next to each item to show how well they think they know it.

B Students do the self-check in the Workbook on page 49.

C Divide the class into pairs or groups of three or four.

Students compare their answers. Go round the class and check for any common problems.

Students compare their self-check results with the faces they drew.

In the whole class ask *What problems did you find with the self-check?* Students suggest problem areas.

Take remedial action, as necessary. (See Introduction page vii for possible strategies.)

Ask What did you like best in this unit? What didn't you like? Students give their responses. Ask *Why?* Take note of student responses. They can help you to adjust your teaching towards the things that motivate the students most.

CULTURE SPOT

Workbook page 49

- Divide the class into pairs or groups of three or four.
- Students look quickly at the table.
- Ask *What does the table show?*
- Students give their ideas.
- Ask *What do you already know about this topic?*
- Students give their ideas. Discuss these ideas.
- Say *Read the Culture spot text. Note anything that you find interesting or unusual.*
- Ask *Did you find anything interesting or unusual?*
- Students give their ideas.
- Read each comparison question in turn.
- Discuss each question. Encourage students to compare their situation with the one in the text.

UNIT 8 Time out

This unit serves as a consolidation unit. Unit 7 introduced a major grammar area (the present simple tense) and Unit 9 introduces another major area (the present continuous tense). This unit, therefore, deals with a few smaller items of grammar and consolidates the present simple.

The new grammar in the Victoria Road section of this unit should not require pre-teaching. Allow the students to work out the new grammar points for themselves, as they read the story. You can therefore start the Victoria Road story now.

PROJECT

A sports survey

Conduct a sports survey in your class.

a Make a questionnaire. Use the questionnaire opposite to help you.

b Use your questionnaire. Interview people in your class.

c Make graphs to show your results. Write about your results. The graphs below will help you.

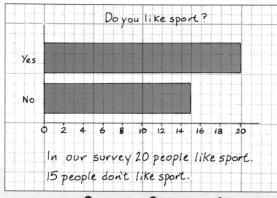

In our survey 20 people like sport.
15 people don't like sport.

SPORTS QUESTIONNAIRE

Name ....

Address ....
....
....

*Do you like sport? Yes ☐ No ☐

*Do you play a sport in your free time?
Yes ☐ No ☐

What do you play? ....
....

*Do you watch sport on TV? Yes ☐ No ☐
*Do you go to sports events? Yes ☐ No ☐

*please put a tick in the appropriate box

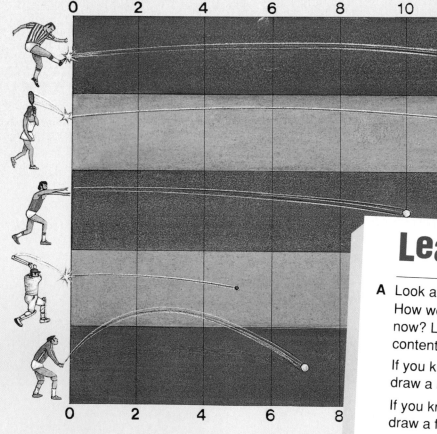

What sports do you play?

Twelve people in our class play football.

Fifteen people in our class play ....

Learning diary

A Look at the first page of this unit. How well do you know these things now? Look at each point in the contents list.

If you know it well, draw a happy face.

If you know it fairly well, draw a face like this.

If you don't know it well, draw a sad face.

B Try the self-check in the Workbook.

C Compare your answers with a partner. Discuss any problems with your teacher.

▶ Pronunciation: page 113

8 time out

Contents

Grammar points

56	**Victoria Road:** Kamala misses the bus	object pronouns
58	**Reading:** Paradise island	to / at
60	**Listening:** A radio programme	some / any
61	**Interaction:** Making suggestions	Let's.... Do you want to...?
62	**Project:** Holiday	

The main grammar point in this unit is:

some / any

HAVE YOU GOT ANY MONEY?

VICTORIA ROAD

Kamala misses the bus

- Books closed. Ask *What happened in the last episode of 'Victoria Road'?*
- Students give their responses. Ask follow-up questions.

Answer key
Darren Tooley is angry with Terry, because of what happened at the dance and at the cafe. He and his friends came looking for Terry. They met Casey and found out where Terry lives and when he comes home from school. They found out that Terry comes home alone on Wednesdays, because he plays table tennis after school. They told Casey not to tell Terry, because they wanted to give him a 'surprise'.

- Students open their books and read the questions.
- Choose students to read the questions aloud. Make sure everyone understands the questions.
- Students look through the picture story to find the answers to the questions. They can refer to the full text, too.
- Students give their answers to the questions.

Answer key
*Kamala, Sue and two of their friends
They are at school.
They are talking about going to the cinema after school.
She doesn't want to take them to the cinema.
She misses the bus.*

- Ask *What happens in this episode?* Using the pictures students give a summary of the story. (Students use the mother tongue, if necessary at this stage.)
- Explain any new vocabulary that students need to understand the dialogue.

Answer key
Two girls at school ask Sue and Kamala if they want to go to the cinema after school. Sue decides to go, but Kamala says that she can't, because she helps in her parents' shop after school. After school Sue asks Kamala to take her coat and bags home for her, because she doesn't want to take them to the cinema with her. Then Sue goes off to the cinema with her friends. The bags are very heavy. While Kamala is struggling to pick them up, the bus arrives. Kamala tries to run for the bus, but she misses it.

- Say *Now look at the full dialogue.*
- Play the tape. Students listen and follow in their books.
- Play the tape again, if necessary.

Notes
I help in the shop after school. Kamala's parents own a newsagent's shop. Small shops like this are often run by Asian families. All members of the family will usually help in the shop.

You do your community work at the hospital on Wednesday. British school pupils often do community work. It may be voluntary work for a church or it may be part of their school curriculum. In such work, pupils help in local hospitals or do small jobs for old people living alone. Sue helps in a hospital on Wednesdays after school or on Saturdays.

- Students read the statements and tick the boxes.
- Choose students to read each statement and give the answer.
- Ask *How do you know?* Students use the dialogue to justify their answers.

Note
This is a very important stage, because it shows whether students have understood the dialogue.

Answer key

a	W	d	W	g	W	j	D
b	W	e	D	h	D	k	R
c	D	f	R	i	D		

- Books closed. Play the tape again. Stop after each utterance. Students repeat.
- Repeat any utterances that students find difficult.

Useful expressions

- Divide the class into pairs.

- Students look at the list of expressions. They write a translation in the boxes. They use the story and context to work out an appropriate mother-tongue expression.

> **Note**
> A lot of these expressions are idioms and cannot be translated word for word. Make sure students understand this.

- Students give their answers. Discuss as necessary.

Object pronouns

BUILD UP

a
- Divide the class into pairs.

- Students look at the examples.

- Copy the examples onto the board.

- Make sure students understand the difference between object and subject.

b
- Students look at the story and find the missing words. They complete the list.

- Copy the gapped lists onto the board.

- Choose students to come out and complete the lists.

- Students find examples in the story to justify their choice.

> **Answer key**
> | | |
> |---|---|
> | me | us |
> | him | you |
> | her | them |

- Divide the class into pairs.
- Students choose their roles.
- Students read the dialogue.
- If time, change roles and do the dialogue again.
- Choose one pair to act the dialogue in front of the class.

FOLLOW UP

- Students answer the questions in class or at home.

> **Answer key**
> a *They want to go to the cinema.*
> b *She helps in her parents' shop after school.*
> c *She does her community work at the hospital.*
> d *She doesn't want to take them to the cinema.*
> e *She's in a hurry.*
> f *He plays football.*
> g *She's got a driving lesson.*
> h *She misses the bus.*

Kamala misses the bus

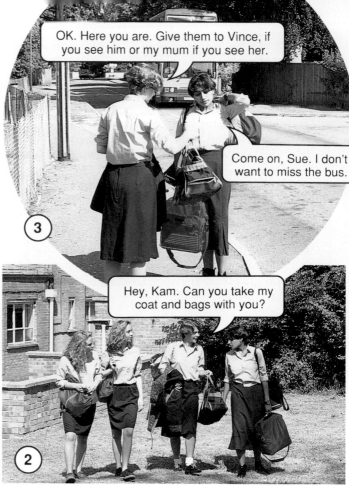

OK. Here you are. Give them to Vince, if you see him or my mum if you see her.

Come on, Sue. I don't want to miss the bus.

③

Hey, Kam. Can you take my coat and bags with you?

1 ▼ Look at the story.

- Who are the people?
- Where are they?
- What is happening?
- Why does Sue give her bags to Kamala?
- What happens to Kamala?

There's a good film at the cinema this week.

Let's go after school.

OK. What about you, Kam?

I can't. I help in the shop after school.

①

②

Kamala Come on, Sue. I don't want to miss the bus.

Sue OK. Here you are. Give them to Vince, if you see him or my mum if you see her. Thanks, Kam. Bye.

Kamala Blimey, Sue. These bags are heavy. Oh no. There's the bus.

Kamala Stop. Wait. Oh, damn!

 2 ▶ Listen and follow in your book.

Girl 1 There's a good film at the cinema this week.

Girl 2 Let's go after school. Do you two want to join us?

Sue OK. What about you, Kam?

Kamala I can't. I help in the shop after school. Anyway, you do your community work at the hospital on Wednesday, Sue.

Sue Oh, it's all right. I can go on Saturday.
Later

Sue Hey, Kam. Can you take my coat and bags with you? I don't want to take them to the cinema.

Kamala Oh, all right, but I can't take them to your house. I'm in a hurry.

Sue It doesn't matter. There's nobody at home. Mum has got a driving lesson and Vince plays football on Wednesday.

3 ▼ Right, Wrong or Don't know?

		✓	✗	?
a	It's Monday.	☐	☐	☐
b	Sue goes to the cinema after school every Wednesday.	☐	☐	☐
c	Kamala wants to go to the cinema.	☐	☐	☐
d	Kamala goes to dance classes after school.	☐	☐	☐
e	Kamala doesn't want to take Sue's coat and bags.	☐	☐	☐
f	Sue works at the hospital on Wednesday.	☐	☐	☐
g	Sue's mother is at work.	☐	☐	☐
h	Mr Scott comes home at six o'clock.	☐	☐	☐
i	Vince plays football with Casey.	☐	☐	☐
j	Kamala's bags are very heavy.	☐	☐	☐
k	Kamala misses the bus.	☐	☐	☐

VICTORIA ROAD   56

 Listen again and repeat.

Useful expressions

 How do you say these in your language?

Let's ....

you two

What about you?

It's all right.

I'm in a hurry.

It doesn't matter.

There's nobody at home.

There's the bus.

Oh, damn!

Object pronouns

BUILD UP

 a Look.

I	love	her.
She	loves	me.

This is a subject pronoun.   **This is an object pronoun.**

b Find the other object pronouns in the Victoria Road story. Complete this list.

subject	object
I	....
he	....
she	....
it	it

subject	object
we	....
you	....
they	....

7 Work with a partner. One person is Sue and one of the other girls, and one person is Kamala and the second girl. Read the dialogue.

FOLLOW UP

8 Answer these questions.

a What do the girls want to do after school?
b Why can't Kamala go to the cinema with the other girls?
c What does Sue do on Wednesday?
d Why doesn't Sue want to keep her coat and bags?
e Why can't Kamala take them to Sue's house?
f What does Vince do on Wednesday?
g Why isn't Sue's mother at home?
h Why is Kamala angry?

READING

Paradise Island

In this activity students use the texts and the picture to work out the meaning of the new words.

- Divide the class into pairs or groups of three.
- Students look at the pictures. Ask *What can you see in the pictures?* Encourage the students to look for the name in English.

> **Answer key**
> *an island*

- Students look at the texts. Ask *What is it about? Where is it from?*
- Encourage students to look through the text for the words they need to give the answers.

> **Answer key**
> *It's about a holiday island for young people. The island is called Paradise Island.*
> *It's from a holiday advertisement.*

- Students look at the list of words. Don't give their meanings.
- Explain the activity.
- Students read the texts and label the items on the map.
- If possible, copy the map on the board. Or, hold up the book and point to the items.
- Choose students to give their answers.
- Students justify their answers from the texts.

- Divide the class into pairs.
- Choose one pair. Demonstrate the activity.
- Repeat with another pair.
- All pairs do the activity.
- They reverse roles and repeat.

> **Answer key**
> *Can you buy clothes?*
> *No, you can't.*
>
> *Can you have a picnic?*
> *Yes, you can. You can have a picnic in the forest.*
>
> *Can you go to a museum?*
> *No, you can't.*
>
> *Can you watch television?*
> *No, you can't.*
>
> *Can you go to the cinema?*
> *Yes, you can.*
>
> *Can you fish?*
> *Yes, you can. You can fish in the river or in the sea.*
>
> *Can you buy food?*
> *Yes, you can. You can buy food at the supermarket.*
>
> *Can you send a letter?*
> *Yes, you can. You can send a letter at the post office.*
>
> *Can you go skating?*
> *No, you can't.*
>
> *Can you go skiing?*
> *No, you can't.*
>
> *Can you swim?*
> *Yes, you can. You can swim in the sea or in the swimming pool.*
>
> *Can you dance?*
> *Yes, you can. You can dance at the disco.*
>
> *Can you go walking?*
> *Yes, you can. You can go walking in the hills.*
>
> *Can you go climbing?*
> *Yes, you can. You can go climbing in the hills.*

to/at

BUILD UP

a
- Students look at the examples.
- Ask *What is the difference between 'to' and 'at'?*

> **Answer key**
> *We use 'to' when there is movement. We use 'at' when there is no movement.*

- If this difference does not exist in the students' mother tongue, ask the students to translate the sentences. Point out the difference.

b
- Students complete the sentences.
- Students give their answers.

> **Answer key**
> *at   at   to   at   at   to   to   to*

• Divide the class into groups of three or four.

• Each group decides what it will do for the first three days.

• Students give their ideas.

FOLLOW UP

 • Students can do this exercise at home or in class.

> **Answer key**
> *Island   holiday   people   lot   do*
> *beaches   pool   tennis court   hills   have*
> *in   evening   Sharks   There's   show*
> *film*

READING

1 Read the information about Paradise Island. Label these things on the map.

beach	souvenir shop
island	tennis court
forest	swimming pool
river	sea
disco	restaurant
cinema	supermarket

Come to Paradise Island – the holiday island for young people. Paradise Island has got two beautiful beaches. You can swim in the sea or go windsurfing.

You can have a picnic the forest. You can cli the hills. You can fis in the river.

Or you can swim in our Olympic swimming pool.

There are lots of things to do on Paradise Island. There's a tennis court.

58

the evenings you can dance at Sharks Disco. There's a cinema too. We show a new film every day.

You sleep in huts in Paradise Village.

You can buy food at the ~~su~~permarket or you can eat at ~~the~~ Blue Dolphin restaurant.

There's a souvenir shop, too, and a post office.

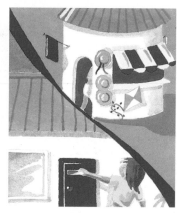

Come to Paradise Island for a wonderful holiday.

2 What can you do on Paradise Island? Ask and answer.

Example
Can you go windsurfing?
Yes, you can. You can go windsurfing in the sea.

Use these cues.

go windsurfing	go to the cinema	go skiing
buy clothes	fish	swim
have a picnic	buy food	dance
go to a museum	send a letter	go walking
watch television	go skating	go climbing

to/at

BUILD UP

3 **a Look.**

Let's go **to** the cinema.   We're **at** the cinema.

b Write 'to' or 'at'.

Where's Jane? She's .... the tennis court.

We have lunch .... the restaurant.

I go .... the beach every day.

There's a good film .... the cinema.

Can you buy postcards .... the shop?

Let's go .... the disco.

Can I send this letter .... Greece, please?

Come .... Paradise Island for your holiday.

4 **You are on Paradise Island. Plan your first three days.**

	morning	afternoon	evening
Day 1			
Day 2			
Day 3			

FOLLOW UP

5 **Here's a postcard from someone on Paradise Island. Complete it.**

Paradise Island

Dear Jane,
I'm on Paradise .... It's a ....
island for young .... There are a .... of
things to .... here. There are two beautiful
.... and a swimming .... too. You can
play tennis at the .... and you
can climb the .... or .... a picnic ..... the
forest. And in the .... there's a disco. It's
called .... a cinema, too. They
.... a new........... every day. Hope you're well.
*   Love, Pete*

59

LISTENING

Paradise Island

 In this activity students learn to connect the sound of new words to the written form.

- Revise the Reading section on pages 58 and 59.

- Divide the class into pairs.

- Students look at the labelled pictures. Allow the students two minutes to study the pictures and their names.

- Explain the activity.

- Play the tape. Students listen and tick the things that are mentioned. Stop after each interview to give students time to check their answers.

- Students give their answers.

- Play the tape again, if there are problems.

 Paradise Island

Presenter Hi, our programme this week comes from Paradise Island. It's a holiday island for young people. What do people think of it?

Girl 1 I think it's great.

Presenter What is there to do here?

Girl 1 We always go to the beach in the morning. The beaches are very clean.

Presenter Can you swim in the sea?

Girl 1 Yes, you can and you can go windsurfing, too.

Presenter What do you usually do in the evening?

Girl 1 There's a good disco. It's called Sharks. We usually go there, but we sometimes go to the cinema. They show some good films.

Presenter Do you like Paradise Island?

Boy 1 No. It's boring. There isn't a lot to do.

Presenter Why?

Boy 1 Well, you can go to the beach and to the disco, but that's all. There aren't any interesting buildings – museums, churches or castles.

Presenter Do you like the forest?

Boy 1 Yes, but it's very small. You can see everything on the island in one day.

Presenter Do you like Paradise Island?

Boy 2 It's OK.

Presenter What do you like?

Boy 2 It's very quiet. There aren't any cars on the island.

Presenter Do you like that?

Boy 2 Yes. I live in a big city at home.

Presenter What don't you like?

Boy 2 The shops. There's a supermarket and some small shops. But they're expensive and they haven't got a lot of things.

Presenter Do you like the beach?

Girl 2 Yes, but I don't swim in the sea. I go to the swimming pool.

Presenter Why?

Girl 2 I'm afraid of sharks.

Presenter Are there any animals on the island?

Girl 2 There aren't any snakes or tigers or animals like that. But there are insects and some big spiders. Ugh, I don't like them.

Presenter Do you like the huts?

Girl 2 They're small and they haven't got bathrooms. But they're OK.

- Students draw two columns in their books.

- Explain the activity.

- Play the tape again. Stop after each activity. Students complete their charts.

- Draw two columns on the board.

- Students give their answers. Write them on the board.

- Play the tape again if there are disagreements.

 • Students give their ideas.

some/any

BUILD UP

 a • Students look at the examples.

 b • Students complete the rule.

 • Students give their answers.

Answer key
some
any
any

- Students look at the sentences.

- Get one student to give the first sentence.

- Students make the remaining sentences.

- Students give their answers.

Answer key			
a	*any*	f	*some*
b	*any*	g	*any*
c	*any*	h	*some*
d	*some*	i	*some*
e	*any*		

- Divide the class into pairs.

- Students choose their roles.

- Explain the activity.

- Pairs make their dialogues. Go round and help with any problems.

- Students reverse roles and repeat.

- Get two pairs to demonstrate their dialogues in front of the class.

the evenings you can dance at Sharks Disco. There's a
cinema too. We show a new film every day.

You sleep in huts in Paradise Village.

You can buy food at the
ermarket or you can eat at
Blue Dolphin restaurant.

There's a souvenir shop,
too, and a post office.

*Come to Paradise Island
for a wonderful holiday.*

to/at

BUILD UP

3 a **Look.**

Let's go **to** the cinema.   We're **at** the cinema.

b **Write 'to' or 'at'.**

Where's Jane? She's …….. the tennis court.

We have lunch …….. the restaurant.

I go …….. the beach every day.

There's a good film …….. the cinema.

Can you buy postcards …….. the shop?

Let's go …….. the disco.

Can I send this letter …….. Greece, please?

Come …….. Paradise Island for your holiday.

4 **You are on Paradise Island. Plan your first
three days.**

	morning	afternoon	evening
Day 1			
Day 2			
Day 3			

2 **What can you do on Paradise Island? Ask and
answer.**

Example
Can you go windsurfing?
Yes, you can. You can go windsurfing in the sea.

Use these cues.

go windsurfing	go to the cinema	go skiing
buy clothes	fish	swim
have a picnic	buy food	dance
go to a museum	send a letter	go walking
watch television	go skating	go climbing

FOLLOW UP

5 **Here's a postcard from someone on Paradise
Island. Complete it.**

Paradise Island

Dear Jane,
I'm on Paradise ……………. It's a ……………
island for young ……………. There are a …….. of
things to …….. here. There are two beautiful
……………… and a swimming ………… too. You can
play tennis at the ……………. …………… and you
can climb the …………. or ………… a picnic ….. the
forest. And in the …………… there's a disco. It's
called …………… . …………… a cinema, too. They
………… a new………… every day. Hope you're well.
Love, Pete

59

LISTENING

Paradise Island

In this activity students learn to connect the sound of new words to the written form.

- Revise the Reading section on pages 58 and 59.
- Divide the class into pairs.
- Students look at the labelled pictures. Allow the students two minutes to study the pictures and their names.
- Explain the activity.
- Play the tape. Students listen and tick the things that are mentioned. Stop after each interview to give students time to check their answers.
- Students give their answers.
- Play the tape again, if there are problems.

 Paradise Island

Presenter Hi, our programme this week comes from Paradise Island. It's a holiday island for young people. What do people think of it?

Girl 1 I think it's great.

Presenter What is there to do here?

Girl 1 We always go to the beach in the morning. The beaches are very clean.

Presenter Can you swim in the sea?

Girl 1 Yes, you can and you can go windsurfing, too.

Presenter What do you usually do in the evening?

Girl 1 There's a good disco. It's called Sharks. We usually go there, but we sometimes go to the cinema. They show some good films.

Presenter Do you like Paradise Island?

Boy 1 No. It's boring. There isn't a lot to do.

Presenter Why?

Boy 1 Well, you can go to the beach and to the disco, but that's all. There aren't any interesting buildings – museums, churches or castles.

Presenter Do you like the forest?

Boy 1 Yes, but it's very small. You can see everything on the island in one day.

Presenter Do you like Paradise Island?

Boy 2 It's OK.

Presenter What do you like?

Boy 2 It's very quiet. There aren't any cars on the island.

Presenter Do you like that?

Boy 2 Yes. I live in a big city at home.

Presenter What don't you like?

Boy 2 The shops. There's a supermarket and some small shops. But they're expensive and they haven't got a lot of things.

Presenter Do you like the beach?

Girl 2 Yes, but I don't swim in the sea. I go to the swimming pool.

Presenter Why?

Girl 2 I'm afraid of sharks.

Presenter Are there any animals on the island?

Girl 2 There aren't any snakes or tigers or animals like that. But there are insects and some big spiders. Ugh, I don't like them.

Presenter Do you like the huts?

Girl 2 They're small and they haven't got bathrooms. But they're OK.

- Students draw two columns in their books.
- Explain the activity.
- Play the tape again. Stop after each activity. Students complete their charts.
- Draw two columns on the board.
- Students give their answers. Write them on the board.
- Play the tape again if there are disagreements.

- Students give their ideas.

some/any

BUILD UP

 a • Students look at the examples.

b • Students complete the rule.
- Students give their answers.

Answer key
some
any
any

- Students look at the sentences.
- Get one student to give the first sentence.
- Students make the remaining sentences.
- Students give their answers.

Answer key

a	*any*	**f**	*some*
b	*any*	**g**	*any*
c	*any*	**h**	*some*
d	*some*	**i**	*some*
e	*any*		

- Divide the class into pairs.
- Students choose their roles.
- Explain the activity.
- Pairs make their dialogues. Go round and help with any problems.
- Students reverse roles and repeat.
- Get two pairs to demonstrate their dialogues in front of the class.

FOLLOW UP

7 • Students write a postcard. They use the postcard on page 59 as a model.

INTERACTION

Making suggestions

1 • Students look at the Victoria Road story and complete the sentences.

> **Answer key**
> *Let's*
> *Do you want to*

- Ask *When do we use these expressions?*
- Students give their ideas.

2 • Divide the class into pairs.

- Students read the items in A and B.
- Choose one pair. Demonstrate the activity with the example.
- Repeat with another pair.
- All pairs do the activity.
- They reverse roles and repeat.

> **Answer key**
> Answers depend on students' choice.

A GAME

3 • Divide the class into groups of five or six. Groups sit in a circle.

- Students suggest things to have.
- Demonstrate the game with one group. Students say the sentence in turn. They must remember what everyone has added to the list so far and then add another item, so the list gets longer all the time. If a student misses something from the list, can't add a new item or gets *some* and *any* wrong, he/she is out. The game continues until only one student is left.
- Students play the game in their groups.

FOLLOW UP

4 • Students write their dialogues. They use 'Let's' for five suggestions and 'Do you want to . . . ?' for five suggestions.

LISTENING

Paradise Island

1 📼 Listen. You will hear part of a radio programme about Paradise Island. Which of these do the people mention? Tick them.

churches

horses

snakes

sharks

lions

tigers

spiders

dogs

cars

swimming pool

castles

cinema

tennis

insects

beach

bathrooms

rivers

shops

2 What do people like about Paradise Island? What don't they like? Make a chart like this. Write what people say.

+	−
Example *The beaches are very clean.*	*There isn't a lot to do.*

3 Do you agree with the people in the interviews? What do you like on your holidays?

some / any

4 **a** Look at this dialogue.

Are there **any** animals on the island?
There aren't **any** snakes or tigers. But there are **some** big spiders.

b When do we use 'some'? When do we use 'any'? Complete this rule.

> We use .... in positive statements.
>
> We use .... in negative statements.
>
> We use .... in questions.

5 Here are some more things from the interviews about Paradise Island. Complete them with 'some' or 'any'.

a Are there .... shops here?

b There aren't .... cars on the island.

c Have you got .... friends here?

d They've got .... souvenirs in the shop.

e There aren't .... museums.

f There are .... interesting people here.

g Are there .... sharks in the sea?

h There are .... beautiful birds on the island.

i We usually have lunch with .... people from Greece.

6 Work with a partner. One person is the interviewer, one is a person on Paradise Island. Use the information in your chart. Make the dialogues.

Here are some questions to help you.

Do you like Paradise Island?
What do you usually do here in the morning?
Do you like the . . . ?
Are there any . . . ?
Can you . . . ?
What do you like about Paradise Island?
What don't you like about Paradise Island?

FOLLOW UP

7 Write a postcard from someone who doesn't like the island.

INTERACTION

Making suggestions

1 Look at the Victoria Road story on page 56. Complete these sentences.

.... go to the cinema after school.

.... join us?

2 Make dialogues. Choose from A and B.

Example
A Do you want to *go to the cinema?*
(Let's *go to the cinema.*)

B *No, I can't. I haven't got any money.*

A	B
go to the cinema	No, I can't. I must go home.
go to the beach	No, I don't want to.
go to the cafe	No, I can't. I must do my homework.
watch a video	Let's have a rest first.
listen to a record	I'm sorry. I help my parents after school.
go to the shops	No, I can't. I've got an appointment at the dentist.
play football	No, I can't. I haven't got a ticket.
go swimming	No, I can't. I haven't got any money.
go to the dance	No, I want to stay here.
climb the hill	No, I want to watch the football match on TV.

3 **A GAME**

A 'I haven't got any pens.'
B 'I've got some pens, but I haven't got any pencils.'
C 'I've got some pens and some pencils, but I haven't got any apples.'
D 'I've got some pens and some pencils and some apples, but I haven't got any . . .'

Continue.

FOLLOW UP

4 Write your dialogues for Exercise 2.

61

PROJECT

Holiday

This project can be done as an individual project or as a group project.

It can be done in class or at home.

The project has three different parts: a labelled map, an illustrated leaflet and a postcard. You can adjust the project to fit the time available or the level of the students by doing one, two or all of these parts. In a mixed ability class you can choose different parts for different groups or individuals.

- Students look at the map and pictures of Kenya.
- Say *What things can you do there? Have you ever been to Africa? Kenya?*
- Students give their ideas and talk about places they have visited or know something about in Africa, etc.
- Decide which project tasks students will do (see above).
- Students decide what their ideal holiday location is.
- Students plan their project.
- Students produce a rough draft of their project. They use the map, text and postcards on this page and on pages 58 and 59 as models.
- Discuss the rough drafts and suggest corrections.
- Students find pictures to illustrate their projects. Travel agencies usually have brochures that students can get pictures from.
- Students produce a finished project. Students can do their project either on a large poster or in a book. This project will work best as a poster.
- Students display their projects.
- Discuss the projects. Ask:
  What did you like or dislike about doing the project? What new language have you learnt in doing this project?

▶ **Pronunciation: page T113a**

LEARNING DIARY

Note
Discuss in the mother tongue.

A Students look at the contents list on page 55.

They draw a face next to each item to show how well they think they know it.

B Students do the self-check in the Workbook on page 58.

C Divide the class into pairs or groups of three or four.

Students compare their answers. Go round the class and check for any common problems.

Students compare their self-check results with the faces they drew.

In the whole class ask *What problems did you find with the self-check?* Students suggest problem areas.

Take remedial action, as necessary. (See Introduction page vii for possible strategies.)

Ask What did you like best in this unit? What didn't you like? Students give their responses. Ask *Why?* Take note of student responses. They can help you to adjust your teaching towards the things that motivate the students most.

CULTURE SPOT
Workbook page 58

- Divide the class into pairs or groups of three or four.
- Students look quickly at the text.
- Ask *What is the text about?*
- Students give their ideas.
- Ask *What do you already know about this topic?*
- Students give their ideas. Discuss these ideas.
- Say *Read the Culture spot text. Note anything that you find interesting or unusual.*
- Ask comprehension questions about the text.
- Students give their answers. Explain any words that students need.
- Ask *Did you find anything interesting or unusual?*
- Students give their ideas.
- Read the comparison question.
- Discuss the question. Encourage students to compare their situation with the one in the text.

You can start immediately with the Victoria Road story on page 64, or you can pre-teach the present continuous first. If you wish to pre-teach the language, use the following procedure.

> **Note**
> At this stage you only need to introduce the grammar items, so that students can understand the story more easily. There are exercises later for more concentrated practice. Spend no more than 10 minutes on the pre-teaching.

1   Introduce the positive form of the present continuous.

- Open the door. Say *I'm opening the door.* Repeat.
- Choose a student. Ask *What am I doing?*
- Elicit the answer *You're opening the door.*
- Repeat with another student.
- Choose a student. Say *Read your book.*
- Ask *What are you doing?*
- Elicit the answer *I'm reading a book.*
- Ask another student *What is he/she doing?*
- Elicit the answer *He/She's reading a book.*
- Repeat procedure for other activities. Use *open/close the door/window/book, write* and *sing.*

2   Introduce the question form of the present continuous.

- Say *I'm wearing . . . .*
- Choose a student. Ask *What am I wearing?*
- Elicit the answer *You're wearing . . . .*
- Choose other students. Ask *What are you wearing? What is he/she wearing?* Introduce names of clothes, as necessary.

> **Note**
> Students should already know *T-shirt* and *tracksuit.*

3   • Books open. Students look at the picture and the text on page 63.

- Say *We call this the present continuous tense. We use it to describe what is happening now.*

4   • Start the Victoria Road story on page 64.

PROJECT

Holiday

**What is your ideal place for a holiday?
It can be a real or an imaginary place.**

- Draw a map of your place.
- Label the buildings and other features.
- Write a leaflet about the place. Say what you can do there.
- Illustrate your leaflet with some pictures.
- Write a postcard from there to someone you know.

KENYA
Come to Kenya for an
unforgettable holiday.

 Stay in one of the fine hotels on the Kenyan coast. Don't worry about the language. Everybody here speaks English. You can sunbathe on the beautiful beaches. Lie on the white sand. Swim in the warm blue water of the Indian Ocean. Or, you can spend a day on a dhow.

Dear Carol and Peter
Kenya is great! The beaches
are beautiful. At the
moment, we're on safari.
There are lots of animals —
Lions, giraffes, zebras.
Hope you're well. Bye.
   love Alan and Mary

Carol and Peter Long
42 Walton Street
OXFORD
OX7 3BT
ENGLAND

But don't spend all your time on the beach. This is Africa and Africa means safaris. You can go on safari to one of the national parks. Here you can see lions, elephants, giraffes, zebras, flamingoes

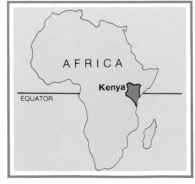

AFRICA

Kenya

EQUATOR

and many other animals. And from the Amboseli national park you can see Africa's highest mountain, Mt. Kilimanjaro. Don't forget your camera!

Learning diary

A Look at the first page of this unit. How well do you know these things now? Look at each point in the contents list.

If you know it well, draw a happy face.

If you know it fairly well, draw a face like this.

If you don't know it well, draw a sad face.

B Try the self-check in the Workbook.

C Compare your answers with a partner. Discuss any problems with your teacher.

8

▶ Pronunciation: page 113

Contents

Grammar points

64	**Victoria Road:** A strange girl	
66	**Language work**	the present continuous tense
68	**Reading:** Fashion parade	clothes
70	**Listening:** A new pair of jeans	the present simple and the present continuous tense
71	**Interaction:** At the clothes shop	words with no singular
72	**Project:** Fashion page	

The main grammar point in this unit is:

the present continuous tense

She's wearing jeans.
She isn't wearing a dress.
Is she wearing a blouse?

She's wearing jeans today.
But she doesn't wear jeans
when she goes to school.
She wears a school uniform.

VICTORIA ROAD

A strange girl

- Books closed. Ask *What happened in the last episode of 'Victoria Road'?*

- Students give their responses. Ask follow-up questions, for example *What does Terry do on Wednesdays? When does he come home? Who knows this?*

Answer key
It was Wednesday. Sue and Kamala were at school. Some friends asked if they wanted to go to the cinema after school. Sue decided to go, but Kamala couldn't, because she helps in her parents' shop after school. After school Sue asked Kamala to take her coat and bags home for her, because she didn't want to take them to the cinema. Then Sue left with her friends. The bags were heavy and while Kamala was picking them up, the bus arrived. Kamala tried to run for the bus, but she missed it.

- Students open their books and read the questions.

- Choose students to read the questions aloud. Make sure everyone understands the questions.

- Students look through the picture story to find the answers to the questions. They can refer to the full text, too.

- Students give their answers to the questions. (Students use the mother tongue, if necessary at this stage.)

- Explain any new vocabulary that students need to understand the dialogue.

Answer key
Terry, Kamala, Darren Tooley and his friends
They are in Victoria Road.
Sue has gone to the cinema with some friends.
They're waiting for Terry. Darren Tooley is angry with Terry, because he spilt a drink down his back and he is planning his revenge.
He puts on Sue's coat. He is trying to hide from the three boys.

- Say *Now look at the full dialogue.*

- Play the tape. Students listen and follow in their books.

- Play the tape again, if necessary.

Notes
It's Wednesday. Terry plays table tennis after school on Wednesdays. That's why he is on the same bus as Kamala. Darren Tooley and his friends found out from Casey in Unit 7 that Terry comes home alone that day.

- Students read the statements and tick the boxes.

- Choose students to read each statement and give the answer.

- Ask *How do you know?* Students use the dialogue to justify their answers.

Note
This is a very important stage, because it shows whether students have understood the dialogue.

Answer key
a	R	d	W	g	R	j	R
b	R	e	R	h	W		
c	W	f	W	i	R		

- Books closed. Play the tape again. Stop after each utterance. Students repeat.

- Repeat any utterances that students find difficult.

Useful expressions

- Divide the class into pairs.
- Students look at the list of expressions. They write a translation in the boxes. They use the story and context to work out an appropriate mother-tongue expression.

> **Note**
> A lot of these expressions are idioms and cannot be translated word for word. Make sure students understand this.

- Students give their answers. Discuss as necessary.

- Divide the class into pairs.
- Students choose their roles.
- Students read the dialogue.
- If time, change roles and do the dialogue again.
- Choose one pair to act the dialogue in front of the class.

FOLLOW UP

a • Students can complete their sentences in class or at home.

> **Answer key**
> *The three boys (guys)/Darren Tooley and his friends*
> *Terry*
> *The three boys (guys)/Darren Tooley and his friends*
> *Kamala*
> *Kamala and Terry*
> *The wind*
> *Terry*
> *The three boys (guys)/Darren Tooley and his friends*
> *Kamala*

b • Students match the sentences with the correct picture.

> **Answer key**
> | | |
> |---|---|
> | *2* | *5* |
> | *4, 5, 6* | *2* |
> | *6* | *2* |
> | *1* | *3* |
> | *1* | |

A strange girl

1 Look at the story.

- Who are the people?
- Where are they?
- Why is Kamala carrying Sue's coat and bags?
- What are the three boys doing? Why?
- What does Terry do? Why?

2 🎧 Listen and follow in your books.

Terry Hi, Kam. Why are you carrying those bags and that coat?

Kamala They're Sue's. But I can't explain now. I'm in a hurry.

Kamala What's the matter, Terry? What are you doing?

Terry I'm hiding from those three guys round the corner.

Terry What are they wearing?

Kamala Well, one of them is wearing a red sweater and jeans; one is wearing a black jacket and grey trousers.

Terry Is the other guy wearing a blue sweatshirt?

Kamala Yes, he is.

Terry It's them. What are they doing?

Kamala Well, they aren't doing anything. They're sitting on a wall.

Kamala Look, Terry, I must go. I'm late.

Terry Wait a minute, Kam. Give me Sue's coat and bags. I can take them.

Terry Good, the big guy isn't looking at me. But the wind is blowing the hood.

Terry Oh no!

Darren There he is. Quick. Chase him.

VICTORIA ROAD   64

3 **Right, Wrong or Don't know?**

	✓	✗	?
a In picture 1, Terry and Kamala are arriving at Victoria Road.	❑	❑	❑
b Kamala is carrying Sue's bags.	❑	❑	❑
c Three boys are waiting at the bus stop.	❑	❑	❑
d The three boys are Terry's friends.	❑	❑	❑
e In picture 2 Terry is hiding from the three boys.	❑	❑	❑
f The three boys are all wearing sweatshirts.	❑	❑	❑
g One of the boys is Darren Tooley.	❑	❑	❑
h The three boys are talking to a man.	❑	❑	❑
i In picture 4 Terry is wearing Sue's coat.	❑	❑	❑
j In the last picture, the three boys are chasing Terry.	❑	❑	❑

4 Listen again and repeat.

Useful expressions

5 How do you say these in your language?

I can't explain.

What's the matter?

round the corner

It's them.

What are they doing?

I'm late.

Wait a minute.

There he is.

6 **Work with a partner. One person is Terry, one is Kamala and Darren Tooley. Read the dialogue.**

FOLLOW UP

7 What is happening in each picture in the story?

a Complete the sentences.

.... are sitting on a wall.

.... is wearing Sue's coat.

.... are chasing Terry.

.... is carrying Sue's bags and coat.

.... are arriving at Victoria Road.

.... is blowing the hood.

.... is hiding from the three boys.

.... are waiting for Terry.

.... is giving Sue's coat and bags to Terry.

b Which picture does each sentence describe? Put a number next to each sentence.

LANGUAGE WORK

The present continuous tense

BUILD UP

a • Divide the class into pairs.

• Students complete the sentences. While they are doing this, copy the gapped sentences onto the board.

• Choose students to come out and complete the sentences.

> **Answer key**
> *'m*
> *is wearing*
> *'re sitting*
> *aren't doing*
> *isn't looking*

b • Students complete the table. They use the dialogue to help them. While they are doing this copy the table onto the board.

• Choose students to come out and complete the table.

• Students quote examples from the dialogue to justify the rule in the table.

• Students make ten sentences using the table.

> **Answer key**
>
> | | | |
> |---|---|---|
> | I | am
'm
am not
'm not | |
> | He
She
It | is
's
is not
isn't | eating.
sitting on the wall.
hiding.
wearing trousers.
carrying two bags.
waiting for the bus. |
> | We
You
They | are
're
are not
aren't | |

2 • Students look at the picture. Ask *Who are the people?*

• Students give their answers.

• Get one student to give the first sentence.

• Students make the remaining sentences.

• Students give their answers.

> **Answer key**
> (possible answers)
> *Mr Moore is cooking.*
> *Mrs Moore is cutting some rolls.*
> *Terry and Casey are playing football.*
> *Vince is sitting on a picnic box. He's watching Terry and Casey.*
> *Sue and Kamala are talking.*
> *Mr Scott is eating a hamburger.*
> *Mrs Scott is reading a magazine.*

3 • Divide the class into pairs.

• Students look at the picture.

• Choose students to read out the clues.

• Make sure students understand the difference in meaning between 'wearing', 'carrying' and 'have got'. Use the pictures to help you explain.

• Explain the activity.

• Students work out which girl is which from the clues.

• Students give their answers.

• Ask *How do you know?* Students justify their answers from the clues.

> **Note**
> This is an important stage. Students should be able to explain fully in English.

> **Answer key**
> (Left to right) *Olivia, Rebecca, Angela, Jean, Lisa*

The present continuous tense: questions

BUILD UP

a • Divide the class into pairs.

• Students complete the questions. While they are doing this, copy the sentences and the question openers onto the board.

• Choose students to come out and complete the questions.

> **Answer key**
>
> *Is the other guy wearing a blue sweatshirt?*
> *Why are you carrying those bags?*

b • Students find the questions in the Victoria Road story and check them.

c • Students complete the table. They use the questions in **a** to help them. While they are doing this copy the table onto the board.

• Choose students to come out and complete the table.

• Students quote examples from the Victoria Road story to justify the rule in the table.

• Students make ten sentences using the table.

> **Answer key**
>
> | | | | |
> |---|---|---|---|
> | | *am* | *I* | |
> | *What* | *is* | *he*
she
it | *doing?* |
> | | *are* | *you*
we
they | |

5 • Students look at the picture and the example.

• Get one student to read the example aloud.

• Get another student to give the next sentence.

• Students make the remaining sentences.

• Students give their answers.

> **Answer key**
>
> **b** *What are Sue and Kamala doing?*
> **c** *What is Mr Scott eating?*
> **d** *Where is Vince sitting?*
> **e** *What is Mrs Scott reading?*
> **f** *Is Mr Moore cutting rolls?*
> **g** *What is Sue wearing?*

A MIME GAME

6 • Demonstrate the activity.

• Divide the class into two teams, A and B.

• Students think of possible mimes.

• One student from team A does a mime. Team B must guess what he/she is doing. They have five guesses. If they guess correctly, they get one point.

• Teams reverse roles.

• Each team does six mimes. The team with most points is the winner. (The game can also be played in groups, if preferred.)

FOLLOW UP

7 • Students write their descriptions of what the people are doing in the picture in Exercise 2. This can be done in class or at home.

> **Answer key**
>
> (See Exercise 2.)

LANGUAGE WORK

The present continuous tense

BUILD UP

1 **a** Complete these sentences from the Victoria Road story.

I .... hiding.

One of them .... a red sweater.

They .... on a wall.

They .... anything.

The big guy .... at me.

This is the present continuous tense. It describes something that is happening at the moment.

b Complete this table.

I	am 'm am not 'm not	eating.
		sitting on a wall.
He She It	....	hiding. wearing trousers.
		carrying two bags.
We You They	....	waiting for the bus.

2 Look at the picture. What are the people doing?

3 Who is who? Work out which girl is Rebecca, which is Angela, which is Jean, which is Olivia and which is Lisa. Use these clues.

Lisa isn't wearing jeans.
Angela and Olivia haven't got bags.
Olivia isn't wearing a sweatshirt.
Jean and Angela aren't wearing T-shirts.

Note:

She is **wearing** a coat.

She is **carrying** a coat.

The present continuous tense: questions

BUILD UP

 a Make these into questions.

The other guy is wearing a blue sweatshirt

Is .... ?

You are carrying those bags.

Why .... ?

b Check your answers in the Victoria Road story.

c Complete this table with these words.

it   is   she   they   am   he   you   are   we   I

	....	....	....
		....	
What	....	....	doing?
		....	
	....	....	
		....	

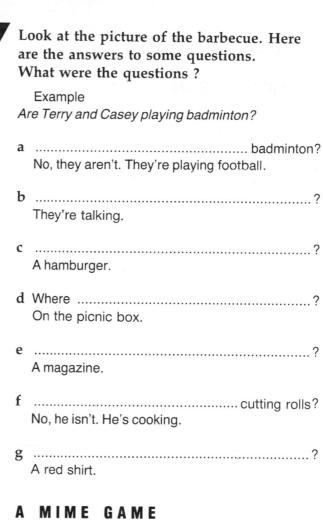

5 Look at the picture of the barbecue. Here are the answers to some questions. What were the questions ?

Example
Are Terry and Casey playing badminton?

a .... badminton?
No, they aren't. They're playing football.

b .... ?
They're talking.

c .... ?
A hamburger.

d Where .... ?
On the picnic box.

e .... ?
A magazine.

f .... cutting rolls?
No, he isn't. He's cooking.

g .... ?
A red shirt.

A MIME GAME

 A Mime an action.
B Ask what A is doing.

Example
B *'Are you cooking?'*
A *'No, I'm not.'*
B *'Are you washing a car?'*
A *'Yes, I am.'*

FOLLOW UP

7 Write your answers to Exercise 2.

✳ *Teacher*: Jane, name seven animals that live in Africa.
Jane: A giraffe and six elephants.

✳ *Mother*: Jane! Why are you writing on your T-shirt?
Jane: The teacher said we've got to write a project on clothes.

READING

Fashion parade

For Exercises 1–5 divide the class into groups of three or four. This activity works in two stages. First, students use their existing vocabulary and grammatical knowledge (clothes and colours; *he/she*) to match texts to pictures. Then, they use the pictures to work out the meanings of the new words in each text.

1
- Students look at page 68.

a • Ask *Which outfit do you like best? Why?*
- Students give their ideas.

b • Read the instructions aloud.
- Make sure students understand the activity.
- Students read the six texts and match them to the correct models. They write the model's name on the correct picture.
- Students give their answers.
- Ask *How do you know?* Students justify their choice by quoting from the texts.

Answer key
1 *Liz*
2 *Ben*
3 *Katy*
4 *Colin*
5 *Sharon*
6 *David*

2
- Read out the list of words.
- Explain the activity. Point out that now that they know which pictures goes with which text, they should be able to work out what the unknown words mean.
- Students label an example of each thing in the pictures.
- Students give their answers. They hold up their books to point to the item and give its name.

3 a • In their groups students design a new outfit, using the items in the pictures. If you wish they can make one outfit for boys and one for girls.

b • Choose groups to describe their ideas.

4
- Students give their ideas.
- Ask *Why?* Students explain their choice. (This discussion can be carried out in English.)

5
- Students draw a chart.
- Ask *What do you think 'unisex' means?*

Answer key
Can be worn, by either sex, for example, jeans.

- Students fill in their chart.
- Copy the chart onto the board.
- Students call out words for the lists. Write them on the board. (Or choose three students. Each one completes the list for boys, girls or unisex on the board. Other students add more words.)

6
- Students choose their six favourite items of clothing.
- Choose students to read out their lists.

FOLLOW UP

7   Students write a description of their clothes.

READING

1 **a** Look at the pictures. Which outfit do you like best? Why?

b Read the texts. Match them to the correct pictures and write the names of the people.

Sharon's wearing a pink jumper, a dark brown skirt, brown tights and brown shoes. Her jumper is £12.99 from 'Dorothy Perkins'. The jacket is grey with pink buttons and is £49.99 from 'Warehouse'. Sharon's also wearing a purple headband and pink gloves.

Ben's suit is by Dior. What do you call that colour? Brown? Pink? You describe it. With his suit Ben's wearing a brown and white shirt, a brown belt and brown shoes. He's carrying a black coat.

Where's **Katy** going in this outfit? She's wearing a black dress, tights and black shoes. Her earrings and bracelet are from 'The Jewel Shop'. The brooch on her dress is her grandmother's! Katy's carrying a black and silver bag.

Now what's **Colin** wearing? Is it a suit? Maybe, but it hasn't got trousers. It's got shorts. Colin is also wearing an orange shirt, a grey waistcoat and canvas shoes. Colin's outfit is by Byblos.

Is **David** a sports fan? He's wearing a white cricket sweater and black and white baseball boots, and he's holding a red baseball cap in his hand. The cricket sweater is £28 from 'Sportif' and the baseball cap is £8.50 from 'You'. David is also wearing jeans, red and grey socks and a black watch.

Liz's outfit is cheap and sporty. She's wearing a black sweatshirt with a hood (£18 from 'French Connection'), red shorts, black tights and black and red trainers. What has she got in that bag?

fashion parade

1

4

3

2

5

 a Use the things in the pictures. Choose different items to make a new outfit.

b Describe your new outfit.

Which outfit would you choose for these occasions?

a You are going to a friend's birthday party.
b You are going for a picnic.
c You are going to the cinema.
d You are visiting your grandparents.
e You are helping with the housework.
f You are going to a wedding.

W	O	R	D		W	O	R	K

How many names of clothes do you know? Put them in a chart like this. Who can make the longest list?

boys	girls	unisex

You are going on holiday. You can only take six things. Choose six things from your own clothes.

Example
My blue trousers.

FOLLOW UP

Describe the clothes that you are wearing now.

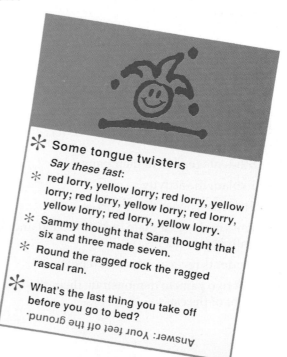

※ Some tongue twisters
Say these fast:
※ red lorry, yellow lorry; red lorry, yellow lorry; red lorry, yellow lorry; red lorry, yellow lorry; red lorry, yellow lorry.
※ Sammy thought that Sara thought that six and three made seven.
※ Round the ragged rock the ragged rascal ran.
※ What's the last thing you take off before you go to bed?
Answer: Your feet off the ground.

6

Find one example of each of these things in the pictures.

shirt	dress	shorts	trousers	waistcoat
belt	socks	cap	brooch	headband
suit	shoes	coat	jacket	
skirt	earrings	gloves	sweater	
tights	trainers	bag	bracelet	

69

LISTENING

A new pair of jeans

 a • Divide the class into pairs.

  • Students look at the pictures.

  • Ask *Who is in the pictures? What is he/she doing? What is he/she wearing?*

  • Students give their answers.

  • Students number the pictures to make a story.

  • Choose one pair to give their order. They explain their story.

  • Other students suggest different orders.

b • Play the tape.

  • Students listen and check their order.

  • Ask *What is the correct order?*

  • Students give their ideas and tell the story.

> **Answer key**
> The pictures should be numbered down the page as follows:
> 2   4   5   1   3

  • Play the tape again.

 A new pair of jeans

Mother Why are you wearing those old jeans, Cliff?
Boy People always wear old jeans. You can't wear new jeans, Mum.
Mother Here's £20. Go and buy some new jeans.

Boy How much are these jeans?
Assistant They're £19.99.

Mother Have you got your new jeans?
Boy Yes, they're in this bag. Where are the scissors?

Mother Cliff! What are you doing?
Boy I'm cutting these jeans.
Mother But they're your new jeans!
Boy People always cut their jeans. You can't wear new jeans, Mum.
Mother Kids! I don't understand you!

2 • Students remain in their pairs.

  • Explain the activity.

  • Students choose their roles.

  • Pairs make their dialogues. Go round and help with any problems.

  • Students reverse roles and repeat.

  • Get two pairs to demonstrate their dialogues in front of the class.

The present continuous and the present simple tense

BUILD UP

 a • Students look at the sentences.

  • Choose students to read the sentences aloud.

b • Ask *What are the two tenses?*

  • Students give their answers.

> **Answer key**
> **A** *the present continuous*
> **B** *the present simple*

  • Students study the rule.

 • Students look at the sentences.

  • Get one student to give the first sentence.

  • Students make the remaining sentences.

  • Students give their answers.

> **Answer key**
> **a** *'re having*
> **b** *have*
> **c** *'re doing*
> **d** *'m wearing*
> **e** *wear*
> **f** *'s looking*
> **g** *looks*

5 • Students give their ideas.

FOLLOW UP

6 • Students can complete the sentences at home or in class.

> **Answer key**
> (See tapescript.)

INTERACTION

At the clothes shop

 a • Divide the class into pairs.

  • Students look at the picture. Ask *Who is in the picture? Where are they? What are they doing?*

  • Students give their answers.

> **Answer key**
> *A boy and a girl*
> *The boy is a customer and the girl is a shop assistant.*
> *They're in a shop.*
> *The boy is buying a pair of jeans.*

b • Students look at the dialogue.

   • Make sure everyone understands the task.

   • Students write numbers in the boxes.

c • Play the tape. Students listen and check their order.

   • Discuss any problems.

   • Play the tape again.

How much are these jeans?
They're £18.95.
Can I try them on?
Of course. There's a changing room over there.
Are they all right?
Yes, they're fine.
Do you want anything else?
No, thank you.
That's £18.95, then, please.
Here you are.
That's £1.05 change. Thank you.
Thank you. Goodbye.
Goodbye.

 • Demonstrate the activity with one pair.

   • Students read the dialogue in pairs.

   • They reverse roles and repeat.

Words with no singular

BUILD UP

3 **a** • Students look at the examples.

   • Choose one student to read out the examples.

   • Explain *Clothes which go on the legs are plural, because they have two parts – one for each leg. Scissors is plural, because it has two parts.* (However, 'suit' and 'tracksuit' have a singular, even though they have two parts.)

b • Choose one pair. Demonstrate the activity with the examples.

   • Repeat with another pair.

   • All pairs do the activity. Go round and check for correct use of *is this* and *are these*.

   • They reverse roles and repeat.

   • Choose pairs to read each dialogue aloud.

 • Divide the class into new pairs.

   • Explain the activity. Students can use the dialogue from Exercise 1 to help them.

   • Students choose their roles.

   • Pairs make their dialogues. Go round and help with any problems.

   • Students reverse roles for alternate items.

   • Get two pairs to demonstrate their dialogues in front of the class.

FOLLOW UP

5 • Students write their dialogues at home or in class.

LISTENING

A new pair of jeans

1 a Look at these pictures. Number them in the correct order to make a story.

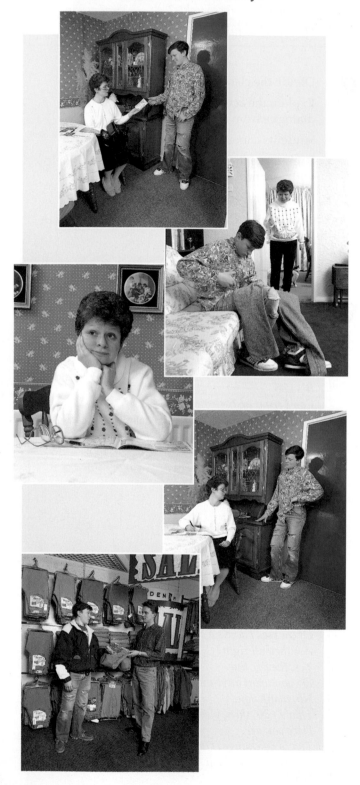

b Listen and check your order.

2 Work with a partner. Act the dialogue.

The present continuous and the present simple tense

3 a Look.

A	B
Why **are you wearing** those old jeans?	People always **wear** old jeans.
I'm cutting these jeans.	People always **cut** their jeans.

b What are these two tenses?

> The present continuous tense describes what is happening now, at the moment.
> The present simple tense describes the usual situation, or what happens regularly.

4 Complete these sentences. Put the verb in brackets into the correct tense.

a We .... an English lesson at the moment. (have)

b We .... English every day. (have)

c We .... an exercise about the present continuous tense. (do)

d I .... jeans today. (wear)

e I .... jeans to school every day. (wear)

f The teacher .... at my book now. (look)

g Our teacher .... at our books every lesson. (look)

5 'Kids! I don't understand you!' Do your parents ever say this to you? What about?

FOLLOW UP

6 Complete this dialogue.

Mother Cliff! ....?

Boy .... cutting these jeans.

Mother But they're your .... jeans.

Boy People .... jeans. .... new jeans, Mum.

Mother Kids! I .... understand you!

70

INTERACTION

At the clothes shop

1

a Look at the pictures.

- Where are the people?
- What are they doing?

b Number the questions and answers in the correct order to make the dialogue.

☐ Goodbye.

☐ Are they all right?

☐ They're £18.95.

☐ Thank you. Goodbye.

☐ Yes, they're fine.

☐ That's £1.05 change. Thank you.

☐ Of course. There's a changing room over there.

☐ That's £18.95, then, please.

☐ Do you want anything else?

☐ How much are these jeans?

☐ Here you are.

☐ No, thank you.

☐ Can I try them on?

c 📼 **Listen and check your answers.**

2 **Work with a partner. Act the dialogue.**

Words with no singular

BUILD UP

3 **a Look.**

this T-shirt   these jeans

These words are always plural.

jeans   trousers   tights   scissors

b Look at these clothes. Make dialogues.

Example
How much are these jeans?
They're £16.99.

How much is this T-shirt?
It's £7.30.

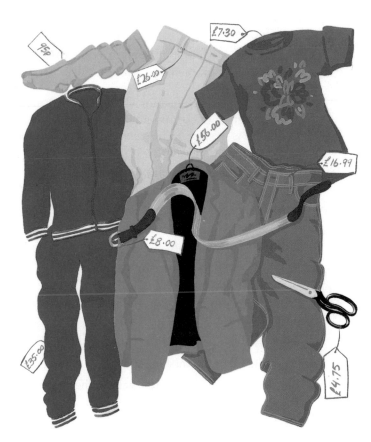

4 **Make shopping dialogues for these things in the pictures.**

T-shirt   tracksuit   trousers   jacket

Use the dialogue in Exercise 1 to help you.

FOLLOW UP

5 **Write your dialogues from Exercise 4 for the tracksuit and the trousers.**

PROJECT

Fashion page

This project can be done as an individual project or as a group project.
It can be done in class or at home.

- Students look at the pictures.
- Read out each word in turn. Students point to the correct item in their books.
- Explain the activity.
- Students look at the texts on page 68. Ask *What kind of information do the texts give?*
- Students give their ideas.
- Students plan their project.
- Students produce a rough draft of their project.
- Discuss the rough drafts and suggest corrections.
- Students can present their projects in two possible ways:
- 1 Students produce a finished project either on a large poster or in a book. Students display their projects.
  2 Students put on a fashion show. Students act as models and a commentator describes what he/she is wearing. This can be done as well as, or instead of, the written project.
- Discuss the projects. Ask *What problems did you find with vocabulary in this project? How did you find the words you needed?*

SONG: BE BOP-A-LULA

(First recorded by Gene Vincent on Capitol Records 1956)

 Students look at the song: Ask *What do you think the missing words are?*

- 🔲 Play the tape. Students listen.
- Students fill in the missing words.
- Play the tape again. Students check their answers.
- Students give their answers.
- Play the tape again. Students sing along.

Answer key

She's	don't	my	baby	doll	girl
dress	can	blue	queen	with	that

▶ **Pronunciation: page T113a**

LEARNING DIARY

Note
Discuss in the mother tongue.

A Students look at the contents list on page 63.

They draw a face next to each item to show how well they think they know it.

B Students do the self-check in the Workbook on page 67.

C Divide the class into pairs or groups of three or four.

Students compare their answers. Go round the class and check for any common problems.

Students compare their self-check results with the faces they drew.

In the whole class ask *What problems did you find with the self-check?* Students suggest problem areas.

Take remedial action, as necessary. (See Introduction page vii for possible strategies.)

Ask *What did you like best in this unit? What didn't you like?* Students give their responses. Ask *Why?* Take note of student responses. They can help you to adjust your teaching towards the things that motivate the students most.

CULTURE SPOT
Workbook page 67

- Divide the class into pairs or groups of three of four.
- Students look quickly at the text and pictures.
- Ask *What do you already know about this topic?*
- Students give their ideas. Discuss these ideas.
- Students look more closely at the text and pictures. Explain any words that students need.
- Ask *Did you find anything interesting or unusual?*
- Students give their ideas.
- Read each comparison question in turn.
- Discuss each question. Encourage students to compare their situation with the one in the text.

READING

- Divide the class into pairs.
- Students look at the pictures.
- Students write what each girl is doing, next to each picture.
- Students give their answers.

> **Answer key**
> 1 *She is getting up.*
> 2 *She is having a shower.*
> 3 *She is having her breakfast.*
> 4 *She is going to school.*
> 5 *She is watching a film at the cinema.*
> 6 *She is walking.*
> 7 *She is getting up.*
> 8 *She is getting some water.*
> 9 *She is carrying the water on her head.*
> 10 *She is working.*

- Choose one student to read out the questions.
- Students read the text and find the girls' names.

> **Answer key**
> *Selina, Kelly*

- Students draw two columns in their exercise books. They write **Selina** at the top of one column and **Kelly** at the top of the other.
- Students read the text and find the answers to the other questions. They write them in the columns.
- Students give their answers.

> **Answer key**
> (possible answers)
> **Selina**
> *She lives in a village in Africa.*
> *She gets up at 4 o'clock.*
> *She fetches water from the river three times a day.*
> *She helps her mother in the house.*
> *She goes to bed at 8 o'clock.*
>
> **Kelly**
> *She lives in a city in Britain.*
> *She gets up at 8 o'clock.*
> *She has a shower.*
> *She goes to school by car.*
> *She watches television or goes to the cinema in the evening.*

PROJECT

Fashion page

Make a fashion page for a magazine.

- Collect or draw pictures of clothes that you like.
  Or use photographs of yourself and your friends.
- Write what each model is wearing. Use the texts
  on page 68 to help you. There are some more useful
  words on this page.

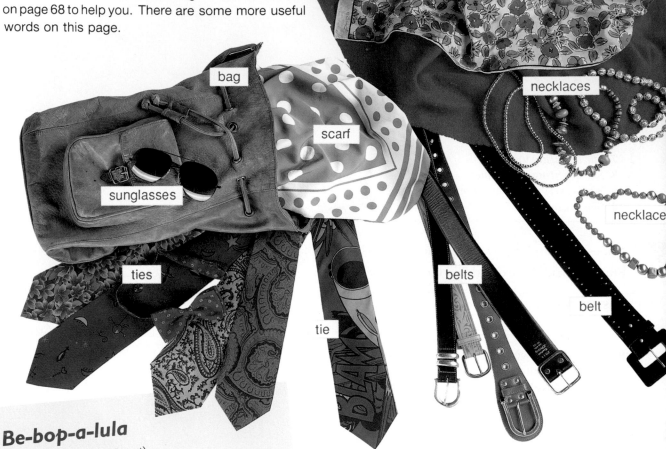

scarves

necklaces

bag

scarf

necklace

sunglasses

ties

tie

belts

belt

Be-bop-a-lula

(first recorded by Gene Vincent)

Chorus

    Be-bop-a-lula
    .... my baby.
    Be-bop-a-lula
    I .... mean maybe.
    Be-bop-a-lula
    She's .... baby.
    Be-bop-a-lula
    I don't mean maybe.
    Be-bop-a-lula
    She-e-e's my .... doll, my baby doll, my baby ....

1 See the .... with the red .... on.
    She .... do the boogie all night long.

2 See the girl in the tight, ... jeans.
    She's the .... of all the teens.

3 See the girl .... the diamond ring.
    She knows how to shake .... thing.

Learning diary

A Look at the first page of this unit.
How well do you know these things
now? Look at each point in the
contents list.

If you know it well,
draw a happy face.

If you know it fairly well,
draw a face like this.

If you don't know it well,
draw a sad face.

B Try the self-check in the Workbook.

C Compare your answers with a
partner. Discuss any
problems with your teacher.

9

▶ Pronunciation: page 113

READING

1 Look at these pictures. What are the two girls doing in each picture? Write your answer next to each picture.

2 Read the texts.

- What are the two girls' names?
- Where do they live?
- What does each girl do every day?

Selina lives in a village in Africa. Her day starts at 4 o'clock. She gets up and she walks three miles to the river. She collects some water and she carries it back to her house. It's very heavy. The water isn't clean, but there isn't any water in the village. Selina doesn't go to school. She can't read or write. She helps her mother in the house. She fetches water from the river three times every day. She goes to bed at 8 o'clock.

Kelly lives in a city in Britain. She gets up at 8 o'clock. She has a shower every morning. She eats her breakfast and then she goes to school. Her father takes her to school in his car. In the evening Kelly watches television or goes to the cinema with her friends. When Kelly wants some water, she goes to the kitchen or the bathroom.

Selina and Kelly live in different worlds. But Kelly knows Selina and Selina knows Kelly. At Kelly's school there is a photograph of Selina. In Selina's village there is a photograph of Kelly's class. Why?

73

3
- Students look at the example.
- Get one student to read the examples aloud.
- Students make the remaining sentences.
- Students give their answers.

Answer key

Kelly gets up at eight o'clock.
Selina doesn't get up at eight o'clock.

Kelly doesn't live in a village.
Selina lives in a village.

Kelly doesn't carry water.
Selina carries water.

Kelly doesn't walk eighteen miles each day.
Selina walks eighteen miles each day.

Kelly travels by car.
Selina doesn't travel by car.

Kelly watches television.
Selina doesn't watch television.

Kelly goes to the cinema.
Selina doesn't go to the cinema.

 4 a
- Divide the class into pairs.
- Choose one student to read the instructions.
- Choose another student to give the first question.
- Pairs write the remaining questions.
- Choose pairs to give their answers.

Answer key

When do you get up?
How do you travel (go) to school?
What do you do in the evening?
Where does Selina live?
When does she get up?
Why does she fetch water from the river?
Does she go to school?
When does she go to bed?

b
- Demonstrate the activity with one pair.
- In pairs students read the dialogue.
- They reverse roles and repeat.

 5 a
- Students look at the pictures.
- Ask *Who are the people? Where are they?*
- Students give their ideas.
- Ask *What do you think the people are doing?*
- Students say what the people are doing in each picture.
- Ask *Why do you think the people are doing these things?*
- Students give their ideas.

b
- Play the tape. Students listen and number each picture.
- Play the tape again. Students check their answers.

Answer key
4 2 5 6 7 3 1

- Point to each picture. Ask *What is happening?*

 One World

Selina and Kelly live in different worlds. But Kelly knows Selina and Selina knows Kelly. At Kelly's school there is a photograph of Selina. In Selina's village there is a photograph of Kelly's class. Why? Kelly and her friends collect things. They collect stamps, bottles, cans, old clothes. They take these things to school. At the school there is a bottle bank, a stamp bank, a can bank and a clothes bank. The boys and girls put their things in the banks. When there a lot of things in the banks, they sell them. They send the money to Selina's village. The people in the village buy tools and materials. They are building a pipe from the river to the village.

6
- Students look at the example.
- Get one student to read the example aloud.
- Get another student to give the next dialogue.
- Students make the remaining dialogues.
- Students give their answers.

Answer key

1 *What are you doing?*
  We're building a pipe.
2 *What are you doing?*
  I'm taking the bottles to school.
3 *What are you doing?*
  We're buying tools.
5 *What are you doing?*
  We're putting bottles into the bottle bank.
6 *What are you doing?*
  I'm selling the bottles.
7 *What are you doing?*
  I'm sending the money to Selina's village.

7
You can do this activity as a whole class discussion if you prefer.
- Divide the class into groups of five or six.
- Ask *How can you help other people?*
- Students suggest ideas:
  (possible ideas)
  helping parents in the home
  helping younger brothers and sisters
  helping old people
  collecting or giving money to charities
  helping at church or in a club

- Groups write down what they do to help other people.
- Groups report their findings.

FOLLOW UP

8 Students use the pictures in Exercise 5. They describe what Kelly and her friends do.

> **Answer key**
> (See tapescript for **5a**: students' answer should reproduce the information on the tape.)

Selina and Kelly: Different worlds or one world?

 3 Do Kelly and Selina do these things? Write sentences.

Example
Kelly goes to school.
Selina doesn't go to school.

go to school
get up at eight o'clock
live in a village
carry water
walk eighteen miles each day
travel in a car
watch television
go to the cinema

4 A local radio station is making a programme called 'One World'. An interviewer is talking to Kelly about her life and Selina's life.

a Here are Kelly's answers. What are the questions?

Interviewer ....?
Kelly I get up at eight o'clock.

Interviewer How ....?
Kelly My father usually takes me in his car.

Interviewer ....?
Kelly I watch TV or I go to the cinema with my friends.

Interviewer ....?
Kelly In a village in Africa.

Interviewer ....?
Kelly At four o'clock. And then she collects water from the river.

Interviewer Why ....?
Kelly Because there isn't any water in her village.

Interviewer ....?
Kelly No, she doesn't. She helps her mother in the house.

Interviewer ....?
Kelly At eight o'clock in the evening.

b Work with a partner. Role play the interview.

 5 Why do Selina and Kelly know each other?

a Look at these pictures. What are the people doing in each picture?

b 🔊 Listen to part of the radio programme about Kelly and Selina. Put the pictures in the correct order.

6 Interview the people in the pictures. Ask them what they are doing.

Example
What are you doing?
I'm collecting bottles.

7 Do you help other people? Ask people in your class. Write what they do.

FOLLOW UP

8 Describe how Kelly and her friends help Selina.

✳ What is a frog's favourite drink?
Answer: Croaka Cola.

✳ What do you get after someone has taken it?
Answer: A photograph.

✳ Where does Friday come before Thursday?
Answer: In the dictionary.

LANGUAGE WORK

- Divide the class into eight groups
- Groups make their lists.
- Draw eight columns on the board.
- Get someone from each group to complete one of the lists on the board.
- Other groups add further items to the list.

- Students look at the sentences.
- If necessary, revise the rule for *some* and *any*.
- Get one student to give the first sentence.
- Students make the remaining sentences.
- Students give their answers.

> **Answer key**
>
> **a** *any*   **d** *any*   **g** *some, some*
>
> **b** *some*   **e** *some*   **h** *any*
>
> **c** *any*   **f** *any*

GRAMMAR GAME

In this game, students practise grammar in an enjoyable context. As they move around the board, each student builds up a list of words. They must try to make a grammatically correct sentence from any four or more of their words. In playing this game, students use a lot of grammar. Although they only make one final sentence, they will make a lot of possible sentences in their head as they try to make the winning sentence, so they are constantly practising grammar rules as they play.

Here are some additional rules:
You can only use your own words.
You can't add any words.
You can use your words in any order, as long as it is correct grammar.
Your sentence can be a statement, a question or an imperative.
If you make a wrong sentence, you miss a turn.
If there is any doubt about a sentence, the group decides whether it is correct or not.
(optional) If you don't speak English, you miss a turn.

Procedure

- Divide the class into groups of four or five. Groups sit round a table with one copy of the game in the middle.
- If necessary, get students to make a dice using a pencil. Most pencils have six sides. Students scratch numbers 1–6 on each side. They roll the pencil as a dice.
- Demonstrate the game with one group.

- Groups play the game. Go round and deal with any problems or disputes.
- Groups check their winning sentences with you. Then they can play another round.
- If you notice any problems with grammar, revise the grammar point.

This activity is a mini-project. Students describe their daily life. They illustrate it with some pictures.

- Students look at the instructions.
- Say *Imagine you were writing to Kelly or Selina about your life. What would you say?*
- Students give their ideas.
- Make sure everyone understands the task.
- Students write their essays.
- Check essays for the correct use of present tenses.

▶ **Pronunciation: page T114**

You can start immediately with the Victoria Road story on page 78, or you can pre-teach the past tense of *to be*, using the material on page 77. If you wish to pre-teach the language, use the following procedure.

> **Note**
> At this stage you only need to introduce the grammar items, so that students can understand the story more easily. There are exercises later for more concentrated practice. Spend no more than 10 minutes on the pre-teaching.

1 Introduce *yesterday*.

- Ask *What day is it today?*
- Elicit response.
- Say *Today is (Tuesday). Yesterday was (Monday).*

2 Introduce *was*.

- Say *I'm at school today. I was at school yesterday, too.* (If it's Monday, say *I'm at school today, but I was at home yesterday.*)
- Choose a student. Ask *Where were you yesterday?*
- Elicit the answer *I was ... .*
- Repeat with other students.
- Choose another student. Point to a student who has answered your question. Ask *Where was he/ she yesterday?*
- Repeat with other students.

3 Introduce *were*.

- Point to two students. Say *They were at school (at home) yesterday.*
- Choose another student. Ask *Where were they yesterday?*
- Elicit the response *They were at school (at home).*
- Repeat with other students.

4 • Students open their books and look at the examples for the past tense of *to be*.

- Choose students to read the examples.

5 Start the Victoria Road story on page 78.

LANGUAGE WORK

1 **Write down these things.**

5 sports
6 kinds of clothes
3 things that you do in the morning
3 things that you don't do in the morning
3 things that you do at the weekend
3 things that you don't do at the weekend
5 buildings
6 things that you see on a map

2 **Complete these sentences from the radio programme about Selina and Kelly. Use 'some' or 'any'.**

a There isn't .... water in the village.

b There is .... water in the river, but it isn't clean.

c There aren't .... bathrooms in the huts in the village.

d The people in the village haven't got .... money for their pipe.

e Kelly's friends send them .... money.

f Have you got .... bottles for the bottle bank?

g I've got .... cans and .... stamps.

h Has Selina got .... brothers or sisters?

GRAMMAR GAME

3 Move round the board. When you land on a word, write it down. The first person to make a correct sentence with four or more of the words is the winner.

FOLLOW UP

4 Write to someone in another country.

- Tell them about your life.
- Say how often you do things.
- Add some pictures. Say what you are doing in the pictures.

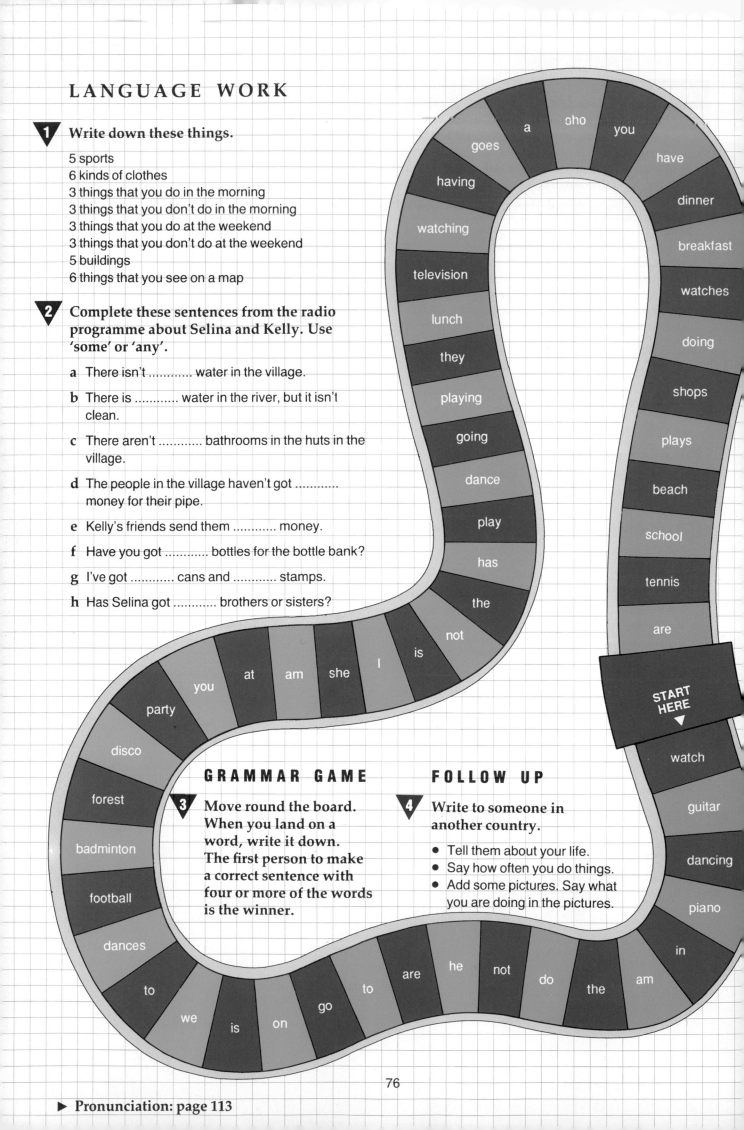

START HERE

76

▶ Pronunciation: page 113

11 mystery

the past simple: to be / regular verbs

Contents

Grammar points

78 **Victoria Road:** In the park

80 **Language work**   the verb 'to be': past tense

82 **Reading:** Was it Nessie?   the past simple tense: regular verbs

84 **Listening:** The Grey Lady   past tense verbs with /ɪd/ endings

85 **Interaction:** Write a play

86 **Project:** Mysteries

The main grammar points in this unit are:

the past simple tense: 'to be'

Yesterday in Victoria Road . . .

Sue wasn't at the hospital.
She was at the cinema.
Was Kamala at the cinema, too?

Casey and Vince weren't at the cinema.
They were in the park.
Where were Terry and Darren Tooley?

the past simple tense: regular verbs

Now   *In 1988*
Alan lives in Scotland. *He **lived** in Scotland.*
He works in a hotel.   *He **worked** in a hotel.*

VICTORIA ROAD

In the park

- Books closed. Ask *What happened in the last episode of 'Victoria Road'?*
- Students give their responses. Ask follow-up questions.

Answer key

Sue went to the cinema with some friends. She gave her bags and coat to Kamala. Kamala missed the bus. She caught a later bus. Terry was on the bus, because he played table tennis after school. When they arrived at Victoria Road, Terry saw Darren Tooley and his friends. They were waiting for Terry. Terry offered to take Sue's coat and bags home for Kamala. Then Kamala went home. Terry put Sue's coat on and walked past Tooley and his friends, hoping they would not recognize him, but the wind blew the hood of the coat down. Tooley saw Terry. He and his friends chased Terry.

- Students open their books and read the questions.
- Choose students to read the questions aloud.
- Students look through the picture story to find the answers to the questions. They can refer to the full text, too.
- Students give their answers to the questions.

Answer key

Casey, Vince, Mrs Scott
Vince and Casey are in the park. Later Vince and his mother are at home.
Vince and Casey are walking through the park. They find Sue's bags.
Sue's coat
Sue does her community work at the hospital on Wednesdays.

- Ask *What happens in this episode?*
- Using the pictures, students give a summary of the story.
- Explain any new vocabulary that students need to understand the dialogue.

Answer key

Vince and Casey are in the park. They find Sue's books and bags. Then they see a coat in the lake. They jump in the water and get the coat. It's Sue's coat. Vince telephones the hospital, but Sue isn't there. When his mother comes home, she telephones the police.

- Say *Now look at the full dialogue.*
- Play the tape. Students listen and follow in their books.
- Play the tape again, if necessary.
- Ask the 'What do you think?' questions.
- Students give their ideas.

Notes

4–nil This is a football score. To give football scores, we just give the number of goals for each side (for example, *two–one, three–two*) *Nil* means no goals. If the score is a draw, we say 'four–all' (4–4) or one–all (1–1).

brilliant The normal meaning of this word is 'very bright' or, metaphorically, very clever (a brilliant scientist). Today among young people it is used as a general word for 'very good'.

We'd better . . . This means 'I think we should . . .'.

- Students answer the questions.
- Choose students to read each question and give the answer. Pay particular attention to the use of the past tense of *to be*.
- Ask *How do you know?*
- Students use the dialogue to justify their answers. (This is a very important stage, because it shows whether students have understood the dialogue.)

Answer key

They were in the park.
They were on their way back from football.
Sue's books were on the grass.
It was in the lake.
No, it wasn't. It was under a bench.
No, she wasn't.
No, she wasn't.

- Books closed.
- Play the tape again. Stop after each utterance. Students repeat.
- Repeat any utterances that students find difficult.

Useful expressions

- Divide the class into pairs.
- Students look at the list of expressions. They write a translation in the boxes. They use the story and context to work out an appropriate mother-tongue expression.

> **Note**
> A lot of these expressions are idioms and cannot be translated word for word. Make sure students understand this.

- Students give their answers. Discuss as necessary.

- Divide the class into pairs.
- Students choose their roles.
- Students read the dialogue.
- If time, change roles and do the dialogue again.
- Choose one pair to act the dialogue in front of the class.

FOLLOW UP

- Say *Casey told his mother what happened*.
- Students fill in the gapped story.
- In pairs, students compare answers.
- Check answers.

> **Answer key**
> *Vince   way   from   in   There   grass*
> *lake   Sue's   under   coat   in   there*
> *at   Wednesdays   she*

In the park

1 Look at the story.

- Who are the people?
- Where are they?
- What are they doing?
- What is in the lake?
- Why does Mrs Scott think Sue is at the hospital?

> 4-nil. You were great, Casey. Your second goal was brilliant. I...

> Hey, look at all those books on the grass near the lake.

> These are Sue's books.

> There's someone in the water. Come on.

2 🔊 Listen and follow in your books.

Vince 4-nil. You were great, Casey. Your second goal was brilliant. I . . .

Casey Hey, look at all those books on the grass near the lake.

Casey These are Sue's books. What are they doing here?

Vince And here's her bag under this bench.

Casey What's that over there?

Vince There's someone in the water. Come on.

Vince Oh my God. It's Sue's coat. But where's Sue?

Casey She isn't here. Sue! Sue!

Later

Mrs Scott Now tell me again, Vince.

Vince I was in the park with Casey. We were on our way back from football.

Mrs Scott Where was Sue's coat?

Vince It was in the lake.

Mrs Scott Were the books in the water, too?

Vince No, they weren't. They were on the grass.

Mrs Scott But it's Wednesday. Sue must be at the hospital today.

Vince Well, she wasn't at the hospital half an hour ago.

Mrs Scott Oh dear! We'd better call the police.

What do you think?

- Where is Sue?
- What do Vince and Mrs Scott think?
- Why was Sue's coat in the lake?

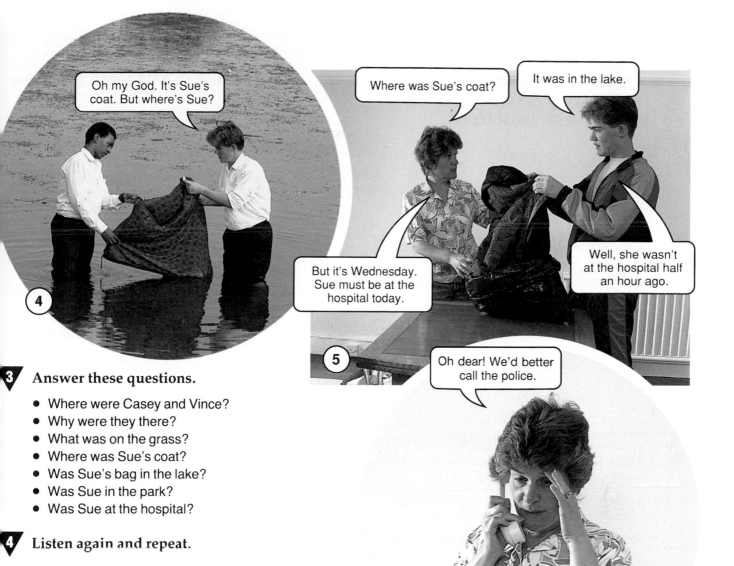

Oh my God. It's Sue's coat. But where's Sue?

④

Where was Sue's coat?

It was in the lake.

But it's Wednesday. Sue must be at the hospital today.

Well, she wasn't at the hospital half an hour ago.

⑤

Oh dear! We'd better call the police.

⑥

3 Answer these questions.

- Where were Casey and Vince?
- Why were they there?
- What was on the grass?
- Where was Sue's coat?
- Was Sue's bag in the lake?
- Was Sue in the park?
- Was Sue at the hospital?

4 Listen again and repeat.

Useful expressions

How do you say these in your language?

4–nil
You were great!
Brilliant!
What are they doing here?
Oh my God!
on our way back from …
She must be at the hospital.
half an hour ago
Oh dear!
We'd better …
call the police

6 Work with a partner. One person is Vince, one person is Casey and Mrs Scott. Read the dialogue.

FOLLOW UP

7 Casey is talking to his parents. Complete what he says.

.... and I were on our ....
back .... football. We were
.... the park. .... were
some books on the .... near the
.... They were .... books.
Her bag was .... a bench and her
.... was .... the water. But
Sue wasn't .... She usually does her
community work .... the hospital on
.... But .... wasn't there
today.

LANGUAGE WORK

The verb 'to be': past tense

BUILD UP

 a • Divide the class into pairs.

• Students complete the sentences. While they are doing this, copy the sentences onto the board.

• Choose students to come out and complete the sentences.

Answer key
was
was
wasn't
were
were
were
weren't

b • Students complete the table. They use the Victoria Road story to help them. While they are doing this copy the table onto the board.

• Choose students to come out and complete the table.

• Students quote examples from the story to justify the rule in the table.

• Students make ten sentences using the table.

Answer key		
I		
He	*was*	
She	*wasn't*	*in the park.*
It		
		great.
We		
You	*were*	*at the hospital.*
They	*weren't*	

 a • Students complete the dialogue, in the same pairs as before.

• Choose pairs to read out parts of the dialogue. Other students compare their answers.

Answer key				
were	*was*	*were*	*was*	*Were*
wasn't	*was*	*was*	*was*	*Were*
weren't	*were*	*was*	*was*	*wasn't*
wasn't	*wasn't*	*wasn't*	*Was*	*was*

b • In pairs students read the dialogue.

• They reverse roles and repeat.

The verb 'to be': past tense questions

BUILD UP

 a • Students complete the table.

• Copy the table onto the board.

• Choose students to complete the table on the board.

Answer key
The books were on the grass.   Were the books on the grass?
Sue was at school.   Was Sue at school?

b • Ask *How do we make questions with the past tense of the verb 'to be'?*

• Students complete the rule.

• Choose one student to read out the rule.

Answer key
was   were   (either order)

• Demonstrate the rule with the table on the board.

Years

BUILD UP

 a • Students look at the examples.

• Choose one student to read the examples.

b • Choose students to say the years.

Answer key
nineteen seventy-two
nineteen forty-five
fourteen ninety-two
eighteen oh one
ten sixty-six

• Write more examples on the board, if you wish. Use these: *1567, 1820, 1995, 1909, 1705, 1666.*

A GENERAL KNOWLEDGE QUIZ

 a • Divide the class into groups of three or four.

• Students read the questions and choose the correct answer. Explain any vocabulary, as necessary.

• Read out the questions and answers in turn. Groups say whether the answer is correct or not. Write on the board how many groups agree with each possible answer.

b • ▣ Play the tape. Stop after each question. Students check their answers.

(The questions are given in the Student's Book.)
 1 The first man on the moon was Neil Armstrong.
 2 The first man in space was from Russia. His
    name was Yuri Gagarin.
 3 The 'King of Rock and Roll' was Elvis Presley.
 4 The Beatles were from Liverpool in England.
 5 The First World War was from 1914 to 1918.
    (The Second World War was from 1939 to 1945.)
 6 Christopher Columbus was from Genoa in Italy.
 7 The World football champions in 1986 were
    Argentina.
 8 In 1988 the Olympics were in Seoul in Korea.
 9 The first president of the United States of
    America was George Washington.
10 Superman was from Krypton.

- Groups add up their totals. See which group
  got the most correct.

- Discuss each question. Find out what the
  students know about each of the possible
  answers, for example, what they know about
  Kennedy, Lincoln and Reagan.

FOLLOW UP

6

> **Answer key**
> (See tapescript for **5b**: students' answers
> should reproduce the information on the tape.)

LANGUAGE WORK

The verb 'to be': past tense

BUILD UP

 a Complete these sentences from the Victoria Road story.

I .... in the park with Casey.

It .... in the lake.

She .... at the hospital half an hour ago.

You .... great, Casey.

We .... on our way back from football.

They .... on the grass.

No, they ....

This is the past tense of 'to be'.

b Complete this table. Use these words.

were   weren't   was

I He She It	.... wasn't	in the park. great.
We You They	....	at the hospital.

 2 A policewoman is interviewing Vince.

a Complete their conversation with 'was', 'wasn't', 'were' or 'weren't'.

Policewoman Where .... you?

Vince I .... in the park.

Policewoman Why .... you in the park?

Vince I .... on my way back from football.

Policewoman .... you alone?

Vince No, I .... My friend Casey .... with me.

Policewoman Where .... the bag?

Vince It .... under a bench.

Policewoman .... the books under the bench, too?

Vince No, they .... They .... on the grass.

Policewoman And where .... the coat?

Vince It .... in the lake.

Policewoman But your sister .... there. Is that right?

Vince No, she .... in the park. She .... at home and she .... at the hospital.

Policewoman .... she at school in the afternoon?

Vince Yes, she ....

b Work with a partner. Act the conversation.

The verb 'to be': past tense questions

BUILD UP

 3 **a** Put these words in the correct order to make a statement and a question.

	statement	question

on were
  the grass
  books the
school
  Sue at was		

b How do we make questions with the verb 'to be' in the past tense? Complete the rule.

> To make questions in the past tense of the verb 'to be', we put .... or .... in front of the subject.

Years

BUILD UP

 4 **a** Look.

1914 = nineteen fourteen
1885 = eighteen eighty-five

b Say these years.

1972   1945   1492   1801   1066

a **Answer the questions.**

A GENERAL KNOWLEDGE QUIZ

1 Who was the first man on the Moon?

  a John Glenn
  b Yuri Gagarin
  c Neil Armstrong
  d Buzz Aldrin

2 Where was the first man in space from?

  a Russia
  b America
  c Germany
  d Japan

3 Who was the 'King of Rock and Roll'?

  a James Dean
  b Elvis Presley
  c Bob Dylan
  d John Lennon

4 Where were the Beatles from?

  a San Francisco
  b London
  c New York
  d Liverpool

5 When was the First World War?

  a 1914–18
  b 1939–45
  c 1910–1915
  d 1885–1900

6 Where was Christopher Columbus from?

  a Portugal
  b Spain
  c Italy
  d Brazil

7 Who were the world football champions in 1986?

  a Argentina
  b West Germany
  c the Netherlands
  d Denmark

8 Where were the Olympics in 1988?

  a Japan
  b America
  c Korea
  d Greece

9 Who was the first president of the United States?

  a John F. Kennedy
  b George Washington
  c Abraham Lincoln
  d Ronald Reagan

10 Where was Superman from?

  a Tristan
  b Saturn
  c the Moon
  d Krypton

b **Listen and check your answers.**

FOLLOW UP

6 Write the correct answers to the quiz in full.

READING

Was it Nessie?

 a • Students look at the questions.

• Choose one student to read out the questions.

• Students look at the text and the pictures to find the answers.

• Students give their answers.

Answer key
1 *Alan Cockerell*
2 *It was 1988.*
3 *He was at Loch Ness in Scotland.*
4 *It's about the Loch Ness monster.*

b • Students give their ideas.

Notes
Loch Ness is in Scotland. It is the deepest lake in Britain. Many people believe that there is a prehistoric monster living in the lake. Some people have seen things that look like possible monsters (see the photographs), but no one has ever taken a conclusive photograph. The monster is often called 'Nessie'.

 In this activity students are encouraged to work out a grammar rule for themselves.

a • Divide the class into pairs.

• Students look at the table.

• Explain the activity.

• Students read the first paragraph and complete the table.

• Copy the table onto the board.

• Choose students to complete the table on the board.

Answer key
worked
finished
walked

b • Students look at the table. Ask *What do you notice about all the verbs in the 'past' column?*

• Students give their ideas.

• Students complete the rule.

Answer key
-ed

c • Students look through the story and find more past tense verbs.

• Students give their ideas.

Answer key
happened
appeared
stopped
looked
moved
watched
hurried
grabbed
returned

 • Students look at the pictures.

• Students read the text and number the pictures in the correct order.

• Students give their order.

• Ask *How do you know?* Students quote from the text to justify their order.

Answer key

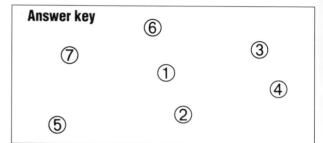

 • Students use the pictures to tell the story.

Answer key
(possible answer)
Alan Cockerell finished work at two o'clock. He walked home alone.
While he was on his way home, something happened in the lake.
He stopped and looked at it.
Then he hurried to his cottage.
He grabbed his camera.
He returned to the lake, but there was nothing there.

 • Students answer the questions.

• Students give their answers.

• Students quote from the text to justify their answers.

Answer key
Nessie is the Loch Ness monster.
He's a waiter.
He worked late. His friends were already at home.
It was large and black.
He didn't have his camera. He fetched his camera, but when he returned to the lake, the thing wasn't there.

• Students look at the pictures.

• Students give their opinions.

FOLLOW UP

Answer key
(See Exercise 4.)

READING

Was it Nessie?

a **Look quickly at the story and the pictures. Answer these questions.**

- What is the man's name?
- What year was it?
- Where was he?
- What is the story about?

b **What do you know about this topic?**

My name is Alan Cockerell. I'm a waiter. I work at a hotel near Loch Ness. I live in a cottage near the hotel. I finish work in the hotel at one o'clock in the morning. Then I walk home with two friends. They work at the hotel, too.

One night in 1988 I worked late. I finished work at two o'clock. I walked home alone, because my friends were already at home. It was a clear night and there was a full moon.

While I was on my way to my cottage, something happened. Something appeared in the lake. It was large and black. I stopped and looked at it. The thing moved along the lake. I watched it for about a minute. Then I hurried to my cottage and grabbed my camera.

But when I returned to the lake, there was nothing there.

I'm sure it was the Loch Ness monster. It was Nessie. I know it was.

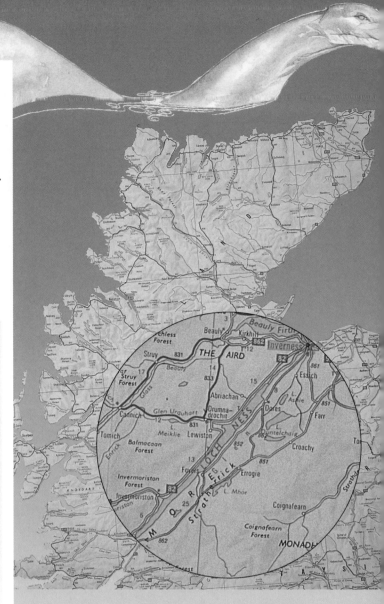

The past simple tense

BUILD UP

a **Read the first two paragraphs. Complete this table with the correct form of the verbs.**

1988 past	now present
....	work
....	finish
....	walk

b **How do we make the past tense? Complete this rule.**

> To make the past tense, we add .... to the verb.

c **Find more examples of past tense verbs in the story.**

3 Read the story and number these pictures in the correct order.

4 Use the pictures. Tell the story.

5 Answer these questions.

- Who is Nessie?
- What is Alan Cockerell's job?
- Why was he alone that night?
- What was the thing like?
- Why hasn't Alan got a photograph of the thing?

6 What do you think?

- Is this the Loch Ness monster?
- Do you believe Alan Cockerell's story?

FOLLOW UP

7 Write Alan's story. Write one sentence about each of the pictures in Exercise 3. Start like this.

Alan finished work at two o'clock. He walked home alone . . .

83

LISTENING

The Grey Lady

 • Students look at the picture.
- Ask *What do you think the story is about?*
- Students give their ideas.

> **Answer key**
> *a ghost*

- Ask follow-up questions *What kind of ghost was it? Who saw it?*

 • Students read the questions.
- Play the first part of the tape. Students listen.
- Students give their answers. Ask questions to get all the information, for example, *What was his/her name? When did she live there? What did she do first? What did she shout?*

> **Answer key**
> *The Grey Lady. Her name was Lucy Loxley. She lived in the house a long time ago. Her father was Sir Roger Loxley. He owned the house. She appeared in the room. She started to cry. She shouted 'No, no, never!' Then she walked through the wall.*

- Play the tape again, if necessary.
- Ask *What do you think happened to Lucy?* Students give their ideas.

📼 The Grey Lady: part 1
Woman Who are you?
Ghost No! no! Never!
Man What's the matter? What's the matter?
Woman There was someone here in the room. A ghost.
Man Oh, don't be silly. It . . .
Housekeeper Was it a young woman?
Woman Yes, it was.
Man Well, what happened?
Woman This young woman. She just appeared. She started to cry. Then she shouted 'No! No! Never!' and she . . . she walked through that wall and she disappeared.
Man Walked through the wall? Oh, that's silly!
Housekeeper It isn't silly, sir. That was the Grey Lady.
Man The Grey Lady. Who was she?
Housekeeper A long time ago a man called Sir Roger Loxley owned this house. He had a daughter. Her name was Lucy. She was the Grey Lady.

 • Divide the class into groups of three or four.
- Students look at the pictures. Ask *Who are the people?*
- Students read the cues. Explain any new vocabulary.
- Explain the activity.
- Students use the cues to decide what happened to Lucy.
- Choose one group to tell the story. Encourage students to use the correct past form of the cues.
- Other groups suggest different stories.

 • 📼 Play the second part of the tape.
- Students listen and check their ideas.

📼 The Grey Lady: part 2
Housekeeper A long time ago a man called Sir Roger Loxely owned this house. He had a daughter. Her name was Lucy. She was the Grey Lady.
Man What happened to her?
Housekeeper You see, Sir Roger gambled. He needed money. A rich neighbour, Lord Griston, wanted to marry Lucy. He was old and ugly. He offered Sir Roger a lot of money.
But Lucy refused to marry Lord Griston. She wanted to marry Thomas Mowbray. He lived in the village. He was young and handsome and he loved Lucy. But he was poor.
Woman Did Lucy marry Lord Griston?
Housekeeper No. She refused to marry him. Sir Roger locked Lucy in this room. Lucy cried and cried. Then, one night she jumped out of that window and died.
Man But there isn't a window there. It's a wall.
Housekeeper Look again. You see? There was a window there. Sir Roger filled it up.
Woman Look! She's right. You can see where the old window was. Oh, poor Lucy!

- In their groups students write the cues under the pictures.
- Draw four columns on the board.
- Choose four students to write the cues in the columns.
- Students correct the position of the cues, if necessary.
- Play both parts of the tape again.

> **Answer key**
> **Sir Roger Loxley**
> *gamble*
> *own the house*
> *need money*
> *accept Lord Griston's money*
> *lock Lucy in a room*

Lucy Loxley
refuse to marry Lord Griston
want to marry Thomas Mowbray
cry
jump out of a window

Thomas Mowbray
love Lucy
live in the village
young and handsome
poor

Lord Griston
offer Sir Roger a lot of money
want to marry Lucy
old and ugly
rich

Lord Griston
He offered Sir Roger a lot of money.
He wanted to marry Lucy.
He was old and ugly.
He was rich.

FOLLOW UP

 7 • Students use the cues to write the story.

Answer key
(possible answer)
Sir Roger Loxley owned the house. He had a daughter. Her name was Lucy. Sir Roger gambled. He needed money. A rich neighbour, Lord Griston, wanted to marry Lucy. He offered Sir Roger a lot of money. Sir Roger accepted the money, but Lucy refused to marry Lord Griston. She wanted to marry Thomas Mowbray. He lived in the village. He was young and handsome and he loved Lucy, but he was poor. Sir Roger locked Lucy in a room. She cried and cried. One night she jumped out of a window and died.

INTERACTION

 1 a • Revise the story of the Grey Lady again. Play the tape again or choose a student to read his/her story.

• Divide the class into groups of four.

• Students read the instructions. Make sure everyone understands the activity.

• Students write their dialogue. The play should last only 3–4 minutes.

• Go round and help students with any problems.

b • Students choose their roles.

• In groups, students practise their dialogue.

c • Choose groups to perform their play in front of the class. Don't worry if not every group has a turn.

FOLLOW UP

 2 • Students memorize their play.

 5 a • Briefly revise regular past tenses. Use *lived, worked, appeared.*

• Students look at the sentences.

b • Play the tape again. Stop after each of the verbs in the sentences.

• Ask *What do you notice about the verbs?*

• Students give their ideas.

Answer key
The '-ed' ending is pronounced /ɪd/.

c • Students complete the rule.

Answer key
d   t

d • Choose students to read out the verbs. Correct the pronunciation of the *-ed* ending.

 6 • Students look at the cues.

• Choose students to say what each person did.

Answer key
Sir Roger Loxley
He gambled.
He owned the house.
He needed money.
He accepted Lord Griston's money.
He locked Lucy in a room.

Lucy Loxley
She refused to marry Lord Griston.
She wanted to marry Thomas Mowbray.
She cried.
She jumped out of a window.

Thomas Mowbray
He loved Lucy.
He lived in the village.
He was young and handsome.
He was poor.

1 Look at the picture. What do you think the story is about?

2 🔊 Listen to the first part of the tape. Answer these questions.

- Who was the ghost?
- What did it do?

3 What do you think happened a long time ago? Look at these pictures and the cues to help you decide.

offer Sir Roger a lot of money
love Lucy
gamble
live in the village
old and ugly
want to marry Lucy
lock Lucy in a room
refuse to marry Lord Griston
own the house
cry
poor
want to marry Thomas Mowbray
need money
jump out of a window
accept Lord Griston's money
young and handsome
rich

4 🔊 Listen to the second part and match the cues to the correct picture.

Lucy Loxley

refuse to marry
Lord Griston
. . . .
. . . .
. . . .
. . . .
. . . .

/ ɪd / **endings**

BUILD UP

 a Look at these sentences.

She **shouted** 'No! No! Never!'
He always **needed** money.
Lord Griston **wanted** to marry Lucy.

b Listen to the story of the Grey Lady again.
What do you notice about the verbs?

c Complete this rule.

> When the verb ends in .... or ...., we
> pronounce the -ed ending / ɪd /.

d Say these verbs.

watched	wanted	offered	refused
arrested	locked	jumped	needed
shouted	cried	lived	gambled

 6 Use the cues. Say what each person did in the
story.

FOLLOW UP

 7 Write the story of the Grey Lady.

INTERACTION

 1 Make a play about Lucy Loxley. Your play
should have four acts.

Act 1: Thomas and Lucy fall in love.
Act 2: Lord Griston and Sir Roger arrange the
marriage.
Act 3: Lucy refuses to marry Lord Griston.
Act 4: Sir Roger locks Lucy up and she jumps out
of the window.

a Work in a group of four. Write the
dialogue.

b Each person takes one of the roles.

Lucy Loxley	Lord Griston
Sir Roger Loxley	Thomas Mowbray

c Act your play.

FOLLOW UP

2 Learn your play.

Sir Roger Loxley

gamble
....
....
....
....
....

Lord Griston

offer Sir Roger
a lot of money
....
....
....
....

Thomas Mowbray

love Lucy
....
....
....
....
....

PROJECT

Mysteries

This project can be done as an individual project or as a group project. It can be done in class or at home. It will require some research.

- Students look at the pictures.
- Ask *What do you think the pictures show? Do you know anything about them?*
- Students give their ideas.
- Students look at the list of topics and match them to the pictures.
- Students give their ideas.
- Students choose a topic and plan their project.
- Students find information and produce a rough draft about their topic.
- Discuss the rough drafts and suggest corrections.
- Students produce a final version. They illustrate it.
- Students present their projects.
- Discuss the projects. Ask *What did you find easy or difficult in doing the project? How did you find information for your topic ?*

▶ **Pronunciation: page T114**

LEARNING DIARY

Note
Discuss in the mother tongue.

A Students look at the contents list on page 77.

 They draw a face next to each item to show how well they think they know it.

B Students do the self-check in the Workbook on page 77.

C Divide the class into pairs or groups of three or four.

 Students compare their answers. Go round the class and check for any common problems.

 Students compare their self-check results with the faces they drew.

 In the whole class ask *What problems did you find with the self-check?* Students suggest problem areas.

 Take remedial action, as necessary. (See Introduction page vii for possible strategies.)

Ask *What did you like best in this unit? What didn't you like?*
Students give their responses. Ask *Why?* Take note of student responses. They can help you to adjust your teaching towards the things that motivate the students most.

CULTURE SPOT
Workbook page 76

- Divide the class into pairs or groups of three or four.
- Students look quickly at the text.
- Ask *What is the text about?*
- Students give their ideas.
- Ask *What do you already know about this topic?*
- Students give their ideas. Discuss these ideas.
- Say *Read the Culture spot text. Note anything that you find interesting or unusual.*
- Ask comprehension questions about the text.
- Students give their answers. Explain any words that students need.
- Ask *Did you find anything interesting or unusual?*
- Students give their ideas.
- Read each comparison question in turn.
- Discuss each question. Encourage students to compare their situation with the one in the text.

You can pre-teach the main grammar points (irregular verbs and the past tense negative) in this unit when you discuss the story so far.

Note

At this stage you only need to introduce the grammar items, so that students can understand the story more easily. In particular, you only need to introduce the concept of irregular past forms, not all the irregular verbs in the story. There are exercises later for more concentrated practice.

---

1 • Books closed. Ask questions to revise the Victoria Road story so far.
   Ask:
   Where did Sue go after school?
   Did Kamala go with her?
   What did Sue do with her coat and her bags?
   What happened to Kamala?
   Who did she meet on the bus?
   Who did Terry see in Victoria Road?
   What did Kamala do with Sue's things?
   What did Terry do?
   What happened?
   Who found Sue's coat?
   Where did they find it?
   Did they find Sue?
   What did Mrs Scott do?

   • Students answer in English. When students give their answers, introduce the correct past tense form of the verb.

Answer key

It was Wednesday. Sue went to the cinema with some friends after school. Kamala didn't go with her. Sue didn't want to take her coat and bags to the cinema, so she gave them to Kamala. Kamala missed the bus. She got a later bus and she met Terry. When they arrived at Victoria Road, Darren Tooley and his friends were there. Terry took Sue's coat and bags. He put the coat on, but Tooley and his friends saw Terry. They chased him.
Later Vince and Casey were in the park. They found Sue's books on the grass and her coat in the lake. But Sue wasn't there. Vince telephoned the hospital, but she wasn't there. When Vince's mother came home, she telephoned the police.

---

2 • Students look at the example sentences on page 87.

   • Choose students to read the sentences.

   • Explain 'irregular verbs'. Give examples from the students' own language, if it has irregular verbs, too.

PROJECT
Mysteries

Collect information about some famous mysteries. Here are some topics.

- monsters like the yeti
- UFOs
- ghosts
- mysterious disappearances
- lost cities

Write about the mysteries and illustrate them with pictures and maps.

Learning diary

A Look at the first page of this unit. How well do you know these things now? Look at each point in the contents list.

If you know it well, draw a happy face.

If you know it fairly well, draw a face like this.

If you don't know it well, draw a sad face.

B Try the self-check in the Workbook.

C Compare your answers with a partner. Discuss any problems with your teacher.

11

► Pronunciation: page 113

Contents

Grammar points

88 **Victoria Road:** Sue's coat — the past simple tense: irregular verbs

91 **Language work** — the past simple tense: negative

92 **Reading:** Amazing escapes — more irregular verbs

94 **Listening:** Band Aid

95 **Interaction:** An interview — the past simple tense: questions

96 **Project:** A class newspaper

The main grammar points in this unit are:

the past simple tense: irregular verbs

Sue went to the cinema.

Casey and Vince found Sue's coat.

the past simple tense: negatives

Sue didn't bring her coat home. Kamala brought it home.

Terry didn't find Sue's coat. Vince and Casey found it.

the past simple tense: questions

What did Terry do with Sue's coat?

Did Vince and Terry find Sue's coat on the grass?

VICTORIA ROAD

Sue's coat

- Students open their books and read the questions.
- Choose students to read the questions aloud. Make sure everyone understands the questions.
- Students look through the picture story to find the answers to the questions. They can refer to the full text, too.
- Students give their answers to the questions.

Answer key

A policewoman, Kamala, Vince, Casey, Sue, Terry
They are in Kamala's parents' shop.
They are talking about Sue's coat.
He runs away from his friends.

- Ask *What happens in this episode?* Using the pictures, students give a summary of the story. Encourage students to use the past tense.
- Explain any new vocabulary that students need to understand the dialogue.

Answer key

A policewoman comes to Kamala's shop. She asks Kamala some questions. Suddenly, Sue arrives. Kamala tells the policewoman about Terry and the coat. Sue is very sorry. Then Terry appears at the window. But, when he sees his friends, he runs away. They chase him. Sue says she is sorry. Terry doesn't want to see his friends.

- Say *Now look at the full dialogue.*
- Play the tape. Students listen and follow in their books.
- Play the tape again, if necessary.
- Ask *Why didn't Terry want to see his friends?* Students give their ideas.

Notes

What's going on? This means 'What's happening?' It implies that something strange or unusual is happening.

I bet This means 'I think that'. It means that you are so sure that you would gamble money on it.

the rat This is not very polite. It means someone who can't be trusted.

you lot This is an informal way of showing that you mean the whole group, not just one person.

That's funny 'Funny' has two meanings. It can mean humorous or strange. Here it means strange. 'That's funny' means 'That's strange. I don't understand it.'

- Students answer the questions.
- Choose students to read each question and give the answer.
- Ask *How do you know?*
- Students use the dialogue to justify their answers. This is a very important stage, because it shows whether students have understood the dialogue.

Answer key

a *No, she didn't. She came home alone.*
b *She went to the cinema.*
c *Vince and Casey found it.*
d *She wanted to collect her coat and bags from Kamala.*
e *She gave it to Terry.*
f *He put it on.*
g *He saw him at the window.*
h *He ran away.*

Sue's coat

1 Look at this episode of the story.

- Who are the people?
- Where are they?
- What are they talking about?
- What does Terry do at the end?

Speech bubbles (photo 1):
> You come home with Sue Scott every day. Did you come home with her today?

> No, I didn't. I came home alone. Sue didn't come home.

Speech bubbles (photo 2):
> Hi, Kam. What's going on? There's a police car outside. Have you got my coat and...?

> Sue! You're alive!

2 🔊 Listen and follow in your book.

Policewoman You come home with Sue Scott every day. Did you come home with her today?

Kamala No, I didn't. I came home alone. Sue didn't come home. She went to the cinema with some friends. Why?

Casey We found her coat in the lake.

Kamala But Sue didn't have her coat. I had it. I brought it home for her. But I haven't got it now. I . . .

Sue Hi, Kam. What's going on? There's a police car outside. Have you got my coat and . . . ?

Vince and Casey Sue! You're alive!

  Later

Policewoman Well, what did you do with the coat?

Kamala I gave it to Terry.

Policewoman And what did he do with it?

Sue I bet he took it to the park and threw it in the lake – the rat!

Kamala No, he didn't do that, Sue. He did something strange. You see, I left him at the corner. When I got to the shop, I could still see him. And he, well . . . he put your coat on. Oh no! Now I understand. Those three boys. They wanted Terry.

Speech bubbles (photo 3):
> Oh no! Now I understand. Those three boys. They wanted Terry.

> You'd better tell us about the three boys, I think.

Policewoman You'd better tell us about the three boys, I think.

Later

Kamala So, that's what happened.

Sue Oh, it's all my fault. Poor Terry. Why did I do it?

Vince There he is! At the window.

Casey That's funny. When he saw us, he ran away.

Sue Terry, Terry.

Sue Terry, I'm sorry. I'm sorry.

Terry Oh, hi, you lot.

Why didn't Terry want to see his friends?

3 Answer these questions.

a Did Kamala come home with Sue today?
b Where did Sue go after school?
c Who found the coat?
d Why did Sue come to the shop?
e Why didn't Kamala have the coat?
f What did Terry do with the coat?
g Where did Vince see Terry?
h What did Terry do when he saw the others?

The past tense: irregular verbs

BUILD UP

- Students look at the examples.
- Choose one student to read the examples.
- Students look through the story and complete the table.
- Copy the table onto the board.
- Choose students to come out and complete the table.

Answer key

came	had	saw	took	went	found
gave	left	ran	threw	did	got
could					

- Books closed.
- 📼 Play the tape again. Stop after each utterance. Students repeat.
- Repeat any utterances that students find difficult.

Useful expressions

- Divide the class into pairs.
- Students look at the list of expressions. They write a translation in the boxes. They use the story and context to work out an appropriate mother-tongue expression.

Note
A lot of these expressions are idioms and cannot be translated word for word. Make sure students understand this.

- Students give their answers. Discuss as necessary.

- Divide the class into groups of three.
- Students choose their roles.
- Students read the dialogue.
- If time, change roles and do the dialogue again.
- Choose one group to act the dialogue in front of the class.

FOLLOW UP

Answer key

got	saw	was	had	gave	left
went	put	walked	saw	took	
wanted	escaped	did			

LANGUAGE WORK

 a
- Divide the class into pairs.
- Students find and complete the sentences. While they are doing this, copy the sentences onto the board.
- Choose students to come out and complete the sentences.

Answer key
came
didn't come
didn't have
had
didn't do
did

b
- Students complete the rule.

Answer key
didn't

- Ask *What form of the verb is used after 'didn't?'*
- Students look at the sentences in **a** and give their answer.

Answer key
*The stem (or infinitive) form **not** the past tense form*

- Students complete the table. While they are doing this, copy the table onto the board.
- Choose students to come out and complete the table.
- Students quote examples from the Victoria Raod story to justify the rule in the table.
- Students make six sentences using the table.

Answer key

I		
He		*run away.*
She		
It	*didn't*	*find the coat.*
We		
You		*jump out of the window.*
They		

- Students look at the example.
- Get one student to read the example aloud.
- Get another student to give the next sentence. Make sure students give full sentences, as in the example. In this way students must give the negative and the positive of the same verb.
- Students make the remaining sentences.
- Students give their answers.

3

a
- Explain the activity.
- Students write down their ideas. They write them in full sentences.

b
- Divide the class into groups of four.
- Students read their answers to the group.
- Each group chooses the two most interesting ideas for **did** and **didn't do**.
- Groups report their ideas to the class.

FOLLOW UP

The past tense: irregular verbs

BUILD UP

 This is the regular past tense.

present	past
look	look**ed**

But some verbs have an irregular past tense.

Example

present	past
come	*came*
bring	*brought*
put	*put*

Find the past tense of these verbs in the Victoria Road story.

present	past
come	
have	
see	
take	
go	
find	
give	
leave	
run	
throw	
do	
get	
can	

 Listen to the story again and repeat.

Useful expressions

 How do you say these in your language?

What's going on?

I bet . . .

The rat!

something strange

You'd better . . .

So that's what happened.

It's all my fault.

There he is!

That's funny.

7 **Work in a group of three. One person is Sue and Casey, one is the policewoman and Vince, one is Terry and Kamala. Read the dialogue.**

FOLLOW UP

8 **Terry is telling the others what happened. Complete his description with these words.**

was	had	walked	went
gave	left	did	saw
took	saw	wanted	
got	put	escaped	

When I .... off the bus, I .... these three guys. Kamala .... on the bus, too. She .... Sue's coat and bags. She .... me the coat and bags. She .... me at the corner and then she .... to her shop. I .... Sue's coat on and .... round the corner. But the three guys .... me. They .... me to the park. They .... to throw me in the lake, but I ....

How .... you escape?

Well ....

90

LANGUAGE WORK

The past simple tense: negative

BUILD UP

 a **Look at the Victoria Road story. Complete these sentences.**

I .... home alone.

Sue .... home.

Sue .... her coat.

I .... it.

He .... that, Sue.

He .... something strange.

b **How do we make the past simple negative? Complete this rule.**

> To make the past simple negative we put
> .... in front of the infinitive.

c **Complete this table of the past simple negative. Use the correct words from this list.**

find   jumped   didn't   ran   found
did   jump   run

| I He She It We You They | .... | .... away. .... the coat. .... out of the window. |

2 **These statements about the Victoria Road story are all wrong. Correct them.**

Example
Sue didn't go to the hospital after school. She went to the cinema.

a Sue went to the hospital after school.
b Kamala brought Vince's coat home.
c She gave the coat to Mrs Scott.
d Terry threw the coat in the lake.
e Vince and Casey found Sue's coat in a tree.
f Terry telephoned the police.
g The policewoman asked Sue about the three boys.
h Vince said, 'It's all my fault'.
i Kamala saw Terry at the shop window.
j Terry came into the shop.

3 **Imagine that yesterday was the best day of your life.**

a **Write down:**
  ● six things that you did.
  ● six things that you didn't do.

b **Compare your ideas with other people in the class.**

FOLLOW UP

4 **Write your answers to Exercise 2.**

JOKE OF THE WEEK

IT FOOLS EVERYONE!

LOCH NESS

READING

Amazing escapes

In this activity students use textual clues to help them sort out three stories. Students don't need to understand every word (see Exercise 2).

Note
These are all true stories.

- Divide the class into pairs.
- Explain the activity.
- Students read the clues and put A, B or C in the boxes. They use the pictures to help them.
- Students give their answers.

Answer key
ABC
CBA
BAC
BCA
ACB
CAB

 In this activity students reflect on what clues they used to sort out the stories. Use this to show students how much knowledge they can use to help them work out the meaning when they don't know every word.

- Choose one student to read out story **A**. After each line ask *How do you know that that is the correct line for story A?*
- Students give their answers.
- Repeat for **B** and **C**.

Answer key
(possible clues)
the pictures: for example, *the same man in each picture*

repeated vocabulary: *window, jump, television/TV, crash*

derivatives: *German, Germany*

semantic fields: *sea, sank, swam; gun, explode; building, window*

logic: *became unconscious/woke him up; fell 5485 m/didn't break any bones*

 a • Students underline all the verbs.
- Students give their answers. Make a list on the board. (Show the whole of phrasal verbs to get students used to them.)

Answer key
*was   went up   had   became
jumped out of   didn't die   hit   caught
blew   exploded   flew   crashed   landed
woke up   fell   didn't have   climbed out of
sank   interviewed   swam away   rescued
didn't break   said   changed   jumped*

b Students come out and underline the regular verbs.

Answer key
*jumped   exploded   crashed   landed
climbed   interviewed   rescued   changed*

c • Students complete the table with the irregular verbs from the list.

Note
It is important that students do this on their own. They can then see that the irregular verbs are not totally irregular, but are similar in form to the stem of the verb.

- Copy the table onto the board.
- Students come out and complete it.

Answer key
*swam   fell
caught   became
said   flew
woke up   sank
hit*

FOLLOW UP

 Answer key
*was   exploded   fell   landed   broke
became   was*

Note
This is from the Guinness Book of Records. Vesna Vulovic holds the record for surviving the longest fall without a parachute.

READING

Amazing escapes

1 Look at the sentences below. There are three stories here. The sentences are all in the correct order, but the three stories are mixed up. Put A, B or C next to each sentence to make the three stories.

- [ ] In 1944 Nicholas Alkemade was in a plane over Germany.
- [ ] A New York man went up the Empire State Building.
- [ ] In 1989 Thomas Root was on his way from Washington to Florida in a small plane.

- [ ] He had a heart attack and became unconscious.
- [ ] He jumped out of a window. But he didn't die.
- [ ] The German guns hit the plane.

- [ ] The wind caught him and blew him through another window.
- [ ] He jumped out of the plane before it exploded.
- [ ] The plane flew for 1000 miles and then crashed into the sea.

- [ ] He landed in the NBC television studio in the middle of a programme.
- [ ] The crash woke him up.
- [ ] He fell 5485m. He didn't have a parachute.

- [ ] He landed in some snow in a forest.
- [ ] He climbed out of the plane before it sank.
- [ ] The TV presenter interviewed him.

- [ ] He swam away and a helicopter rescued him.
- [ ] He didn't break any bones.
- [ ] He said, 'I changed my mind after I jumped.'

2 | How did you sort out the stories? What clues did you use?

I CHANGED MY MIND AFTER I JUMPED

W O R D   W O R K

3 a Underline all the verbs in the stories.

   b Which verbs are regular?

   c Write the past tenses of these irregular verbs.

swim ....   fall ....

catch ....   become ....

say ....   fly ....

wake up ....   sink ....

hit ....

92

FOLLOW UP

4 **Complete this story.**

Vesna Vulovic .... an air stewardess for

Yugoslav Airlines. In 1972 her DC9 plane

.... over Czechoslovakia. She ....

10,160 metres. She .... in a forest. She

.... a lot of bones and ....

unconscious. She .... in hospital for 16

months. But she survived.

LISTENING

Band Aid

• Students look at the pictures and read the questions.

• Students say what they know.

Answer key
(See tapescript in 3.)

• Students look at the text. They try to complete it. Students should be able to guess a lot of the words. Even if they can't guess the exact word, they can guess what kind of word is missing.

• Students give their ideas.

• Make sure everyone understands the task.

• Play the tape. Students listen and check their ideas.

 Band Aid

Interviewer When did Band Aid start?

Band Aid spokesman It started in October 1984.

Interviewer Why did Band Aid start?

Band Aid spokesman Bob Geldof saw pictures of the famine in Ethiopia on the television news, and he wanted to help.

Interviewer What did Bob Geldof do before he started Band Aid?

Band Aid spokesman He was the singer with the Boomtown Rats.

Interviewer What did Band Aid do first?

Band Aid spokesman A group of famous pop stars made a record. It was called 'Feed the World'.

Interviewer How much money did 'Feed the World' make?

Band Aid spokesman It made £8 million.

Interviewer Did Band Aid stop after 'Feed the World'?

Band Aid spokesman No, it didn't. In July 1985 Band Aid held a pop concert in Britain and America.

Interviewer What was the pop concert called?

Band Aid spokesman It was called Live Aid. It made over £60 million.

Interviewer What did Band Aid buy with the money?

Band Aid spokesman They bought food, medicine and lorries for the people of Africa.

Interviewer What did Bob Geldof do after Live Aid?

Band Aid spokesman He visited Africa.

Interviewer How many countries did he visit?

Band Aid spokesman Six – Mali, Burkina Fasso, Niger, Chad, Sudan and Ethiopia.

• Students fill in the missing words.

• Play the tape again. Students check their texts.

• Choose students to read their completed text. Other students compare their answers.

Answer key

was	*changed*	*saw*	*wanted*	*formed*
made	*expected*	*made*	*didn't stop*	
held	*made*	*bought*		

FOLLOW UP

• Students find some information.

• Students report what they have found to the class.

Notes
• The famine affected the area known as the Sahel, which is the southern edge of the Sahara Desert. The desert appears to be getting larger. Nobody knows exactly why there was a drought, but it is probably caused by the destruction of the rainforests in the region. In Ethiopia the famine was made worse by the civil war in the country.

• Band Aid was an international enterprise. People from many countries were involved. Students may know about efforts in their own country to help with famine relief in Africa.

INTERACTION

The past simple: questions

BUILD UP

 1 a • Divide the class into pairs.

• Students find and complete the sentences. While they are doing this, copy the sentences onto the board.

• Choose students to come out and complete the sentences.

> **Answer key**
> *Did you come*
> *came*
>
> *did he do*
> *did*

• Ask *What form of the verb is used after 'did'?*

• Students look at their sentences and give the answer.

> **Answer key**
> *the stem (or infinitive) form, **not** the past tense form*

b • Students complete the table. They use the sentences to help them. While they are doing this, copy the table onto the board.

• Choose students to come out and complete the table.

• Students make ten sentences using the table.

> **Answer key**
>
> | | | |
> |---|---|---|
> | | *I* | *come home alone?* |
> | | *he* | |
> | | *she* | *crash into the sea?* |
> | *Did* | *it* | |
> | | *we* | *make £8 million?* |
> | | *you* | *go to the cinema?* |
> | | *they* | |

c • Students complete the rule.

> **Answer key**
> *did   verb*

 2 a • Remind students about Band Aid, if necessary. Ask *What do you remember about Band Aid?* Read the text on page 94.

• Divide the class into pairs.

• Students look at the gapped questions.

• ▭ Play the tape. Students listen.

• Students complete the sentences.

• Play the tape again. Stop after each question and answer pair. Students check their questions.

• Students give their questions. Write them on the board.

> **Answer key**
> (See tapescript for **Listening: 3**, page T94.)

b • Students remain in their pairs.

• Students choose their roles.

• Explain the activity.

• Pairs make their dialogues. Go round and help with any problems.

• Students reverse roles and repeat.

• Get two pairs to demonstrate their dialogues in front of the class.

FOLLOW UP

3 • Students write an interview.

LISTENING

Band Aid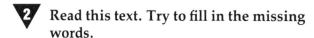

1 Look at these pictures.

- Who is the man? What do you know about him?
- What do you know about Band Aid?

2 Read this text. Try to fill in the missing words.

In the 1970s Bob Geldof .... the singer with the Boomtown Rats. But in October 1984 his life .... On the television he .... pictures of the famine in Ethiopia. Bob Geldof .... to help. He .... Band Aid. A group of famous pop stars .... a record. It was called 'Feed the World'. Bob Geldof .... to make £70,000 from the record. It .... £8 million.

Band Aid .... there. In July 1985 Band Aid .... a pop concert in Britain and America. The Live Aid concert .... over £60 million.

With the money, Band Aid .... food, medicine and lorries for the people of Africa.

3   Listen. You will hear an interview about Band Aid. Complete the text above with the information in the interview.

FOLLOW UP

4   Find out more about Band Aid.

- Why was there a famine in Africa?
- Did people in your country help Band Aid? What did they do?

INTERACTION

The past simple: questions

BUILD UP

1 **a** Look at the Victoria Road Story on page 88. Complete these sentences.

.... home with her today?

I .... home alone.

And what .... with it?

He .... something strange.

b Choose the correct words to complete this table.

went	crashed	go	came
crash	made	come	make

	I		
	he	.... home alone?
	she	.... into the sea?
Did	it	
	we	.... £8 million?
	you	
	they	.... to the cinema?

c Complete the rule.

> To make questions in the past simple we
> use .... + subject + ...

2 **a** 📼 Listen to the interview about Band Aid again. Complete these questions.

When .... ?

Why .... ?

What .... before he started Band Aid?

What .... first?

How much money .... ?

.... after Feed the World?

What .... called?

b Work with a partner. Use your questions and the text on page 94. Role play the interview.

FOLLOW UP

3 Imagine you have done something interesting. A reporter is interviewing you about it. Write the interview. Use these words.

What?   When?   Why?   Where?   Did?

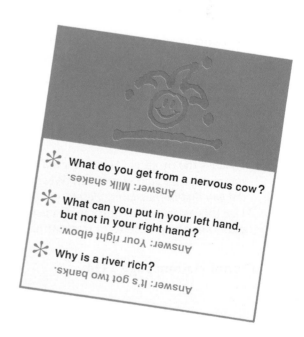

✳ What do you get from a nervous cow?
Answer: Milk shakes.

✳ What can you put in your left hand, but not in your right hand?
Answer: Your right elbow.

✳ Why is a river rich?
Answer: It's got two banks.

95

PROJECT

A class newspaper

This project needs to be done in groups in class, but some of the research and preparation work can be done at home. This project encourages students to:

– take an interest in the news.

– do some realistic and creative translation work. Their sources will all be in the mother tongue, so they will need to summarize the story and present it in English.

• Read the instructions to '... sports news'.

• Students look at the newspaper headlines.

• Ask *What are they about? What kind of news story is each one?*

• Students give their ideas. Students will not understand everything, but they should be able to use a few clues (Graf, EC, Abba, local) to work out what kind of story it is.

• Ask *What kind of stories are in the news here at the moment?*

• Students give their ideas. Ask follow-up questions to get more details.

a • Groups (or individuals) decide which kind of story they will write about. Each area should be covered, but there may be more than one group covering each.

b • Students find a news story and then find out as much as possible about their story from TV or newspapers. They find some pictures for it.

c • Students produce a rough draft of their story.

  • Discuss the rough drafts and suggest corrections.

d • Students produce a finished newspaper article on a sheet of paper and illustrate it.

e • Students put their stories together to make a newspaper.

f • Students give their newspaper a name and display it on the wall.

  • Discuss the projects. Ask *Where did you get information for your story from? What problems did you find in translating the story into English?* Use this as an opportunity to discuss generally the problems of translating.

▶ **Pronunciation: page T114**

LEARNING DIARY

> **Note**
> Discuss in the mother tongue.

A Students look at the contents list on page 87. They draw a face next to each item to show how well they think they know it.

B Students do the self-check in the Workbook on page 87.

C Divide the class into pairs or groups of three or four.

  Students compare their answers. Go round the class and check for any common problems.

  Students compare their self-check results with the faces they drew.

  In the whole class ask *What problems did you find with the self-check?* Students suggest problem areas.

  Take remedial action, as necessary. (See Introduction page vii for possible strategies.)

  Ask *What did you like best in this unit? What didn't you like?*
  Students give their responses. Ask *Why?* Take note of student responses. They can help you to adjust your teaching towards the things that motivate the students most.

CULTURE SPOT
Workbook page 86

• Divide the class into pairs or groups of three or four.

• Students look quickly at the text.

• Ask *What is the text about?*

• Students give their ideas.

• Ask *What do you already know about this topic?*

• Students give their ideas. Discuss these ideas.

• Say *Read the Culture spot text. Note anything that you find interesting or unusual.*

• Ask comprehension questions about the text.

• Students give their answers. Explain any words that students need.

• Ask *Did you find anything interesting or unusual?*

• Students give their ideas.

• Read each comparison question in turn.

• Discuss each question. Encourage students to compare their situation with the one in the text.

You can start immediately with the Victoria Road story on page 98, or you can pre-teach adverbs, using the following procedure.

> **Note**
>
> At this stage you only need to introduce the grammar item, so that students can understand the story more easily. There are exercises later for more concentrated practice. Spend no more than 5 minutes on the pre-teaching.

1 • Write a sentence on the board quickly.
   • Ask *What did I do?*
   • Elicit the answer *You wrote a sentence on the board.*
   • Ask *How did I write it?* Say *I wrote it quickly.*
   • Choose a student. Ask *How did I write it?*
   • Elicit the answer *You wrote it quickly.*
   • Repeat with two more students.
   • Repeat procedure for *slowly.*

2 • Students look at the example on page 97.

3 • Start the Victoria Road story on page 98.

PROJECT

A class newspaper

Some English-speaking people are visiting your country. You want to give them some information about what's in the news in your country at the moment.

Make a class newspaper in English. Your newspaper should include a range of stories, for example:

- the main political news in your country
- a world news story
- a human interest story
- a major event, such as a big robbery or a train crash
- sports news

a Decide which area you will work on.

b Watch the television news and read newspapers. Find a good story.

c Write your story in English.

d Illustrate your story with a picture.

e Put all the stories together to make a class newspaper.

f Give your newspaper a name.

50 Die in Earthquake

★★★

Riots in Two Indian Cities

New Road Opened by Local MP

Prime Minister Resigns

Crisis at EC Summit

ABBA STAR WEDS

Graf Smashes
Way to Second
Grand
Slam
Win

Learning diary

A Look at the first page of this unit. How well do you know these things now? Look at each point in the contents list.

If you know it well, draw a happy face.

If you know it fairly well, draw a face like this.

If you don't know it well, draw a sad face.

B Try the self-check in the Workbook.

C Compare your answers with a partner. Discuss any problems with your teacher.

12

▶ Pronunciation: page 114

13 the movies

adverbs; ordinal numbers; dates

Contents

Grammar points

98   **Victoria Road:** Terry's story

100   **Language work**   **adverbs / ordinal numbers**

102   **Reading:** James Dean   **months of the year**

104   **Listening:** The death of James Dean   **dates**

105   **Interaction:** At the movies   **making arrangements**

106   **Project:** The movies

The main grammar points in this unit are:

Adjectives and adverbs

It was an easy fight.

I escaped easily.

Ordinal numbers

dates

12 September

20 March 1975

VICTORIA ROAD

Terry's story

1
- Students open their books and read the questions.
- Ask the first question.
- Students give their responses. Ask follow-up questions. They can do this entirely in English now.

Answer key
Vince and Casey found Sue's coat in the lake. They didn't know that Sue was at the cinema. Mrs Scott telephoned the police. A policewoman went to Kamala's shop. She asked Kamala about Sue's coat. Suddenly, Sue arrived at the shop. Then Kamala told the policewoman about Terry and Darren Tooley. Sue was very sorry. Then Terry appeared at the window, but when he saw his friends, he ran away. The others chased him. Sue said she was sorry. Terry didn't want to see his friends.

- Choose students to read the remaining questions aloud. Make sure everyone understands the questions.
- Students look through the picture story to find the answers to the questions. They can refer to the full text, too.
- Students give their answers to the question.

Answer key
Terry, Casey, Kamala, Vince, Sue, Darren Tooley and his friends.
They are at the cinema.
Terry is talking about what happened in the park.
Darren Tooley and his friends are very friendly to Terry.

- Ask *What happens in this episode?* Using the pictures, students give a summary of the story.
- Explain any new vocabulary that students need to understand the dialogue.

Answer key
Terry and his friends are going to the cinema. Terry is telling them about his fight with Tooley and his friends. Tooley and his friends come out of the cinema. They are very friendly to Terry. Vince and the others are surprised.

2
- Say *Now look at the full dialogue.*
- Play the tape. Students listen and follow in their books.
- Play the tape again, if necessary.
- Ask *Why do you think Tooley and his friends were friendly to Terry?* Students give their ideas.

Notes
the movies This is an American term for the cinema. It is very commonly used in Britain nowadays, too.

Don't look now, but . . . This means someone that you don't want to see or speak to has appeared.

3
- Students answer the questions.
- Choose students to read each question and give the answer.
- Ask *How do you know?* Students use the dialogue to justify their answers.

Note
This is a very important stage, because it shows whether students have understood the dialogue.

Answer key
a *They're going to the cinema.*
b *He's talking about his fight with Tooley and his friends.*
c *He couldn't run very fast because he had Sue's bags.*
d *He thought quickly and he unbuttoned the coat carefully.*
e *He pulled hard and the coat came off.*
f *He pushed the first boy into the lake, kicked the second boy and hit the third boy with Sue's bag.*
g *Tooley and his friends fought badly.*
h *They said, 'Hi, Terry. It's a great film.'*
i *Tooley and his friends were very friendly.*

4
- Books closed.
- Play the tape again. Stop after each utterance. Students repeat.
- Repeat any utterances that students find difficult.

Useful expressions

- Divide the class into pairs.
- Students look at the list of expressions. They write a translation in the boxes. They use the story and context to work out an appropriate mother-tongue expression.

> **Note**
> A lot of these expressions are idioms and cannot be translated word for word. Make sure students understand this.

- Students give their answers. Discuss as necessary.

- Divide the class into pairs.
- Students choose their roles.
- Students read the dialogue.
- If time, change roles and do the dialogue again.
- Choose one pair to act the dialogue in front of the class.

FOLLOW UP

> **Answer key**
>
> | | | | | | |
> |---|---|---|---|---|---|
> | to | us | Darren | caught | very | took |
> | on | park | carefully | into | hard | off |
> | quickly | first | kicked | hit | bag | |
> | away | brave | easy | badly | friends | |
> | cinema | friendly | ice cream | | | |

Terry's story

1 Look at the story.

- What happened in the last episode?
- Who are the people in this episode?
- Where are they?
- What is Terry talking about?
- Why does Vince say 'That's funny'?

Tell us again, Terry. What happened?

They caught me easily and they took me to the park.

They wanted to throw me in the lake, but I pulled hard and the coat came off.

Then I turned round quickly. I pushed the first boy into the lake. I kicked the second b and hit the third bo with Sue's bag.

2 Listen and follow in your books.

Casey Tell us again, Terry. What happened?

Terry Well, Darren Tooley and his two friends saw me. I couldn't run very fast, because I had the bags. They caught me easily and they took me to the park. I thought quickly and on the way to the park I unbuttoned the coat carefully.

Kamala Ooh, it's exciting. Just like the movies. What did you do when you got to the park?

Terry They wanted to throw me in the lake. But I pulled hard and the coat came off. Then I turned round quickly. I pushed the first boy into the lake. I kicked the second boy and hit the third boy with Sue's bag. Then they ran away.

Kamala You did very well, Terry. You were so brave.

Terry Oh, it was an easy fight. They fought very badly. But I'm sorry about your coat and bags, Sue.

Sue Oh, that's all right, Terry.

Casey Don't look now, but Tooley and his friends are coming out of the cinema.

Darren Hi, Terry. It's a great film.
Terry Oh, er, . . . hi . . ., er . . . thanks. Balcony, please.
Vince That's funny. Why were those guys so friendly?

Terry Oh . . . er . . . I don't know. Would anyone like an ice cream?

3 Answer these questions.

a Where are the group going?
b What is Terry talking about?
c Why did Darren Tooley and his friends catch Terry easily?
d What did Terry do on the way to the park?
e How did Terry escape?
f What did he do to the three boys?
g Why was it an easy fight?
h What did Darren Tooley and his friends do, when they came out of the cinema?
i Why was Vince surprised?

4 Listen again and repeat.

Useful expressions

5 **How do you say these in your language?**

It's exciting.

Just like the movies.

The coat came off.

You were so brave.

I'm sorry about . . .

That's all right.

Don't look now, but . . .

Would anyone like a . . .?

6 Work with a partner. One person is Terry, one person takes all the other parts. Read the dialogue.

FOLLOW UP

7 Complete Kamala's diary.

We went .... the cinema today. Terry told .... what happened in the park. .... Tooley and his two friends .... Terry easily. He couldn't run .... fast with Sue's bags. They .... him to the park, but .... the way to the .... Terry unbuttoned the coat .... They wanted to throw Terry ....the lake, but he pulled .... and the coat came .... Then he turned round .... He pushed the .... guy into the lake, ...the second guy and .... the third guy with Sue's .... Then they ran .... Terry was so .... , but he said it was an .... fight, because they fought very ....

We saw Darren Tooley and his .... They came out of the .... They were very .... It was funny. Terry bought us all an ....

99

LANGUAGE WORK

Adverbs

BUILD UP

 a • Students find and complete the sentences.
   • Copy the sentences onto the board.
   • Choose students to complete the sentences.

> **Answer key**
> *fast*
> *easily*
> *quickly*

   • Explain that adverbs describe the action of a verb.

b • Students look for more adverbs in the Victoria Road story.
   • Students give their answers.

> **Answer key**
> *carefully   hard   well   badly*

 • Students look at the example.
   • Get one student to read the example aloud.
   • Get another student to give the next sentence.
   • Students make the remaining sentences.
   • Students give their answers.

> **Answer key**
> left to right
> *The girl is fighting bravely.*
> *The postman is walking quietly.*
> *Castleford are playing badly.*
> *The boxer is hitting him hard.*
> *Superman is lifting the bus easily.*
> *The man is talking loudly.*
> *The girl is building a card house carefully.*

Adverbs and adjectives

BUILD UP

 a • Write the two sentences on the board.
   • Point to *easy*. Ask *What's this?*
   • Elicit the answer *It's an adjective.*
   • Repeat for *easily* (adverb).
   • Ask *What does an adjective/adverb do?*
   • Students give their ideas.
   • Students look at the rules for adverbs and adjectives.
   • Choose one student to read the rules aloud.

b • Students look at the adverbs in their list and the adverbs in Exercise 2.
   • Students give their ideas.

> **Answer key**
> *-ly*

   • Students complete the list
   • Copy the list onto the board.
   • Choose students to come out and complete it.

> **Answer key**
> *fast   hard   well*

   • Ask *What is different about 'fast' and 'hard'?*

> **Answer key**
> *The adjective and the adverb are the same.*

 • Students complete the sentences.
   • Students give their answers.
   • Ask *Why?*

> **Answer key**
> *well   easily   heavy   bravely   easy*
> *quickly*

T100

Ordinal numbers

BUILD UP

 a • Students complete the gaps.

• Copy the phrases onto the board.

• Choose students to complete them.

> **Answer key**
> *second   third*

• Explain 'ordinal numbers'.

b • Students look at the list.

• Ask *Can you see a pattern in the numbers?*

• Students give their ideas.

> **Answer key**
> *Most of the numbers end in -th.*

• Say *What do you think the missing ordinal numbers are?*

• Students give their ideas.

• Play the tape. Stop after each missing number.

• Students complete the list.

• Write the missing numbers on the board. Choose students to write the words.

c • Play the tape again. Students listen and repeat.

• Write numbers on the board. Students call out the word.

d • Students add the numbers and words to the list.

• Students give their answers.

> **Answer key**
> *twenty-third*
> *twenty-fourth*
> *twenty-fifth*

• Write some higher numbers on the board. Students give the word. Use: *49th, 63rd, 90th, 71st, 28th, 50th, 88th.*

 a • Divide the class into pairs.

• Students read the clues and find the letters.

> **Answer key**
> *a   m   i   n   c   e*

b • Students use the letters to make a word.

> **Answer key**
> *cinema*

c • Divide the class into groups of four.

• Each group chooses a word with five or six letters from the wordlist at the back of the book.

• They mix up the letters and write clues for each letter on a piece of paper.

• Go round and check the clues.

• Groups exchange clues. They try to work out the puzzle.

• Groups compare answers.

FOLLOW UP

7
> **Answer key**
> (See Exercise 2.)

SONG: SAVE ME

• Students look at the song. Ask *What do you think the missing words are?*

• Play the tape. Students listen.

• Students fill in the missing words.

• Play the tape again. Students check their answers.

• Students give their answers.

• Play the tape again. Students sing along.

> **Answer key**
> *sing   make   love   know   come   you*

LANGUAGE WORK

Adverbs

BUILD UP

 a Look at the Victoria Road story. Complete these sentences.

I couldn't run very ....

They caught me ....

I thought ....

These are adverbs. They describe *how* someone did something.

b Find more adverbs in the story.

2 Look at these pictures. Say what the people are doing and how they are doing it. Choose from these adverbs.

quietly	loudly	bravely	sadly
hard	carefully	slowly	badly
easily	fast		

Example
He is driving fast.

Adverbs and adjectives

BUILD UP

 a Look.

It was an **easy** fight.

This is an **adjective**. It describes the noun 'fight'. It tells us *what* the fight was *like*.

They caught me **easily**.

This is an **adverb**. It describes the verb 'caught'. It tells us *how* they caught him.

b Look at the list of adverbs in Exercises 1 and 2. What do most adverbs end with?

But be careful with these adverbs. Complete this list.

adjective	adverb
fast	....
hard	....
friendly	friendly
good	....

4 Choose the correct word from the brackets.

Terry can run .... (good/well)

He couldn't get away from Tooley ....
(easy/easily)

Sue's bags were very ....
(heavy/heavily)

Terry fought .... (brave/bravely)

It was an .... fight. (easy/easily)

Tooley and his friends ran away

.... (quick/quickly)

Ordinal numbers
BUILD UP

5 a Look at the Victoria Road story. Complete
these.

the first boy
the .... boy
the .... boy

We call these ordinal numbers.

b Listen and complete this list.

1st	first	14th	fourteenth
2nd	second	15th	....
3rd	third	16th	....
4th	fourth	17th	seventeenth
5th	fifth	18th	eighteenth
6th	sixth	19th	....
7th	....	20th	twentieth
8th	eighth	21st	twenty-first
9th	ninth	22nd	....
10th	....		....
11th	eleventh		....
12th	twelfth		....
13th	thirteenth		

c Listen again and repeat.

d Add these to the list.

23rd   24th   25th

A PUZZLE

6 a What is the word? Find these letters.

the eighth letter in 'yesterday'
the thirteenth letter of the alphabet
the fourth letter in 'believe'
the third letter in the past tense of 'go'
the fifth letter in the second word of 'post office'
the sixth letter in the plural of 'watch'

b Use your letters to make a word.

c Make a puzzle for another word. Give it to
another group. Can they solve your
puzzle?

FOLLOW UP

7 Write your answers to Exercise 2.

Save Me

Save ....
Oh won't you .... me?
I .... you baby.
Please .... say maybe.

Why won't you save me ....?
.... save me.

.... me.
Please help me, ...
Oh, please, please
Don't .... maybe.

.... won't you save me now?
Please help ....

Tell me.
Oh won't you .... me.
Tell me you love me.
Please don't say ....
Oh why won't .... tell me now?
Please tell me.

.... me.
Oh won't you love me?
.... love you baby.
Please say .... love me, love me.

Why .... you love me now?
I, you .... , I love you.

101

READING

In this section students do a series of activities based on the text. With each activity, they read the text at a deeper level of detail, as follows:

1 They look at the pictures and text briefly to establish the context:
   Who is it about? What do they know about him?

2 They find the main details of his life, using a chart.

3 They look for subsidiary information.

4 They look for specific words.

This sequence of activities gives the learners a model for dealing with a text.

Limit the time for each activity, so that students only look for the information they are asked for.

- Students look at the pictures.
- Ask *Who is this man?*
- Students look at the text, if necessary, to find his name.

Answer key
James Dean

- What do you know about him?
- Students give their ideas. If students don't know anything about him, ask *Who do you think he was?* Students can guess that he was a film star or a pop star; that he was American; that he lived in the 1950s, etc.

 a
- Divide the class into pairs.
- Students look at the chart.
- Explain *event*.

b
- Students read the cues.
- Explain the activity.
- Students look through the text and complete the chart.
- Copy the chart onto the board.
- Students give their answers. Write them on the board.
- Ask *How do you know?*
- Students quote from the text to justify their answers.

Answer key

1931	*Fairmount, Indiana*	*born*
1936	*Los Angeles*	*move*
1939	*Fairmount, Indiana*	*go to live with aunt and uncle*
1952	*New York*	*become an actor*
1954	*Hollywood*	*make films*
1955	*Paso Robles*	*die in a car crash*

- Students read the list of information.
- Students read the text to find the information.
- Students give their answers.

Answer key
basketball   baseball
East of Eden
Rebel Without a Cause   Giant
He made some advertisements for Pepsi-Cola. He appeared on television. He worked in the theatre.

WORD WORK

- Students read the text and make a list of words.
- Students give their ideas. Make a list on the board.

Answer key
(possible words)
James Dean   film   film star   symbol
studio   fan   hero   advertisement
appear   television   programme   work
theatre   Hollywood   star   starred
famous   rich

- Students give their ideas.
- Discuss the students' own favourite film stars.

Dates

BUILD UP

- ▄▄ Play the tape. Students follow in their books and repeat.
- Books closed. Play the tape again. Students listen and repeat.
- Call out the ordinal number of some months. Students give the name. For example: You *the fifth month of the year.* Students *May.*

A BIRTHDAY SURVEY

 a
- Students move around the class. They ask *Which month is your birthday in?* They try to find how many people have a birthday in the same month.

b
- Ask *Which month do you think has most birthdays in it?*
- Students give their ideas.
- Call out each month. Ask *Who has got a birthday in June?* Repeat for each month, but don't call them out in order.
- Make a list on the board.

T102

FOLLOW UP

Answer key

(possible answer)

James Dean was born in Fairmount Indiana in 1931. In 1936 he went to Los Angeles. His mother died in 1939. James went to live with his aunt and uncle in Fairmount. In 1952 he went to New York. He became an actor. In 1954 he went to Hollywood and made his first film. He died in a car crash at Paso Robles in 1955.

READING

1 Look at these pictures.

- Who is the man?
- What do you know about him?

a Look at the chart.

date	place	event
1931		
1936		
1939		
1952		
1954		
1955		

b Look through the text. Put these places and events in the correct order in your chart.

Paso Robles	move
Hollywood	die in a car crash
Fairmount, Indiana	make films
Los Angeles	go to live with aunt and uncle
New York	born
Fairmount, Indiana	become an actor

James Dean was a film star. He made only three films. He died in a car crash in September 1955 near Paso Robles in California. He was only twenty-four years old. But in his short life James Dean became the symbol of young people. He was the teenage rebel. For years after he died his studio received 8000 letters a day. His fans couldn't believe that he was really dead. Today he is still a hero for millions of young people.

James Dean was born in February 1931 in Fairmount, Indiana. When Jimmy was five years old, his father got a job in Los Angeles and the family moved to California. Three years later his mother died. Jimmy went back to Fairmount and lived with his aunt and uncle on their farm.

Jimmy loved sport. He was in the school basketball and baseball teams. He also played the clarinet.

He wanted to be an actor and in January 1952 he went to New York. He made some advertisements for Pepsi-Cola, appeared in some television programmes and he also worked in the theatre.

In 1954 James Dean went to Hollywood and he made his first film. *East of Eden* made him a star. His second film was *Rebel Without a Cause*. In his third and last film, *Giant*, he starred with Elizabeth Taylor and Rock Hudson.

In 1955 James Dean was famous. He was rich too — rich enough to buy a fast sports car.

 Now read the text carefully. Find this information.

- 2 sports that James Dean played
- his first film
- 2 other films that he made
- 3 things that he did in New York

W O R D   W O R K

 Find all the words in the text connected with the word 'actor'.

 What do you think?

- Why was James Dean famous?
- What does 'teenage rebel' mean to you?

Dates

BUILD UP

 📼 **Listen and repeat.**

January	July
February	August
March	September
April	October
May	November
June	December

A BIRTHDAY SURVEY

 a Ask people in your class: 'Which month is your birthday in?'

b Make a chart to show how many people in the class have birthdays in each month. Which month has the most?

FOLLOW UP

Use the information in your chart. Write a short biography of James Dean. Start like this.

James Dean was born in Fairmount, Indiana in 1931. In 1936 he went to Los Angeles. His mother died in . . .

LISTENING

- Revise the lesson on James Dean. Students read the text on pages 102–3.
- Ask questions about the text.

- Divide the class into pairs.
- Students read the text.
- Explain the activity.
- Play the tape. Students listen and underline the parts that are wrong.
- Play the tape again. Students listen.
- Students correct the text.
- Choose one student to give the correct version of the text. Other students say whether they agree or not.

James Dean

James Dean loved motor racing and he often took part in sports car races. He drove well.

On 16th September 1955 he bought a new car. It was a Porsche 550 Spyder. It was silver and he paid $7000 for it. That was a lot of money in those days.

At half past one on Friday 30th September 1955, he left Hollywood with a friend. They were on their way to a race at Salinas.

But they didn't arrive at Salinas. At 5.58 Dean's Porsche crashed into another car. The speedometer stopped at 115 mph. The crash broke Dean's neck. At that moment a film star died and a legend was born.

- Play the tape again. Stop after each sentence. Students check their corrected texts.

3 a • Students look at the example. Read it aloud.

b • Students say the dates. Correct as necessary.
- Ask questions around the class. Ask *When is your birthday? What is the date today? What was the date yesterday? When is (a national/regional holiday)? When is your mother's birthday?*

4 • Divide the class into pairs.
- Explain the activity.
- Pairs suggest questions. Write them on the board.

Answer key
(possible questions)
When were you born?
Where were you born?
Why did you live with your aunt and uncle?
What sport did you play at school?
Can you play a musical instrument?
When did you become an actor?
What did you do in New York?
Why did you go to Hollywood?
What was your first/second/third film?
Who starred in the films with you?
People say that you are a teenage rebel. What do you think of that?
When did you buy your car?
What kind of car is it?
How much did it cost?
Where are you going now?

- Students choose their roles.
- Pairs make their dialogues. Go round and help with any problems.
- Students reverse roles and repeat.
- Get two pairs to demonstrate their dialogues in front of the class.

FOLLOW UP

5 • Students write a dialogue.

INTERACTION

1 **a** • Divide the class into pairs.

• Students look at the posters. Ask *What are they about?*

• Students look at the dialogue.

• Make sure everyone understands the task.

• Students write numbers in the boxes.

b • Play the tape. Students listen and check their order.

• Discuss any problems.

• Play the tape again.

** At the movies**

A Let's go to the movies on Saturday.
B Good idea. What's on?
A Batman III.
B Who's in it?
A Michael Keaton.
B Oh, I like him. Where is it on?
A Studio 2.
B What time does it start?
A On Saturday it starts at five past two, 5.30, or 8 o'clock.
B OK. Let's go at 5.30.
A Fine. See you outside the cinema at 5.15 on Saturday.
B OK. See you there.

c • In pairs students read the dialogue.

• They reverse roles and repeat.

2 **a** • Students look at the posters.

• Ask questions about each poster: *What is the film called? Where is it on? Who's in it? When does it start?*

b • Divide the class into new pairs

• Students choose their roles.

• Explain the activity.

• Pairs make their dialogues. Go round and help with any problems.

• Students reverse roles and repeat.

• Get two pairs to demonstrate their dialogues in front of the class.

FOLLOW UP

3 • Students write one of their dialogues.

LISTENING

The death of James Dean

1 **Here is some more information about James Dean. But a lot of it is wrong. Listen and correct it.**

James Dean loved motor racing and he often took part in sports car races. He drove well.

On 21 August 1954 he bought a new car. It was a Ferrari 590 Spyder. It was gold and he paid $9000 for it. That was a lot of money in those days.

At half past one on Saturday 29 September 1955, he left Hollywood with his new girlfriend. They were on their way to a race at Paso Robles. But they didn't arrive at Paso Robles. At 2.26 Dean's Ferrari crashed into a lorry. The speedometer stopped at 100 mph. The crash broke Dean's neck. At that moment a film star died and a legend was born.

2 Listen again and check your answer.

Dates

3 **a Look.**

> We write 30 September.
>
> But we say *the thirtieth of* September.

b Say these.

16 February	22 June	1 January
20 August	13 September	

4 **You've now got a lot of information about James Dean. Work with a partner. Imagine you are interviewing James Dean on 30 September 1955 before he left Hollywood.**

- Decide what questions you will ask.
- One person is the interviewer, one is James Dean. Act your interview.
- Change roles and ask more questions.

FOLLOW UP

5 Write ten questions and answers from your interview with James Dean.

INTERACTION

At the movies

1 a Put this conversation in the correct order.

- [ ] Batman III.
- [ ] Let's go to the movies on Saturday.
- [ ] Fine. See you outside the cinema at 5.15 on Saturday.
- [ ] What time does it start?
- [ ] Who's in it?
- [ ] Studio 2.
- [ ] OK. See you there.
- [ ] Oh, I like him. Where is it on?
- [ ] OK. Let's go at 5.30.
- [ ] Michael Keaton.
- [ ] On Saturday it starts at five past two, 5.30 or 8 o'clock.
- [ ] Good idea. What's on?

b 📼 Listen and check your answer.

c Act the dialogue.

2 a Look at these film posters.

CANNON MARKET STREET

BACK TO THE FUTURE III

MICHAEL J. FOX
CHRISTOPHER LLOYD
MARY STEENBURGEN

2.15   5.15   8.15

ODEON HIGH STREET

STARTING MONDAY
"CROCODILE" DUNDEE II

PAUL HOGAN AND LINDA KOZLOWSKI
PERFORMANCES DAILY AT: 2.30 5.00 7.30

STUDIO ONE

A CLASSIC STORY OF CONFLICT AND SURVIVAL

LORD of the FLIES

"GRIPS THE IMAGINATION FROM START TO FINISH."

PAUL BALTHAZAR GETTY   CHRIS FURTH

SUN–FRI	2.05	5.35	8.00
SAT	2.15	5.45	8.10

b Make dialogues using the posters. Use the dialogue in Exercise 1 as a model.

FOLLOW UP

3 Write one of your dialogues from Exercise 2b.

PROJECT

The movies

This project can be done as an individual project or as a group project.
It can be done in class or at home.
This project has three parts:
favourite films
a biography of a favourite star
a review of last (or favourite) film
You can choose one, two or all three, depending on time available.

- Students look at the pictures and the texts. They are a model for the students' own projects.

- Ask these questions:
  Who are the stars in this person's project?
  Which films does the writer mention?
  What does the writer say about each film?
  Which film does the writer tell the story of?
  Who is the writer's favourite actress?
  What does the writer say about her?
  Who do you think the writer's favourite actor is? Why?

- Students give their ideas.

- Ask *How often do you go to the cinema? What is your favourite film? Who are your favourite actors and actresses? Why? What do you know about them?*

- Students give their ideas. (You can use this as a basis for forming groups. Form groups of people who like the same film/actor/actress.)

- Students plan their project.

- Students produce a rough draft of their project. Say *Use the project on page 106 as a model.*

- Discuss the rough drafts and suggest corrections.

- Students produce a finished project. Students can do their project either as a large poster or in a book. This project will work best as a poster.

- Students display their projects.

- Discuss the projects. Ask *Look at your rough draft and the final version. What changes did you make? Why did you make them? Did my corrections help?*

▶ **Pronunciation: page T114**

LEARNING DIARY

> **Note**
> Discuss in the mother tongue.

A Students look at the contents list on page 97. They draw a face next to each item to show how well they think they know it.

B Students do the self-check in the Workbook on page 95.

C Divide the class into pairs or groups of three or four.

Students compare their answers. Go round the class and check for any common problems.

Students compare their self-check results with the faces they drew.

In the whole class ask *What problems did you find with the self-check?* Students suggest problem areas.

Take remedial action, as necessary. (See Introduction page vii for possible strategies.)

Ask *What did you like best in this unit? What didn't you like?*
Students give their responses. Ask *Why?* Take note of student responses. They can help you to adjust your teaching towards the things that motivate the students most.

CULTURE SPOT
Workbook page 95

- Divide the class into pairs or groups of three or four.

- Students look quickly at the text.

- Ask *What is the text about?*

- Students give their ideas.

- Ask *What do you already know about this topic?*

- Students give their ideas. Discuss these ideas.

- Say *Read the Culture spot text. Note anything that you find interesting or unusual.*

- Ask comprehension questions about the text.

- Students give their answers. Explain any words that students need.

- Ask *Did you find anything interesting or unusual?*

- Students give their ideas.

- Read each comparision question in turn.

- Discuss each question. Encourage students to compare their situation with the one in the text.

1 **a** • Divide the class into pairs.

   • Students look at the picture. Ask *What can you see in the picture? What rooms can you see? What is in each room?*

   • Write these questions on the board: *Who are the people in the story? What is the story about? When did it happen?*

   • Students read the first two paragraphs to find the answers.

   • Students give their answers.

> **Answer key**
> *Ruth Less, her husband Dennis, her sister Cindy Sweet and her business partner Ken Doe*
> *Someone murdered Ruth Less.*
> *It happened on Wednesday 9 June between 1 and 2 o'clock in the morning.*

b • Explain the activity.

   • Ask *What happened on 8 June?*

> **Answer key**
> *There was a dinner at Ruth Less's house.*

   • Ask *Where were the people on 8 June?*

> **Answer key**
> *They were in the dining room at Ruth Less's house.*

   • Students read the text and draw a line on the picture to show the movements of each person. Each line starts in the dining room at the dinner table.

   • Draw the plan of the house on the board.

   • Choose four students to draw the lines for each person on the board.

Answer key

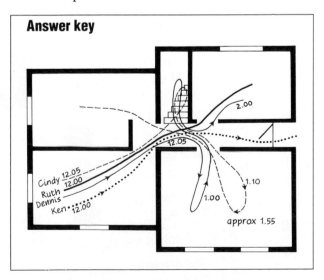

PROJECT

The movies

Make a project about the movies. Describe these.

- Your favourite films.
- Your favourite actors and actresses.
  What do you know about them?
- The last film that you saw.
  Tell the story. Who was in it? Was it good?

Illustrate your project with pictures.

These two actresses are Rosanna Arquette and Madonna in 'Desperately Seeking Susan'. The film was very funny. I didn't really understand it, but I thought Rosanna Arquette was great. She's now officially my favourite film star. So here's some information about her.

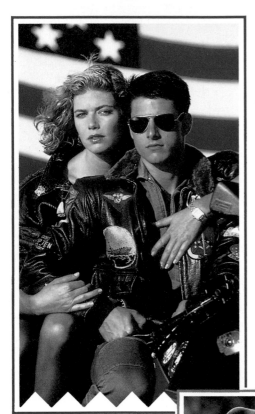

This scene is from 'Top Gun'. The woman is Kelly McGillis and the man is Tom Cruise.

I went to see 'Top Gun' last week. In the film, Tom Cruise was at the United States Navy Fighter Pilots School. He wanted to be the best pilot - the top gun. Kelly McGillis was his teacher at the Pilots School. They fell in love. The story wasn't very good, but the aeroplane scenes were fantastic.

I like Kelly McGillis. I saw her in 'Witness'. It was on the television last year. Harrison Ford was in it, too.

Rosanna Arquette was born in 1959 in the United States. She wasn't the first star in her family. Her grandfather, Clifford Arquette, was an actor, too.

Rosanna became an actress in 1977. She had parts in several TV programmes. She made her first film in 1980. It was called 'More American Graffiti'. Six years later she starred with Madonna in 'Desperately Seeking Susan'.

(I like Madonna, too. She's my favourite singer.)

This is Harrison Ford. I saw him in 'Raiders of the Lost Ark'. I watched it on a video at my friend's house. Harrison Ford played Indiana Jones. It was a great film.

Harrison Ford first became famous, when he played Han Solo in the Star Wars movies. I couldn't find a picture from 'Raiders of the Lost Ark' or 'Star Wars'. So this is Harrison Ford in 'Mosquito Coast'.

Learning diary

A Look at the first page of this unit. How well do you know these things now? Look at each point in the contents list.

If you know it well, draw a happy face.

If you know it fairly well, draw a face like this.

If you don't know it well, draw a sad face.

B Try the self-check in the Workbook.

C Compare your answers with a partner. Discuss any problems with your teacher.

13

▶ Pronunciation: page 114

14 revision

READING

1 a Look at the picture.

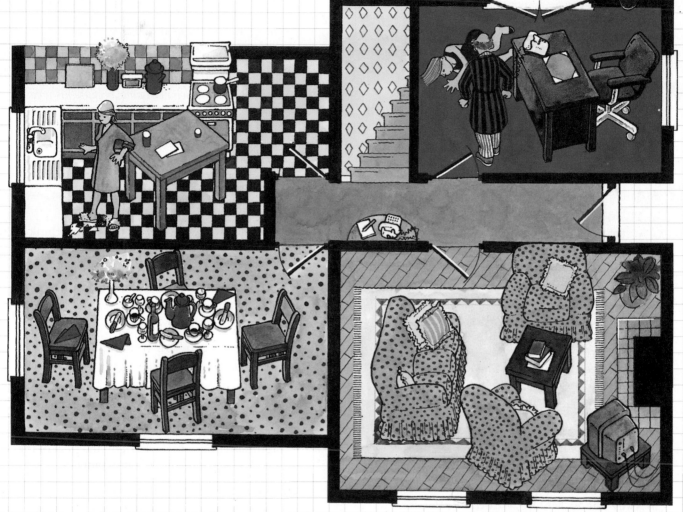

b Read the story. On the picture, draw lines to show the movements of each person between 12 o'clock and 2 o'clock.

Ruth Less is a rich woman – or she *was* a rich woman. On Wednesday 9 June between 1 and 2 o'clock in the morning someone murdered her. The murderer hit her with a heavy baseball bat.

On 8 June there was a dinner in the evening at Ruth Less's house. There were four people at the dinner: Ruth Less; her husband, Dennis; her sister Cindy Sweet and her business partner, Ken Doe.

The dinner finished at twelve o'clock. At five past twelve Ken Doe left. He drove home. Cindy Sweet went to bed. But Ruth Less and her husband didn't go to bed. Ruth went to her office and

worked. Dennis sat in the living room and read a book.

At 1 o'clock Ruth Less telephoned Ken Doe. Dennis Less heard her. He was on his way to bed. At ten past one Cindy Sweet got up. She couldn't sleep. She came downstairs. She went into the living room and watched television.

At 2 o'clock Dennis Less woke up. He heard a crash downstairs. He came downstairs and he went into the office. He found Ruth Less on the floor. She was dead. The French windows were open. Cindy Sweet was in the kitchen.

• Students read the interview.

• Students write the questions.

• Choose students to read out their completed questions. Write them on the board.

Answer key
What time did the dinner finish?
Did your wife go to bed?
Did you go to bed?
Where did you find your wife?
Were the french windows open?
Where was Cindy Sweet?

 • Divide the class into pairs.

• Demonstrate the activity with one pair.

• In pairs students read the dialogue.

• They reverse roles and repeat.

4 a • Students remain in pairs.

• Explain the activity.

• Play the tape. Students listen.

• Students write down the new information.

• Play the tape again. Students check their ideas.

** Who killed Ruth Less?: Part 1**

Mickey Shane Miss Sweet, did you like your sister?

Cindy Sweet No, I didn't. She was a terrible woman. Everybody hated her.

Mickey Shane When you came downstairs, did you see her?

Cindy Sweet No, I didn't.

Mickey Shane Why were you in the kitchen?

Cindy Sweet I went to get a drink. But I dropped the glass.

Mickey Shane Mr Doe, why did Ruth Less telephone you?

Ken Doe She needed some information. It was at my house.

Mickey Shane Was it a good dinner?

Ken Doe No, it wasn't. Ruth and Dennis had an argument. He gambles, you see. Ruth refused to give him any money. But he's a rich man now.

Mickey Shane The dinner finished at 12 o'clock. Did you leave immediately?

Ken Doe No, I didn't. I went into the office and I telephoned the airport.

b • Students give their new information.

Answer key
(possible answers)
Cindy Sweet didn't see Ruth Less when she came downstairs.
She went to the kitchen because she wanted a drink.
She dropped the glass.

Ruth Less telephoned Ken Doe, because she needed some information.
The information was at Ken Doe's house.
Ruth and Dennis had an argument at dinner.
Dennis gambles.
Ruth Less refused to give Dennis any money.
Dennis Less is a rich man now, because his wife is dead.
Ken Doe didn't leave immediately after the dinner.
He went into Ruth's office. He telephoned the airport.

5 • Students give their ideas.

• On the board write how many people think each character is the murderer.

6 • Students read the list of clues. Explain any unknown words.

• Play the tape. Students listen.

• See how many people were right.

• Ask *Who murdered Ruth Less? How did he do it? How did Mickey Shane know?*

• Students give their ideas.

• Play the tape again.

• Students complete the lines on the plan of the house to show Ken Doe's movements.

Who killed Ruth Less?: Part 2

Mickey Shane I know who the murderer is. It was you, Mr Doe.

Cindy Sweet But how did he do it? He was at home. Ruth telephoned him.

Mickey Shane Yes, but Mr Doe has got a telephone in his car. When he left, he waited in his car. He didn't telephone Ruth. So she telephoned him. Then he came back. He came in quietly through the french windows and he killed Ruth. But then you came downstairs, Miss Sweet. So he ran away quickly.

Cindy Sweet But how do you know?

Mickey Shane We found Mr Doe's fingerprints on the handle of the french windows.

Ken Doe But ... but I opened them when I telephoned the airport.

Mickey Shane No, you didn't, Mr Doe. You see, your fingerprints were on the handle outside.

• Students describe how Ken Doe murdered Ruth Less.

> **Answer key**
> (See tapescript for Exercise 6.)

 • Divide the class into groups of four.
- Explain the activity.
- Students plan their whodunnit.
- Students write a story.
- Students draw a plan.
- Students prepare an interview with one of the suspects.
- Go round and help with any problems.
- Groups present their story, plan and interview to the class. The class must work out how the crime was carried out.

Top Twenty

This activity proves an opportunity for a bit of fun in translation.

- Divide the class into groups of four.

a • Read the introduction to the chart.
- Students look at the chart. Ask *Do you know any of these songs?*
- Students give their ideas.
- Explain the activity.
- Students translate the titles. They can use dictionaries for this.
- Groups give their ideas for translations.

b • Explain the activity.
- Each group writes down its own favourite twenty records
  or
  Get each student to write down their favourite five records. Collect their suggestions and compile a class Top Twenty. (This will take a little longer.)
- Groups translate their (or the class's) Top Twenty.
- Groups display their translated charts.

2 Mickey Shane, the detective, interviewed Dennis Less. Here are some of the answers he got. What were his questions?

Mickey Shane What time .... ?

Dennis Less At twelve o'clock.

Mickey Shane .... ?

Dennis Less No, she didn't. Ruth went to her office and worked.

Mickey Shane .... ?

Dennis Less No, I didn't. I sat in the living room and read a book.

Mickey Shane .... ?

Dennis Less On the floor.

Mickey Shane .... the french windows .... ?

Dennis Less Yes, they were but it was a warm night.

Mickey Shane .... ?

Dennis Less She was in the kitchen.

 3 Work in pairs. One person is Mickey Shane, one is Dennis Less. Role play the interview.

 4 a 📼 Listen. You will hear some more information. Write the new information down.

b Say what new information you have got.

Example
Cindy Sweet didn't like Mrs Less.

 5 Can you solve the murder? Who was the murderer? How did he or she do it?

 6 📼 Listen. Mickey Shane is explaining how it happened.

Which of these are important clues?

the glass	a police car
the telephone	the baseball bat
the television	the door handle
fingerprints	

FOLLOW UP

 7 Describe how the murderer killed Ruth Less.

 8 Make your own Whodunnit.

- Describe what happened.
- Draw a plan of the scene.
- Introduce the suspects.
- Make an interview between Mickey Shane and a suspect.

Can other people in the class find the criminal?

a Look at this Top Twenty Chart.
Do you know any of these songs?
Translate the titles into your
own language.

Happy Birthday Radio 581

TOP TWENTY

It's the Hotline programme's birthday today.
Here are our Top Twenty requests.
These are the twenty most-requested
records since Hotline started.

1 MONEY FOR NOTHING
Dire Straits

2 TONIGHT
New Kids on the Block

3 SHE LOVES YOU
The Beatles

4 LIKE A VIRGIN
Madonna

5 A GROOVY KIND OF LOVE
Phil Collins

6 DO THEY KNOW IT'S CHRISTMAS?
Band Aid

7 GOOD VIBRATIONS
The Beach Boys

8 I SHOULD BE SO LUCKY
Kylie Minogue

9 SEALED WITH A KISS
Jason Donovan

10 ITSY BITSY TEENY WEENY YELLOW POLKA DOT BIKINI
Bombalurina

11 BAD
Michael Jackson

12 IMAGINE
John Lennon

13 ANOTHER BRICK IN THE WALL
Pink Floyd

14 WITH A LITTLE HELP FROM MY FRIENDS
Wet Wet Wet

15 I OWE YOU NOTHING
Bros

16 BORN IN THE USA
Bruce Springsteen

17 TWENTY-FOUR HOURS
Betty Boo

18 WILD BOYS
Duran Duran

19 MONEY, MONEY, MONEY
Abba

20 U CAN'T TOUCH THIS
MC Hammer

b Make your own Top Twenty.

● Find out the twenty most popular records in your class or in your group.
● Translate the titles into English.
● Write your chart in English.

109

▶ Pronunciation: page 114

VICTORIA ROAD

The truth

Note

If you don't have time for Exercise 1, have a general classroom discussion about how the story ends. Students suggest possible endings.

- Ask *What happened in the last episode of 'Victoria Road'?*
- Students give their ideas.

Answer key

Terry and his friends went to the cinema. Terry told his friends about his fight with Darren Tooley and his friends. They met Darren Tooley and his friends at the cinema. They were very friendly to Terry. Vince and the others wondered why.

- Divide the class into groups of five.
- Students decide in their groups how the story ends. We must find out what really happened in the park.
- Students write a final episode. It must have a part for each member of the group. It must be no more than three minutes long.
- Groups practise their play in their groups.
- Groups perform their play in front of the class.

- Play the tape. Students listen.
- Ask *What really happened in the park? How did Sue find out?*
- Students give their answers.
- Play the tape again.

VICTORIA ROAD: The truth

Terry Hi, you lot.
Casey Hi, Terry. Oh here's Sue.
Sue Terry. I want to talk to you.
Terry Oh, er. I can't stay, really. I . . .
Sue You rat, Terry Moore. I met Jane Fox today. And she told me what really happened in the park.
Terry Oh, er, well. I must go. See you.
Sue Wait a minute, Terry. You didn't push those boys in the lake. You didn't kick them.
Vince What happened, Sue?
Sue On the way to the lake, our hero, Terry, shouted and kicked and he said it wasn't his fault. He told Darren Tooley and his friends about his blind date and about me in the cafe. And what did they say, Terry?
Terry Well, I don't know, er, well, they said it wasn't my fault.

Sue That's right. They said, 'He's right. It isn't his fault. It's Sue's fault.' Then one of them said, 'Look, these are Sue's things. Let's throw them in the lake.'
Vince So, did you throw Sue's coat in the lake, Terry?
Terry Well, I didn't throw it.
Sue No, but Tooley and his friends threw it in the lake and you watched them. And then you went to the cafe with them.
Kamala Oh, Terry. You didn't!
Sue He did.
Vince So that's why those guys were so friendly at the cinema.
Casey We jumped in the lake and telephoned the police. And you were in the cafe with Tooley!
Terry Wait a minute, you lot. I mean, what could I do? There were three of them.
Casey Come here, Terry!
Terry Er, sorry, I really must go. See you.

Sue Get him!
Terry No. It wasn't my fault. Help!
All Come here!

▶ **Pronunciation: page T114**

LEARNING DIARY

Students look at the Learning diary.

Students do the tasks.

Divide the class into groups of three or four.

Students compare their answers. Go round the class and check for any common problems.

In the whole class discuss students' answers.

Discuss how students can learn the things they are not sure about.

The pronunciation practice sections comprise three elements:

* Units 1 and 2 introduce and practise general concepts.

* Units 3 ,4, 5, 7, 8, 9, 11, 12 and 13 practise individual sounds.

* Units 6, 10 and 14 provide revision practice of the symbols.

Unit 1 Vowels

In this unit, students are introduced to the concept of phonetic symbols and their use. Only a few symbols are introduced at this stage. Students will build up their knowledge of all the symbols as they work through the book.

a • Students look at the two columns.

   • Explain that phonetic symbols show how we pronounce words, not how we write them.

b • Say *You can find phonetic symbols for all the words in this book in the wordlist.*

   • Students turn to the wordlist on page 115 and copy the correct symbols for the words.

   • Copy the list onto the board.

   • Choose students to complete the list.

> **Answer key**
> pop /pɒp/
> desk /desk/
> bag /bæg/
> book /bʊk/
> Britain /ˈbrɪtən/
> door /dɔː(r)/

> **Note**
> The (r) symbol in brackets shows the American English pronunciation of the word.
> This /r/ is not heard in British English.

c • Students work in pairs.

   • Say *Look at the words and symbols in **a** and **b**. Can you guess the missing symbols for the words in **c**? They are all in **a** or **b**.*

   • In pairs, students try to work out the missing symbols.

   • Students check their ideas in the wordlist.

> **Answer key**
> from /frɒm/
> five /faɪv/
> pen /pen/
> we /wiː/
> four /fɔː/
> who /huː/

Consonants

d • Students look at the words.

   • Say *Some consonant symbols are very different.*

   • Read aloud the three words *this, three* and *teacher*. Students repeat.

   • Students look at the list of words with underlined letters.

   • Students turn to the wordlist on page 115 and copy the correct symbols for the underlined letters.

> **Answer key**
> /ʃ/   /j/   /dʒ/   /ks/   /dʒ/

* Students look at the wordlist and find other words with these symbols.

* While they are doing this, draw four columns on the blackboard headed /ʃ/ /j/ /dʒ/ /ks/.

* Students suggest words for the columns.

* Check these suggestions with the phonetic transcription in the wordlist.

* Students look at the cartoon.

* Ask *Do you know what they are saying?*

* Elicit ideas.

> **Answer key**
> *What's your name?*
> *Mary.*

> **Note**
> We do not use punctuation with phonetic symbols.

1 a Look back at the Victoria Road stories.
Make a final episode for it.

b Role play your story

2 🎞 Listen. You will hear how the story
ends. Compare your story to the real one.

Learning diary

You've come to the end of this
book. But it's not the end of
learning English.

14

How do you feel about the things
that you have learnt? Look back at the
Learning diaries in the book. Write down:

- 3 things that you know well now.
- 3 things that you are still not sure about.
- 3 things that you really enjoyed.
- 3 things that you didn't like much.

Discuss your lists with other members of
your class. How do you learn best?

What can you do to learn the things you
are not sure about?

Good luck with your
next year of English!

▶ Pronunciation: page 114   110

PRONUNCIATION PRACTICE

Unit 1 Vowels

a **Look.**

We write	We say
he	/ hi: /
two	/ tu: /
I	/ aɪ /

These are *phonetic* symbols.

b **Use the wordlist on page 115. Write these words with phonetic symbols.**

pop   ....

desk   ....

bag   ....

book   ....

Britain   ....

door   ....

c **Complete these words with phonetic symbols. Check your answers in the wordlist.**

from	/fr .... m/
five	/f ..... v/
pen	/p .... n/
we	/w ... /
four	/f .... /
who	/h .... /

Consonants

Look.

We write	We say
bag	/ bæg /
desk	/ desk /

But some consonants have special phonetic symbols.

this	/ ðɪs /
three	/ θri:/
teacher	/ 'ti:tʃə (r)/

Find the words below in the wordlist on page 115. What are the symbols for the underlined letters?

she   you   orange   six   just

....

Find other words with these symbols.

Unit 2 Spelling

In English the spelling and the sound are not always the same.

Look.

different spelling	same sound
you	/ ju: /
two	/ tu: /

same spelling	different sound
book	/ bʊk /
door	/dɔ:(r)/

Find two more examples.

Compare this to your own language.

/h/

a 🔲 **Listen and repeat.**

he   his   how   her   here   Hartfield
hamburger   hello

b **Say these.**

How old is he?   Can I help you?
Is this her hamburger?   Is he here?

Unit 2 Spelling

In this unit, the relationship between English spelling and sounds is explored. It is important that students understand this relationship.

- Draw students' attention to the two pairs of columns.
- Read the note and the four example words aloud.
- Students find two more words with the same sound but different spelling and two more words with the same spelling but different sounds.
- Check answers.

Answer key

three, we, teacher have the same sound but different spelling.

who and *pop* have the same spelling but different sound.

- Ask *Can you find words like this in our (your) language?*
- Students suggest answers (if any).
- Explain that the phonetic symbols are important because English spelling and sounds are not always the same.

/h/

a
- Make the point that the letter *h* is usually pronounced in English.
- It is pronounced /h/. A word beginning with a vowel is *not* pronounced with /h/ at the beginning.
- Tell students that they are going to practise the /h/ sound.
- Say *I'm going to play the cassette. Listen and repeat the words.*
- ▄▄ Play the tape.
- Students listen and repeat.
- Correct as you go along, as necessary.

b
- Students read the questions.
- Say *I'm going to play the cassette. Listen carefully and repeat what you hear.*
- Students listen and repeat.
- Correct as you go along, making sure that students do not put an /h/ sound in front of *old, is, I, Is* and *Is*.

Unit 3 /ɒ/, /ɔː/

a
- Remind students of these symbols, using the words *pop* and *door*.
- Say *I'm going to play the cassette. You hear a number and then a word. If the word has an /ɔː/ sound, tick the box with that number.*
- Check comprehension.
- ▄▄ Play the tape.
- Students tick boxes when they hear the /ɔː/ sound.
- Stop after 5. Check students are doing the task correctly. Then continue to the end.

▄▄
1 long	8 football
2 short	9 boring
3 blond	10 job
4 doctor	11 from
5 tall	12 four
6 walkman	13 Scotland
7 shop	14 daughter

- Say *Put your pen on the tick with the lowest number and join up all the ticks from the lowest to the highest.*
- Students join the ticks.
- Ask *What shape do you get?*
- Elicit answer.

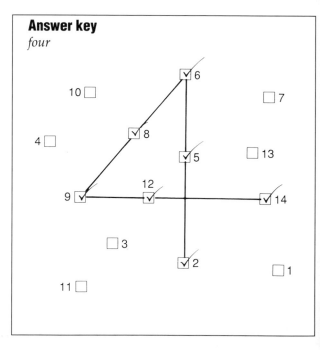

Answer key
four

T112

Unit 4 /æ/, /ɑː/

a
- Students read the list of words.
- Check comprehension.
- Say *Now listen and repeat.*
- ▪▪ Play the tape.
- Students listen and repeat.

b
- Students read the list of words.
- Draw students' attention to the outlines of the van and the car.
- Say *I'm going to play the cassette. Listen carefully and put the words into the van if they have the /æ/ sound and into the car if they have the /ɑː/ sound.*
- Check comprehension.
- ▪▪ Play the tape.
- Students listen and write the words in the correct place.
- Students compare answers in pairs.
- Elicit answers.

> **Answer key**
> **van:** *badge   black   flat   Saturday   can*
> **car:** *dance   class   dark   can't*

c
- Students practise saying all the words. Say *Van* or *Car* and choose a student to say a word from the correct list.

Unit 5 /æ/, /ʌ/

a
- Read aloud the words *back* and *front*.
- Students read the list of words.
- Say *I'm going to play the cassette. Listen carefully and put the words into the back garden if they have the /æ/ sound and the front garden if they have the /ʌ/ sound.*
- Check comprehension.
- ▪▪ Play the tape.
- Students listen and write the words in the correct place.
- Students compare answers in pairs.
- Elicit answers.

> **Answer key**
> **back garden:** *garage   cafe   that   flat   at   badge*
> **front garden:** *cupboard   touch   come   must   up   number*

b
- Play the tape again.
- Students listen and repeat.

Unit 6 Revision

- Students look at the task.
- Explain the activity.
- Students write the sentences in words.
- Students compare their ideas in pairs.

> **Answer key**
> *Can I help you?*
> *A cheeseburger and an orange juice, please.*
> *Anything else?*
> *No, thank you.*
> *That's one pound thirty-two, please.*

Unit 7 /ɒ/, /əʊ/

a
- Students look at the list of words.
- Check comprehension of the words.
- Say *Stop* and *Go. Can you hear the difference? I'm going to play the cassette. If you hear a word with the /ɒ/ sound say 'STOP!' and if you hear a word with the /əʊ/ sound say 'GO!'.*
- Check comprehension. Say *I'll do the first two for you.*
- ▪▪ Play the tape and demonstrate with the first two words.
- ▪▪ Continue with the tape, students call out *STOP!* or *GO!*

▪▪

stop	(STOP)
go	(GO)
shop	(STOP)
close	(GO)
open	(GO)
smoke	(GO)
clock	(STOP)
home	(GO)
watch	(STOP)
goal	(GO)
long	(STOP)
doctor	(STOP)
cola	(GO)
chocolate	(STOP)
not	(STOP)
know	(GO)
on	(STOP)
don't	(GO)
road	(GO)
pop star	(STOP)

- Rewind the tape.

Unit 3 /ɒ/, /ɔː/

a 🔊 Listen to the numbers and the words. If the word has an /ɔː/, tick the box.

b Join up the ticks from the lowest number to the highest number. What shape do you get?

☐6
10☐   ☐7
4☐   ☐8
            ☐5   ☐13
        12
9☐   ☐   ☐14
        ☐3
            ☐2   ☐1
11☐

Unit 4 /æ/, /ɑː/

a 🔊 Listen and repeat.

/æ/	/ɑː/
van	car
Maths	past
apple	answer

b 🔊 Listen and put these words in the van or the car.

badge   dance   black   flat
Saturday   class   dark   can   can't

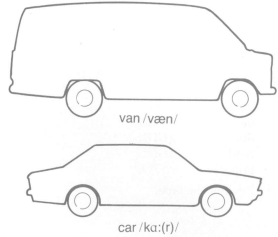

van /væn/

car /kɑː(r)/

c Say all the words.

Unit 5 /æ/, /ʌ/

a Listen and put these words in the front garden or the back garden.

cupboard	come	must	at
touch	cafe	up	number
garage	that	flat	badge

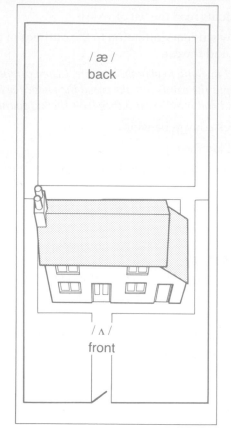

/ æ /
back

/ ʌ /
front

b Listen again and repeat.

Unit 6 Revision

Write this dialogue in words.

ˌkæn aɪ ˈhelp juː

....

ə ˌtʃiːzbɜːgə ænd ən ˈɒrɪndʒ dʒuːs pliːz

....

ˌenɪθɪŋ ˈels

....

nəʊ ˈθæŋk juː

....

ðæts ˌwʌn paʊnd ˈθɜːti tuː pliːz

....

Unit 7 /ɒ/, /əʊ/

a 🔊 **Listen. If you hear the /ɒ/ sound, say STOP. If you hear the /əʊ/ sound, say GO.**

stop	smoke	long	know
go	clock	d**o**ctor	on
shop	home	c**o**la	don't
close	watch	ch**o**colate	road
open	goal	not	p**o**p star

b 🔊 **Listen again. Put the words in the correct box.**

stop / ɒ /	go / əʊ /

c **Say the words.**

Unit 8 /uː/, /juː/

4 a 🔊 **Listen and repeat.**

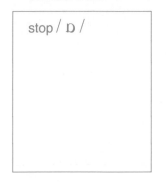

/uː/
s**u**permarket

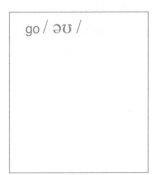

/juː/
m**u**seum

b 🔊 **Listen and put these words under the supermarket or museum.**

do	choose	st**u**dent	exc**u**se me
room	blue	m**u**sic	n**ew**spaper
Tuesday	so**u**venir	f**oo**d	swimming p**oo**l
comp**u**ter	n**ew**	comm**u**nity work	

c **Say all the words.**

Unit 9 Unstressed /ə/

a 🔊 **Listen and repeat.**

scissors trousers sweater summer
souvenir magazine corner photograph
understand hamburger

b **Underline the syllable with the /ə/ sound.**

c **Say the words.**

Unit 10 Revision

Write this dialogue in words.

də jə ˌlaɪk ðɪs ˈtiːʃɜːt

....

nəʊ ˌaɪ ˈdəʊnt bʌt ˌaɪ ˈlaɪk ðəʊz ˈdʒiːnz

....

haʊ ˈmʌtʃ ɑː ðeɪ

....

ðeə ˌθɜːti fɔː ˈpaʊnz

....

əʊ ˌðæts veri ɪkˈspensɪv

....

Unit 11 /ɪ/, /iː/

🔊 **Who is this? Listen and join the dots in the correct order.**

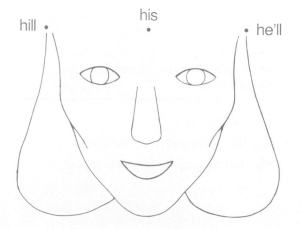

this •   • he's   • live

these •   leave •

hill •   his   • he'll

113

b • Say *Listen again and this time write the words in the correct box.*

    • 📼 Play the tape.

    • Students listen and write the words in the correct box.

    • Students compare answers in pairs.

    • Elicit answers.

> **Answer key**
>
> **stop:** *shop clock watch long doctor chocolate not on pop star*
>
> **go:** *close open smoke home goal cola know don't road*

c • In pairs, students take it in turns to test each other. One student says a word from the list and the other with the book closed must answer *STOP!* or *GO!* (You can, if you prefer, rewind the tape and get students to repeat the words again.)

Unit 8 /uː/, /juː/

a • Draw students' attention to the words under the pictures of the buildings.

    • Say *I'm going to play the cassette. Repeat the words.*

    • 📼 Play the tape.

    • Students repeat the words.

b • Students look at the list of words.

    • Check comprehension of the words.

    • Say *I'm going to play the cassette. Listen carefully and put the words under the supermarket if they have the /uː/ sound and the museum if they have the /juː/ sound.*

    • Check comprehension.

    • 📼 Play the tape.

    • Students listen and write the words in the correct place.

    • Students compare answers in pairs.

    • Elicit answers.

> **Answer key**
>
> **supermarket:** *do choose room blue souvenir food swimming pool*
>
> **museum:** *student excuse me music newspaper Tuesday computer new community work*

c • Rewind the tape.

    • Say *Now listen and repeat the words.*

    • Play the tape again. Students repeat.

Unit 9 Unstressed /ə/

> **Note**
>
> The /ə/ sound is very common in spoken English, and is never stressed. This needs a lot of practice, but make sure that students do not stress the sound when they practise it.

a • Say *The unstressed /ə/ sound is very short. You're going to practise it in these words.*

    • Check comprehension of the words.

    • Say *Listen very carefully to the cassette and repeat the words.*

    • 📼 Play the tape.

    • Students repeat.

    • Rewind the tape and repeat as necessary.

b • Write *scissors* on the board.

    • Ask *Where is the /ə/ sound?*

    • Elicit answer.

> **Answer key**
>
> *sciss**o**rs*

    • Get a student who answers correctly to underline the syllable on the board.

    • Students work in pairs.

    • Students work out where the /ə/ sound comes and underline the correct syllable.

    • While they are doing this, write the words on the board.

    • Elicit answers and get students to come out and underline the correct syllable in each word on the board.

> **Answer key**
>
> *sciss**o**rs trous**e**rs sweat**e**r summ**e**r souv**e**nir mag**a**zine corn**e**r phot**o**graph und**e**rstand hamburg**e**r*

    • Students check their answers.

c • Say *You can always check in a dictionary or in the wordlist to see where the /ə/ sound comes in a new word. Remember not to stress this sound.*

    • Rewind the tape and practise the pronunciation of all the words.

Unit 10 Revision

- Students look at the task.
- Explain the activity.
- Students write the sentences in words.
- Students compare their ideas in pairs.

> **Answer key**
> *Do you like this T-shirt?*
> *No, I don't, but I like those jeans.*
> *How much are they?*
> *They're thirty-four pounds.*
> *Oh, that's very expensive.*

Unit 11 /ɪ/, /iː/

- Read aloud the instructions.
- Say *I'm going to play the cassette with these words on it. Put your pen on 'hill'.*
  *When you hear the next word, connect 'hill' to that word with a line. Continue in the same way and connect the words **in the order that you hear them**.*
- Check comprehension.
- 📼 Play the tape.
- Students listen and connect the words.

  📼
  hill
  this
  these
  he's
  leave
  live
  he'll
  his
  hill
- Ask *What shape do you get?*
- Elicit answer.

> **Answer key**
> *queen*
>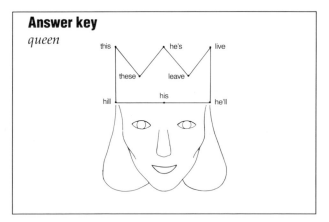

- Ask *Does queen have an /ɪ/ or an /iː/ sound?*
- Elicit answer.

> **Answer key**
> /iː/

Unit 12 /v/

> **Note**
> If your students have difficulty with this sound, tell them to bite their bottom lip with their top teeth, as for /f/.

- Students read the list of words.
- Check comprehension of the words.
- Say *Listen and repeat the words. Be careful with the /v/ sound.*
- 📼 Play the tape.
- Students listen and repeat.
- Rewind the tape for further practice, as necessary.

Unit 13 /ɜː/

- Students look at the list of words.
- Check comprehension of the words.
- Remind students that in English the same sounds can be spelled in different ways.
- Say *All these words have the same vowel sound /ɜː/. Listen and repeat.*

> **Note**
> If the students do this with their books closed, they will have to listen more carefully, so their pronunciation will be better, and they won't be confused by the different spellings.

- 📼 Play the tape.
- Students listen and repeat.
- Rewind the tape for further practice, as necessary. (If students closed their books before, they should open them again now and practise reading and pronouncing correctly.)

Unit 14 Revision

- Students look at the task.
- Explain the activity.
- Students write the sentences in words.
- Students compare their ideas in pairs.

> **Answer key**
> *I saw a ghost in this room yesterday.*
> *What was it like?*
> *It was a young woman with long hair.*
> *What did she do?*
> *She came through that wall but then she disappeared.*
> *Who was she?*
> *I don't know.*

Unit 12 / v /

🔊 **Listen and repeat.**

village	have	visit	give
voice	living room	love	interview
souvenir	river	heavy	favourite

Unit 13 / ɜː /

🔊 **Listen and repeat.**

bird	world	word
first	thirty-first	work
weren't	early	were

Unit 14 Revision

Write this dialogue in words.

ˌaɪ sɔː əˈgəʊst ɪn ðɪs ruːm jestədɪ

....

ˌwɒt wəz ɪt ˈlaɪk

....

ˌɪt wəz ə ˌjʌŋ ˈwʊmən wɪð ˌlɒŋ ˈheə

....

ˌwɒt dɪd ʃiː ˈduː

....

ˌʃiː keɪm θruː ˌðæt ˈwɔːl bʌt ˌðen ʃiː ˌdɪsəˈpɪəd

....

ˌhuː ˈwɒz ʃiː

....

ˌaɪ dəʊnt ˈnəʊ

....

114

WORDLIST

UNIT 1
INTRODUCTION
hello /həˈləʊ/
hi /haɪ/
what /wɒt/
name /neɪm/
from /frɒm/
Britain /ˈbrɪtən/
Australia /ɒˈstreɪlɪə/

the USSR /ðə ˌjuː es es ˈɑː(r)/
the USA /ðə ˌjuː es ˈeɪ/
the States /ðə ˈsteɪts/
the Philippines /ðə ˈfɪlɪpiːnz/
Argentina /ˌɑːdʒənˈtiːnə/
Brazil /brəˈzɪl/
Spain /speɪn/
Germany /ˈdʒɜːmənɪ/
Greece /griːs/
Italy /ˈɪtəlɪ/
famous /ˈfeɪməs/
favourite /ˈfeɪvərɪt/
pop star /ˈpɒp ˌstɑː(r)/
sports star /ˈspɔːts stɑː(r)/

desk /desk/
pen /pen/
pencil /ˈpensl/
window /ˈwɪndəʊ/
blackboard /ˈblækbɔːd/
teacher /ˈtiːtʃə(r)/
book /bʊk/
bag /bæg/
cassette recorder /kəˈset rɪkɔːdə(r)/
door /dɔː(r)/

fast /fɑːst/
alphabet /ˈælfəbet/
car /kɑː(r)/
cabriolet /ˌkæbrɪəˈleɪ/
convertible /kənˈvɜːtəbl/
this /ðɪs/

radio /ˈreɪdɪəʊ/
programme /ˈprəʊgræm/
DJ /ˈdiː ˌdʒeɪ/
on the line /ˌɒn ðə ˈlaɪn/
boyfriend /ˈbɔɪfrend/
girlfriend /ˈgɜːlfrend/
record (noun) /ˈrekɔːd/
birthday /ˈbɜːθdeɪ/
today /təˈdeɪ/
happy /ˈhæpɪ/
Who...? /huː .../
How old...? /haʊ ˈəʊld .../
I don't know. /aɪ ˌdəʊnt ˈnəʊ/
I think... /aɪ ˈθɪŋk .../
thank you /ˈθæŋk juː/

fast food /fɑːst ˈfuːd/
hamburger /ˈhæmbɜːgə(r)/
cheeseburger /ˈtʃiːzbɜːgə(r)/
eggburger /ˈegbɜːgə(r)/
french fries /ˌfrentʃ ˈfraɪz/
juice /dʒuːs/

apple /ˈæpl/
orange /ˈɒrɪndʒ/
cola /ˈkəʊlə/
p (pence) /pens/
£ (pound) /paʊnd/
egg /eg/
Can I help you? /ˌkən aɪ ˈhelp juː/
Anything else? /ˌenɪθɪŋ ˈels/
please /pliːz/

What's this called? /wɒts ˈðɪs kɔːld/
What does... mean? /wɒt dʌz ˈ... miːn/
How do you say...? /ˌhaʊ də juː seɪ ˈ.../
in English /ɪn ˈɪŋglɪʃ/
pronounce /prəˈnaʊns/
spell /spel/
just /dʒʌst/

UNIT 2 YOU
rap /ræp/
Pleased to meet you. /ˌpliːzd tə ˈmiːt juː/
How do you do? /ˌhaʊ də juː ˈduː/
another /əˈnʌðə(r)/
football /ˈfʊtbɔːl/
game /geɪm/
call /kɔːl/
sing /sɪŋ/
song /sɒŋ/
add /æd/

new /njuː/
neighbour /ˈneɪbə(r)/
brother /ˈbrʌðə(r)/
boy /bɔɪ/
girl /gɜːl/
twins /twɪnz/
friend /frend/
best /best/
See you. /ˈsiː juː/
next door /ˌnekst ˈdɔː(r)/
What are they like? /ˌwɒt ɑː(r) ðeɪ ˈlaɪk/
all right /ˈɔːl raɪt/
sister /ˈsɪstə(r)/
a bit /ə ˈbɪt/
bossy /ˈbɒsɪ/
not /nɒt/
You just wait. /ˌjuː dʒʌst ˈweɪt/
quiet /ˈkwaɪət/

good /gʊd/
fan /fæn/
singer /ˈsɪŋə(r)/
great /greɪt/
rubbish /ˈrʌbɪʃ/
wonderful /ˈwʌndəfl/
bad /bæd/
terrible /ˈterəbl/
very /ˈverɪ/
awful /ˈɔːfl/
OK /ˌəʊˈkeɪ/
group /gruːp/

leisure centre /ˈleʒə(r) ˌsentə(r)/

age /eɪdʒ/
address /əˈdres/
road /rəʊd/
telephone /ˈtelɪfəʊn/
number /ˈnʌmbə(r)/
How do you spell ...? /ˌhaʊ də jɔː spel ˈ.../
double /ˈdʌbl/

T-shirt /ˈtiː ʃɜːt/
each /iːtʃ/
How much...? /haʊ ˈmʌtʃ .../
shop /ʃɒp/
postcard /ˈpəʊstkɑːd/
small /smɔːl/
large /lɑːdʒ/
Can I have...? /kən aɪ hæv ˈ.../
I'll take it. /aɪl ˈteɪk ɪt/
altogether /ˌɔːltəˈgeðə(r)/
Here you are. /ˈhɪə juː ɑː(r)/
change /tʃeɪndʒ/
umbrella /ʌmˈbrelə/
badge /bædʒ/
tracksuit /ˈtræksuːt/
watch /wɒtʃ/
red /red/
black /blæk/
green /griːn/
white /waɪt/
yellow /ˈjeləʊ/
blue /bluː/
customer /ˈkʌstəmə(r)/
sales assistant /ˈseɪlz əsɪstənt/

UNIT 3 PEOPLE
fair /feə(r)/
dark /dɑːk/
hair /heə(r)/
eye /aɪ/
brown /braʊn/
tall /tɔːl/
short /ʃɔːt/
date /deɪt/
Saturday /ˈsætədɪ/
colour /ˈkʌlə(r)/
long /lɒŋ/
blond /blɒnd/
pretty /ˈprɪtɪ/
secret /ˈsiːkrɪt/
big /bɪg/
guy /gaɪ/
What are you up to? /wɒt ɑː juː ˈʌp tuː/
school /skuːl/
Wait and see. /ˌweɪt ænd ˈsiː/

son /sʌn/
daughter /ˈdɔːtə(r)/
mother /ˈmʌðə(r)/
father /ˈfɑːðə(r)/
wife /waɪf/
husband /ˈhʌzbənd/
parents /ˈpeərənts/
grandparents /ˈgrændpeərənts/
family /ˈfæməlɪ/

grandmother /ˈgrændmʌðə(r)/
grandfather /ˈgrændfɑːðə(r)/
grandson /ˈgrændsʌn/
granddaughter /ˈgrændɔːtə(r)/
prince /prɪns/
princess /prɪnˈses/
queen /kwiːn/
captain /ˈkæptɪn/

It's time for . . . /ɪts ˌtaɪm fɔː ' . . ./
blind-date /ˌblaɪnd 'deɪt/
ready /ˈredɪ/
possible /ˈpɒsəbl/
job /dʒɒb/
student /ˈstjuːdənt/
shop assistant /ˈʃɒp əsɪstənt/
Scotland /ˈskɒtlənd/
engineer /endʒəˈnɪə(r)/
choose /tʃuːz/
nice /naɪs/
voice /vɔɪs/
boring /ˈbɔːrɪŋ/
fun /fʌn/
bank manager /ˈbæŋk mænɪdʒə(r)/
doctor /ˈdɒktə(r)/
farmer /ˈfɑːmə(r)/
footballer /ˈfʊtbɔːlə(r)/
policeman /pəˈliːsmən/

walkman /ˈwɔːkmən/
house /haʊs/
flat /flæt/
computer /kɒmˈpjuːtə(r)/
dictionary /ˈdɪkʃənrɪ/
often /ˈɒfn/
want /wɒnt/
first /fɜːst/
information /ˌɪnfəˈmeɪʃn/
need /niːd/
photograph /ˈfəʊtəɡrɑːf/
basic /ˈbeɪsɪk/
male /meɪl/
female /ˈfiːmeɪl/
lastly /ˈlɑːstlɪ/
yourself /jɔːˈself/
good-looking /ˌɡʊd 'lʊkɪŋ/
shy /ʃaɪ/
honest /ˈɒnɪst/
strike /straɪk/
once /wʌns/
even /ˈiːvn/
likes and dislikes /ˌlaɪks ən 'dɪslaɪks/
least /liːst/
worst /wɜːst/
food /fuːd/
think /θɪŋk/
world /wɜːld/
idea /aɪˈdɪə/
the opposite sex /ðiː ˌɒpəzɪt 'seks/
ideal /aɪˈdɪəl/
interesting /ˈɪntrəstɪŋ/
intelligent /ɪnˈtelɪdʒənt/
friendly /ˈfrendlɪ/
happy /ˈhæpɪ/
was /wɒz/, /wəz/

writer /ˈraɪtə(r)/
never /ˈnevə(r)/
could /kʊd/, /kəd/

UNIT 4 TIME

dance /dɑːns/
that /ðæt/
over there /ˌəʊvə 'ðeə(r)/
really /ˈrɪəlɪ/
near /nɪə(r)/
see /siː/
with /wɪð/
Go on. /ɡəʊ ɒn/
Excuse me. /ɪksˈkjuːz miː/
Would you like to . . .? /ˌwəd ju: 'laɪk tə . . ./
I'm sorry. /aɪm 'sɒrɪ/
everybody /ˈevrɪbɒdɪ/
I mean . . . /aɪ 'miːn . . ./
hear /hɪə(r)/
stupid /ˈstjuːpɪd/
answer /ˈɑːnsə(r)/
face /feɪs/
so /səʊ/
funny /ˈfʌnɪ/
table /ˈteɪbl/

can /kən/, /kæn/
can't /kɑːnt/
play /pleɪ/
guitar /ɡɪˈtɑː(r)/
speak /spiːk/
English /ˈɪŋglɪʃ/
swim /swɪm/
read /riːd/
music /ˈmjuːzɪk/
badminton /ˈbædmɪntən/
ski /skiː/
drive /draɪv/

timetable /ˈtaɪmteɪbl/
subject (noun) /ˈsʌbdʒɪkt/
period /ˈpɪərɪəd/
homework /ˈhəʊmwɜːk/
RE /ɑː 'riː/
French /frentʃ/
Science /ˈsaɪəns/
Maths /mæθs/
Technology /tekˈnɒlədʒɪ/
History /ˈhɪstrɪ/
Geography /dʒɪˈɒɡrəfɪ/
PE /ˌpiː 'iː/
Art /ɑːt/
lunch /lʌntʃ/
break /breɪk/
assembly /əˈsemblɪ/
registration /redʒɪˈstreɪʃn/

clock /klɒk/
to /tə/, /tuː/
o'clock /əˈklɒk/
past /pɑːst/
minute /ˈmɪnɪt/
time /taɪm/
on /ɒn/
at /ət/, /æt/

appointment /əˈpɔɪntmənt/
dentist /ˈdentɪst/
next /nekst/
afternoon /ˌɑːftəˈnuːn/
morning /ˈmɔːnɪŋ/

come /kʌm/
after /ˈɑːftə(r)/
fine /faɪn/
goodbye /ˌɡʊdˈbaɪ/
van /væn/

UNIT 5 PLACES

go /ɡəʊ/
angry /ˈæŋgrɪ/
still /stɪl/
with /wɪð/
late /leɪt/
tomorrow /təˈmɒrəʊ/
See you. /ˈsiː juː/
chocolate /ˈtʃɒklət/
milk shake /ˈmɪlk ʃeɪk/
talk /tɔːk/
silly /ˈsɪlɪ/
put /pʊt/
tray /treɪ/
touch /tʌtʃ/
careful /ˈkeəfl/
drink /drɪŋk/
again /əˈɡen/
Get out of the way. /ˌɡet aʊt əv ðə 'weɪ/
cafe /ˈkæfeɪ/
seat /siːt/

stand up /stænd 'ʌp/
sit down /sɪt 'daʊn/
write /raɪt/
look /lʊk/
pick up /pɪk 'ʌp/
close /kləʊz/
open /ˈəʊpən/
picture /ˈpɪktʃə(r)/

disk /dɪsk/
disk drive /ˈdɪsk draɪv/
monitor /ˈmɒnɪtə(r)/
screen /skriːn/
keyboard /ˈkiːbɔːd/
part /pɑːt/
keep /kiːp/
envelope /ˈenvələʊp/
ballpoint pen /ˈbɔːlpɔɪnt 'pen/
between /bɪˈtwiːn/
magnet /ˈmæɡnɪt/
carefully /ˈkeəfəlɪ/
must /məst/, /mʌst/
mustn't /ˈmʌsnt/
bit /bɪt/
kilobyte /ˈkɪləbaɪt/
VDU /ˌviː diː 'juː/
visual display unit /ˌvɪʒʊəl dɪˈspleɪ juːnɪt/
hardware /ˈhɑːdweə(r)/
software /ˈsɒftweə(r)/
mouse /maʊs/
floppy disk /ˈflɒpɪ dɪsk/
hard disk /ˈhɑːd dɪsk/
supermarket /ˈsuːpəmɑːkɪt/
disco /ˈdɪskəʊ/
bar /bɑː(r)/
toilet /ˈtɔɪlɪt/
goal /ɡəʊl/
up /ʌp/
shop /ʃɒp/
sandwich /ˈsændwɪdʒ/
jumbo jet /ˌdʒʌmbəʊ 'dʒet/

pizza /ˈpiːtsə/
film /fɪlm/
pop music /ˈpɒp mjuːzɪk/
sport /spɔːt/
hi-fi /ˈhaɪ faɪ/
stereo /ˈsterɪəʊ/
video /ˈvɪdɪəʊ/
jeans /dʒiːnz/
coffee /ˈkɒfɪ/
menu /ˈmenjuː/
restaurant /ˈrestrɒnt/
football /ˈfʊtbɔːl/

dining room /ˈdaɪnɪŋ
  ruːm/
upstairs /ˌʌpˈsteəz/
living room /ˈlɪvɪŋ ruːm/
downstairs /ˌdaʊnˈsteəz/
bathroom /ˈbɑːθruːm/
hall /hɔːl/
stairs /steəz/
garage /ˈgærɑːʒ,
  /ˈgærɪdʒ/
bedroom /ˈbedruːm/
garden /ˈgɑːdn/
front /frʌnt/
back /bæk/
cellar /ˈselə(r)/
toilet /ˈtɔɪlɪt/
kitchen /ˈkɪtʃən/
loo /luː/
cupboard /ˈkʌbəd/
outside /aʊtˈsaɪd/
How many . . .? /haʊ
  ˈmenɪ . . ./
balcony /ˈbælkənɪ/

Have a drink. /ˌhæv ə
  ˈdrɪŋk/
How can you tell
  . . .? /ˌhaʊ kən juː ˈtel
  . . ./
elephant /ˈelɪfənt/
been /biːn/
fridge /frɪdʒ/
footprint /ˈfʊtprɪnt/

UNIT 6 REVISION

dancer /ˈdɑːnsə(r)/
home /həʊm/
lesson /ˈlesn/
only /ˈəʊnlɪ/
both /bəʊθ/
stone /stəʊn/
cold /kəʊld/
baby /ˈbeɪbɪ/
belong to /bɪˈlɒŋ tə/
dream /driːm/
ticket /ˈtɪkɪt/
ride /raɪd/
train /treɪn/
heart /hɑːt/
square /skweə(r)/
try /traɪ/

UNIT 7 SPORT

know /nəʊ/
live /lɪv/
go to school /ˌgəʊ tə ˈskuːl/
other /ˈʌðə(r)/
get /get/
bus /bʌs/
every day /ˌevrɪ ˈdeɪ/

helpful /ˈhelpfl/
about /əˈbaʊt/
surprise /səˈpraɪz/
table tennis /ˈteɪbl tenɪs/

goalkeeper /ˈgəʊlkiːpə(r)/
the rest of . . . /ðə ˈrest əv
  . . ./
week /wiːk/
weekend /ˌwiːˈkend/
go out with . . . /gəʊ ˈaʊt
  wɪð . . ./
go to work /ˌgəʊ tə ˈwɜːk/
work /wɜːk/
bank /bæŋk/
get up /get ˈʌp/
golf /gɒlf/
club /klʌb/
team /tiːm/
practise /ˈpræktɪs/
player /ˈpleɪə(r)/
show /ʃəʊ/
video /ˈvɪdɪəʊ/
manager /ˈmænɪdʒə(r)/
match /mætʃ/
watch /wɒtʃ/
breakfast /ˈbrekfəst/
start /stɑːt/

unusual /ʌnˈjuːʒl/
day /deɪ/
skating rink /ˈskeɪtɪŋ rɪŋk/
ice skater /ˈaɪs skeɪtə(r)/
shower /ˈʃaʊə(r)/
get dressed /get ˈdrest/
tea /tiː/
cinema /ˈsɪnəmɑː/
early /ˈɜːlɪ/
evening /ˈiːvnɪŋ/
take /teɪk/
stay /steɪ/
night /naɪt/
go to bed /ˌgəʊ tə ˈbed/
till /tɪl/
television /ˈtelɪvɪʒn/
disco /ˈdɪskəʊ/
catch /kætʃ/
finish /ˈfɪnɪʃ/
sleep /sliːp/
get out of /get ˈaʊt əv/
same /seɪm/
every /ˈevrɪ/
get home /get ˈhəʊm/
each /iːtʃ/
How long . . .? / haʊ ˈlɒŋ
  . . ./
How often . . .? /haʊ ˈɒfn
  . . ./
grow up /grəʊ ˈʌp/
next /nekst/
first /fɜːst/
last /lɑːst/
get into /get ˈɪntuː/
survey (noun) /ˈsɜːveɪ/
smoke /sməʊk/

sport /spɔːt/
sports event /spɔːts ɪˈvent/
TV /tiː ˈviː/

UNIT 8 TIME OUT

film /fɪlm/

let's /lets/
join /dʒɔɪn/
help /help/
shop /ʃɒp/
community work
  /kəˈmjuːnətɪ wɜːk/
hospital /ˈhɒspɪtl/
coat /kəʊt/
in a hurry /ˌɪn ə ˈhʌrɪ/
It doesn't matter. /ɪt
  ˌdʌznt ˈmætə(r)/
nobody /ˈnəʊbədɪ/
a driving lesson /ə ˈdraɪvɪŋ
  lesn/
give /gɪv/
heavy /ˈhevɪ/
wait /weɪt/
miss /mɪs/
or /ɔː(r)/
if /ɪf/
thanks /θæŋks/
love /lʌv/

beach /biːtʃ/
hill /hɪl/
island /ˈaɪlənd/
forest /ˈfɒrɪst/
bridge /brɪdʒ/
river /ˈrɪvə(r)/
sea /siː/
restaurant /ˈrestrɒnt/
supermarket
  /ˈsuːpəmɑːkɪt/
post office /ˈpəʊst ɒfɪs/
souvenir /ˌsuːvəˈnɪə(r)/
tennis court /ˈtenɪs kɔːt/
swimming pool /ˈswɪmɪŋ
  puːl/
hut /hʌt/
village /ˈvɪlɪdʒ/
wonderful /ˈwʌndəfl/
picnic /ˈpɪknɪk/
climb /klaɪm/
fish /fɪʃ/
send /send/
letter /ˈletə(r)/
buy /baɪ/
food /fuːd/
clothes /kləʊðz/
go windsurfing /gəʊ
  ˈwɪndsɜːfɪŋ/
go walking /gəʊ ˈwɔːkɪŋ/
go skating /gəʊ ˈskeɪtɪŋ/
go skiing /gəʊ ˈskiːɪŋ/

museum /mjuːˈziːəm/
snake /sneɪk/
church /tʃɜːtʃ/
shark /ʃɑːk/
tiger /ˈtaɪgə(r)/
castle /ˈkɑːsl/
insect /ˈɪnsekt/
horse /hɔːs/
dog /dɒg/
lion /ˈlaɪən/
sometimes /ˈsʌmtaɪmz/
always /ˈɔːlweɪz/
usually /ˈjuːʒəlɪ/
interesting /ˈɪntrəstɪŋ/
building /ˈbɪldɪŋ/
city /ˈsɪtɪ/
clean /kliːn/

expensive /ɪk'spensɪv/
spider /'spaɪdə(r)/

ticket /'tɪkɪt/
have a rest /ˌhæv ə 'rest/
go swimming /gəʊ
  'swɪmɪŋ/
unforgettable
  /ˌʌnfə'getəbl/
fine /faɪn/
hotel /həʊ'tel/
Kenyan /'kenjən/
coast /kəʊst/
worry /'wʌrɪ/
sunbathe /'sʌnbeɪð/
beautiful /'bju:tɪfl/
lie /laɪ/
sand /sænd/
warm /wɔ:m/
water /'wɔ:tə(r)/
highest /'haɪɪst/
visit /'vɪzɪt/
Indian Ocean /ˌɪndɪən
  'əʊʃn/
spend /spend/
dhow /daʊ/
safari /sə'fa:rɪ/
Africa /'æfrɪkə/
national park /ˌnæʃnəl
  'pa:k/
elephant /'elɪfənt/
giraffe /dʒɪ'ra:f/
zebra /'zebrə/
flamingo /flə'mɪŋgəʊ/
forget /fə'get/
camera /'kæmrə/
mountain /'maʊntɪn/
newspaper
  /'nju:speɪpə(r)/

UNIT 9 CLOTHES
those /ðəʊz/
carry /'kærɪ/
explain /ɪk'spleɪn/
What's the matter? /ˌwɒts
  ðə 'mætə(r)/
hide /haɪd/
round the corner /ˌraʊnd
  ðə 'kɔ:nə(r)/
sweater /'swetə(r)/
jeans /dʒi:nz/
jacket /'dʒækɪt/
trousers /'traʊzəz/
sweatshirt /'swet-ʃɜ:t/
sit /sɪt/
wall /wɔ:l/
wind /wɪnd/
blow /bləʊ/
hood /hʊd/
quick /kwɪk/
chase /tʃeɪs/
arrive /ə'raɪv/

cook /kʊk/
eat /i:t/
cut /kʌt/
bread /bred/
magazine /ˌmægə'zi:n/

clothes /kləʊðz/
pink /pɪŋk/
jumper /'dʒʌmpə(r)/
skirt /skɜ:t/

tights /taɪts/
shoes /ʃu:z/
purple /'pɜ:pl/
headband /'hedbænd/
gloves /glʌvz/
suit /su:t/
by /baɪ/
shirt /ʃɜ:t/
belt /belt/
dress /dres/
earrings /'ɪərɪŋz/
bracelet /breɪslɪt/
jewel /'dʒu:əl/
silver /'sɪlvə(r)/
sporty /'spɔ:tɪ/
brooch /brəʊtʃ/
price /praɪs/
maybe /'meɪbi:/
shorts /ʃɔ:ts/
orange /'ɒrɪndʒ/
grey /greɪ/
waistcoat /'weɪskəʊt/
canvas /'kænvəs/
outfit /'aʊtfɪt/
cricket /'krɪkt/
socks /sɒks/
baseball /'beɪsbɔ:l/
boots /bu:ts/
hold /həʊld/
cap /kæp/
hand /hænd/
cheap /tʃi:p/
trainers /'treɪnəz/
housework /'haʊswɜ:k/
wedding /'wedɪŋ/
lorry /'lɒrɪ/
thought /θɔ:t/
round /raʊnd/
ragged /'rægɪd/
rock /rɒk/
rascal /'ra:skl/
ran /ræn/
before /bɪ'fɔ:(r)/
go to bed /ˌgəʊ tə 'bed/

these /ði:z/
scissors /'sɪzəz/
understand /ˌʌndə'stænd/
kids /kɪdz/
today /tə'deɪ/

Can I try them on? /kən aɪ
  ˌtraɪ ðem 'ɒn/
of course /əv 'kɔ:s/
changing room /'tʃeɪndʒɪŋ
  ru:m/
fine /faɪn/

sunglasses /'sʌngla:sɪz/
tie /taɪ/
hat /hæt/
scarf /ska:f/
scarves /ska:vz/
necklace /'neklɪs/
baby /'beɪbɪ/
doll /dɒl/
boogie /'bu:gɪ/
all night long /ˌɔ:l naɪt
  'lɒŋ/
teens /ti:nz/
diamond /'daɪəmənd/
ring /rɪŋ/
shake /ʃeɪk/

thing /θɪŋ/

UNIT 10 REVISION
day /deɪ/
miles /maɪlz/
collect /kə'lekt/
water /'wɔ:tə(r)/
clean /kli:n/
fetch /fetʃ/
bottle /'bɒtl/
stamp /stæmp/
sell /sel/
send /send/
money /'mʌnɪ/
tools /tu:lz/
materials /mə'tɪərɪəlz/
build /bɪld/
pipe /paɪp/
frog /frɒg/
after /'a:ftə(r)/
someone /'sʌmwʌn/
before /bɪ'fɔ:(r)/

UNIT 11 MYSTERY
nil /nɪl/
second /'sekənd/
brilliant /'brɪlɪənt/
grass /gra:s/
bench /bentʃ/
park /pa:k/
lake /leɪk/
someone /'sʌmwʌn/
on our way back /ˌɒn a:
  weɪ 'bæk/
ago /ə'gəʊ/
oh dear /əʊ 'dɪə(r)/
we'd better . . . /wi:d
  'betə(r) . . ./
the police /ðə pə'li:s/
policewoman
  /pə'li:swʊmən/

right /raɪt/
alone /ə'ləʊn/
king /kɪŋ/
rock and roll /ˌrɒk ənd
  'rəʊl/
the First World War /ðə
  ˌfɜ:st wɜ:ld 'wɔ:(r)/
champions /'tʃæmpɪənz/
president /'prezɪdənt/
space /speɪs/
the Moon /ðə 'mu:n/
the Netherlands /ðə
  'neðələndz/
the Olympics /ði:
  ə'lɪmpɪks/
first /fɜ:st/

walk /wɔ:k/
waiter /'weɪtə(r)/
hotel /həʊ'tel/
cottage /'kɒtɪdʒ/
story /'stɔ:rɪ/
clear /klɪə(r)/
already /ɔ:'redɪ/
while /waɪl/
full moon /fʊl 'mu:n/
something /'sʌmθɪŋ/
happen /'hæpən/
appear /ə'pɪə(r)/
move /mu:v/
along /ə'lɒŋ/

about /ə'baʊt/
stop /stɒp/
hurry /'hʌrɪ/
grab /græb/
camera /'kæmrə/
return /rɪ't3:n/
nothing /'nʌθɪŋ/
sure /ʃɔ:(r)/
monster /'mɒnstə(r)/

ghost /gəʊst/
young /jʌŋ/
cry /kraɪ/
shout /ʃaʊt/
through /θru:/
disappear /,dɪsə'pɪə(r)/
grey /greɪ/
lady /'leɪdɪ/
a long time ago /ə lɒŋ
  ,taɪm ə'gəʊ/
own /əʊn/
gamble /'gæmbl/
rich /rɪtʃ/
old /əʊld/
ugly /'ʌglɪ/
offer /'ɒfə(r)/
refuse /rɪ'fju:z/
marry /'mærɪ/
handsome /'hænsəm/
poor /pɔ:(r)/
lock /lɒk/
jump /dʒʌmp/
out of . . . /,aʊt əv '. . ./
die /daɪ/
fill up /fɪl ʌp/
arrest /ə'rest/
leave /li:v/

UNIT 12 THE NEWS

What's going on? /wɒts
  ,gəʊɪŋ 'ɒn/
alive /ə'laɪv/
I bet . . . /aɪ bet . . ./
rat /ræt/
strange /streɪndʒ/
put on /pʊt ɒn/
my fault /'maɪ fɔ:lt/
run away /rʌn ə'weɪ/
you lot /'ju: lɒt/

came /keɪm/
had /hæd/
saw /sɔ:/
took /tʊk/
went /went/
brought /brɔ:t/
found /faʊnd/
gave /geɪv/
left /left/
ran /ræn/
threw /θru:/
put /pʊt/
did /dɪd/
got /gɒt/
could /kʊd/

over /'əʊvə(r)/
on his way from . . . to
  . . . /ɒn hɪz weɪ frəm
  '. . . tə '. . ./
plane /pleɪn/
in the middle of . . . /ɪn ðə
  'mɪdl əv . . ./

blew /blu:/
land /lænd/
TV studio /ti: 'vi:
  stju:dɪəʊ/
interview /'ɪntəvju:/
TV presenter /ti: 'vi:
  prɪzentə(r)/
change my mind /,tʃeɪndʒ
  maɪ 'maɪnd/
hit /hɪt/
explode /ɪk'spləʊd/
fell /fel/
parachute /'pærəʃu:t/
said /sed/
snow /snəʊ/
bone /bəʊn/
break /breɪk/
broke /brəʊk/
heart attack /'hɑ:t ətæk/
become /bɪ'kʌm/
became /bɪ'keɪm/
unconscious /ʌn'kɒnʃəs/
wake up /weɪk 'ʌp/
woke up /wəʊk 'ʌp/
sink /sɪŋk/
sank /sæŋk/
helicopter /'helɪkɒptə(r)/
rescue /'reskju:/
flew /flu:/
crash /kræʃ/
caught /kɔ:t/
air stewardess /'eə
  stjʊədes/
airlines /'eəlaɪnz/
survive /sə'vaɪv/
swam /swæm/

change /tʃeɪndʒ/
life /laɪf/
news /nju:z/
famine /'fæmɪn/
famous /'feɪməs/
made /meɪd/
expect /ɪk'spekt/
feed /fi:d/
million /'mɪljən/
hold /həʊld/
held /held/
medicine /'medsn/
lorry /'lɒrɪ/

continent /'kɒntɪnənt/
at the same time /,æt ðə
  seɪm 'taɪm/

UNIT 13 THE MOVIES

easily /'i:zəlɪ/
thought /θɔ:t/
quickly /'kwɪklɪ/
unbutton /ʌn'bʌtn/
exciting /ɪk'saɪtɪŋ/
movies /'mu:vɪz/
hard /hɑ:d/
come off /kʌm 'ɒf/
turn around /t3:n ə'raʊnd/
push /pʊʃ/
kick /kɪk/
well /wel/
brave /breɪv/
easy /'i:zɪ/
badly /'bædlɪ/
friendly /'frendlɪ/
fight /faɪt/

fought /fɔ:t/
anyone /'enɪwʌn/

quietly /'kwaɪətlɪ/
loudly /'laʊdlɪ/
sadly /'sædlɪ/
slowly /'sləʊlɪ/

film star /'fɪlm stɑ:(r)/
symbol /'sɪmbl/
teenage rebel /,ti:neɪdʒ
  'rebl/
receive /rɪ'si:v/
believe /bɪ'li:v/
dead /ded/
hero /'hɪərəʊ/
people /'pi:pl/
born /bɔ:n/
farm /fɑ:m/
basketball /bɑ:skɪtbɔ:l/
baseball /'beɪsbɔ:l/
clarinet /,klærə'net/
five years old /,faɪv jɪəz
  'əʊld/
go back /gəʊ 'bæk/
actor /'æktə(r)/
advertisement
  /əd'v3:tɪsmənt/
theatre /'θɪətə(r)/
last /lɑ:st/
star /stɑ:(r)/
enough /ɪ'nʌf/
sports car /'spɔ:ts kɑ:(r)/
buy /baɪ/

drove /drəʊv/
bought /bɔ:t/
mph /,em pi: 'eɪtʃ/
motor racing /'məʊtə
  reɪsɪŋ/
take part in . . . /teɪk 'pɑ:t
  ɪn . . ./
race /reɪs/
gold /gəʊld/
silver /'sɪlvə(r)/
paid /peɪd/
speedometer
  /spi:'dɒmɪtə(r)/
neck /nek/
legend /'ledʒənd/
bird /b3:d/
word /w3:d/
poster /'pəʊstə(r)/
Top Twenty /tɒp 'twentɪ/
request /rɪ'kwest/
navy /'neɪvɪ/
fighter /'faɪtə(r)/
top gun /tɒp 'gʌn/
fall in love /,fɔ:l ɪn 'lʌv/
scene /si:n/
fantastic /fæn'tæstɪk/
at the bottom of . . . /,æt
  ðə 'bɒtəm əv . . ./
most-requested /,məʊst
  rɪ'kwestɪd/
since /sɪns/
understand /,ʌndə'stænd/
officially /ə'fɪʃəlɪ/
actress /'æktrɪs/
part /pɑ:t/
several /'sevrəl/

UNIT 14 REVISION

murder /ˈmɜːdə(r)/
murderer /ˈmɜːdərə(r)/
bat /bæt/
dinner /ˈdɪnə(r)/
business partner /ˈbɪznɪs
  pɑːtnə(r)/
office /ˈɒfɪs/
heard /hɜːd/
floor /flɔː(r)/
French windows /ˌfrentʃ
  ˈwɪndəʊz/

drop /drɒp/
hate /heɪt/
information /ˌɪnfəˈmeɪʃn/
airport /ˈeəpɔːt/
argument /ˈɑːgjʊmənt/
fingerprints /ˈfɪŋgəprɪnts/
handle /ˈhændl/

met /met/
suspect (noun) /ˈsʌspekt/

USEFUL SETS

Days of the week

Monday /ˈmʌndɪ/
Tuesday /ˈtjuːzdɪ/
Wednesday /ˈwenzdɪ/
Thursday /ˈθɜːzdɪ/
Friday /ˈfraɪdɪ/
Saturday /ˈsætədɪ/
Sunday /ˈsʌndɪ/

Months of the year

January /ˈdʒænjʊərɪ/
February /ˈfebrʊərɪ/
March /mɑːtʃ/
April /ˈeɪprəl/
May /meɪ/
June /dʒuːn/
July /dʒuːˈlaɪ/
August /ˈɔːgəst/
September /sepˈtembə(r)/
October /ɒkˈtəʊbə(r)/
November /nəʊˈvembə(r)/
December /dɪˈsembə(r)/

Cardinal numbers

one /wʌn/
two /tuː/
three /θriː/
four /fɔː(r)/
five /faɪv/
six /sɪks/
seven /ˈsevn/
eight /eɪt/
nine /naɪn/
ten /ten/
eleven /ɪˈlevn/
twelve /twelv/
thirteen /ˌθɜːˈtiːn/
fourteen /ˌfɔːˈtiːn/
fifteen /ˌfɪfˈtiːn/
sixteen /ˌsɪkˈstiːn/
seventeen /ˌsevnˈtiːn/
eighteen /eɪˈtiːn/
nineteen /ˌnaɪnˈtiːn/
twenty /ˈtwentɪ/
twenty-one /ˌtwentɪ ˈwʌn/
twenty-two /ˌtwentɪ ˈtuː/
twenty-three /ˌtwentɪ
  ˈθriː/
twenty-four /ˌtwentɪ
  ˈfɔː(r)/
twenty-five /ˌtwentɪ ˈfaɪv/
twenty-six /ˌtwentɪ ˈsɪks/
twenty-seven /ˌtwentɪ
  ˈsevn/
twenty-eight /ˌtwentɪ ˈaɪt/
twenty-nine /ˌtwentɪ
  ˈnaɪn/

thirty /ˈθɜːtɪ/
forty /ˈfɔːtɪ/
fifty /ˈfɪftɪ/
one hundred /wʌn
  ˈhʌndrəd/
two hundred /tuː
  ˈhʌndrəd/
one thousand /wʌn
  ˈθaʊznd/
two thousand /tuː
  ˈθaʊznd/
ten thousand /ten
  ˈθaʊznd/
one hundred thousand
  /wʌn ˌhʌndrəd ˈθaʊznd/
one million /wʌn ˈmɪljən/

Ordinal numbers

first /fɜːst/
second /ˈsekənd/
third /θɜːd/
fourth /fɔːθ/
fifth /fɪfθ/
sixth /sɪksθ/
seventh /ˈsevnθ/
eighth /eɪtθ/
ninth /naɪnθ/
tenth /tenθ/
eleventh /ɪˈlevnθ/
twelfth /twelfθ/
thirteenth /ˌθɜːˈtiːnθ/
fourteenth /ˌfɔːˈtiːnθ/
fifteenth /ˌfɪfˈtiːnθ/
sixteenth /ˌsɪkˈstiːnθ/
seventeenth /ˌsevnˈtiːnθ/
eighteenth /eɪˈtiːnθ/
nineteenth /ˌnaɪnˈtiːnθ/
twentieth /ˈtwentɪəθ/
twenty-first /ˌtwentɪ ˈfɜːst/
twenty-second /ˌtwentɪ
  ˈsekənd/
twenty-third /ˌtwentɪ
  ˈθɜːd/
twenty-fourth /ˌtwentɪ
  ˈfɔːθ/
twenty-fifth /ˌtwentɪ ˈfɪfθ/
twenty-sixth /ˌtwentɪ
  ˈsɪksθ/
twenty-seventh /ˌtwentɪ
  ˈsevnθ/
twenty-eight /ˌtwentɪ
  ˈeɪtθ/
twenty-ninth /ˌtwentɪ
  ˈnaɪnθ/
thirtieth /ˈθɜːtɪəθ/
thirty-first /ˌθɜːtɪ ˈfɜːst/

Personal pronouns and adjectives

subject pronoun	object pronoun	possessive pronoun
I /aɪ/	me /miː/	my /maɪ/
you /juː/	you /juː/	your /jɔː(r)/
he /hiː/	him /hɪm/	his /hɪz/
she /ʃiː/	her /hɜː(r)/	her /hɜː(r)/
it /ɪt/	it /ɪt/	its /ɪts/
we /wiː/	us /ʌs/	our /ɑː(r)/
they /ðeɪ/	them /ðem/	their /ðeə(r)/

Irregular verbs

Infinitive	Past tense
be /biː/	was /wɒz/, /wɒz/
become /bɪˈkʌm/	were /wə(r)/, /wɜː(r)/
blow /bləʊ/	became /bɪˈkeɪm/
bring /brɪŋ/	blew /bluː/
break /breɪk/	brought /brɔːt/
buy /baɪ/	broke /brəʊk/
can /kən/, kæn/	bought /bɔːt/
catch /kætʃ/	could /kʊd/
come /kʌm/	caught /kɔːt/
do /də/, duː/	came /keɪm/
drive /draɪv/	did /dɪd/
fall /fɔːl/	drove /drəʊv/
feed /fiːd/	fell /fel/
fight /faɪt/	fed /fed/
find /faɪnd/	fought /fɔːt/
fly /flaɪ/	found /faʊnd/
get /get/	flew /fluː/
give /gɪv/	got /gɒt/
go /gəʊ/	gave /geɪv/
have /hæv/	went /went/
have got /hæv ˈgɒt/	had /hæd/
hear /hɪə(r)/	had got /hæd ˈgɒt/
hit /hɪt/	heard /hɜːd/
hold /həʊld/	hit /hɪt/
leave /liːv/	held /held/
make /meɪk/	left /left/
meet /miːt/	made /meɪd/
pay /peɪ/	met /met/
put /pʊt/	paid /peɪd/
read /riːd/	put /pʊt/
run /rʌn/	read /red/
say /seɪ/	ran /ræn/
see /siː/	said /sed/
sink /sɪŋk/	saw /sɔː/
take /teɪk/	sank /sæŋk/
think /θɪŋk/	took /tʊk/
throw /θrəʊ/	thought /θɔːt/
wake up /weɪk ˈʌp/	threw /θruː/
	woke up /wəʊk ˈʌp/

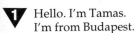

Unit 1

INTRODUCTIONS

 Hello. I'm Tamas.
I'm from Budapest.

Hello. My name's/is Caroline.
I'm from San Francisco.
What's your name?

Hello. I'm Margarita.
I'm from Buenos Aires.

Hi/Hello. My name's Hiroshi.
I'm from Tokyo.
What's your name?

Student's own answer.
Hello. I'm . . .
I'm from . . .

 1 Britain
2 Brazil
3 Italy
4 Russia
5 France
6 Greece
7 Spain
8 USA
9 Belgium

 b
1 I'm from America.
2 Jane is from London.
3 My name is Alan.
4 She's from Japan.
5 I am from Spain.
6 This is Madonna.
7 I'm Jason.
8 Jason's from Australia.

z						
e	t	w	o			t
r	h		n	i	n	e
f	o	u	r			n
i			e			
v			e	i	g	h	t
s	e	v	e	n		
i						
x						

 1 What's this?
It's a pen.
2 What's this?
It's a pizza.
3 What's this?
It's a computer.
4 What's this?
It's a photograph.
5 What's this?
It's a telephone.
6 What's this?
It's a book.

 eleven
twelve
thirteen
fourteen
fifteen
sixteen
seventeen
eighteen
nineteen
twenty

 b
1 her
2 his
3 his
4 her
5 her   his
6 his   Her

 your   record   It's   his   Happy
is   He's   you   for   her

 thirty-nine
twenty-four
one/a hundred
eighty
ninety-nine
sixty-three
forty-one
fifty-five
seventy

 b
1 a   2 an   3 an   4 a   5 a   6 an
7 a   8 a   9 an   10 an   11 a   12 an

 1 Can . . . help . . . A . . . french
2 Anything . . . an . . . juice
3 That's . . . please . . . Thank

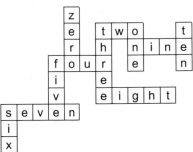 how   what   twenty   you
umbrella   a   apple   eight   two
orange   egg   girl   girlfriend
friend   desk   know   who   old
door

CULTURE SPOT

There is £10.08 on the page
altogether.

Unit 2

VICTORIA ROAD

 1A How do you . . . I'm . . .
. . . to meet you . . . name's . . .
. . . call me . . .
1B Where are you . . .
I'm from . . .

2A . . . What's . . . name?
. . . I'm . . .
. . . do you do . . .
2B . . . please . . . Janet
. . . pleased to . . . you . . . My

 b
1 'm   2 're   3 's   4 're 're 're
5 's   6 're   7 're   8 's   9 'm
10 'm 's

 his
her
our
your
their

 1 Hi   My   I'm
2 friend   sister   Her   twins
3 boy   their   His
4 girl   best friend
5 our   Its

READING

 b
1 Mikhail Gorbachev isn't from
America.
2 I'm not from Hartfield.
3 Madrid and Barcelona aren't in
Italy.
4 You aren't my best friend.
5 This car isn't a Jaguar.
6 I'm not a Madonna fan.
7 Football isn't my favourite game.
8 We aren't from Victoria Road.

 good   **all right**   **bad**
great   OK   terrible
wonderful   not bad   awful
                              rubbish

LISTENING

 b
1 Who's it from?
Are they on holiday?
Where are they?
2 Where's my pen?
Is it in your bag?
3 Where are you from?
Are you from London?
4 Is Terry sixteen?
When is his birthday?
5 Are Vince and Sue in?
Where are they?
Are they with Casey?
Where is the leisure centre?

 What's your name?
How do you spell Wijeratne?
How old are you?
What's your address?
What's your telephone number?

 b
three pens   two boys
a pencil   three cars
four apples   two eggs
two records   a hamburger
a book   two umbrellas
three cassettes
a girl

T121

b

1 This is my new car.
2 Paul McCartney is a great singer.
3 How much is a large hamburger?
4 The green T-shirs are £6 each.
5 This is a terrible book.
6 Where is my old tracksuit?
7 They are an awful group.
8 Kamala is a good friend.
9 Our new telephone number is 629431.
10 My favourite group is Dire Straits.

INTERACTION

11 1 How much is this T-shirt? It's £6.
2 How much are these pens? They're 65p each.
3 How much are these badges? They're 50p each.
4 How much are these pencils? They're 25p each.
5 How much is this book? It's £3.95.
6 How much are these postcards? They're 15p each.
7 How much is this umbrella? It's £4.72.
8 How much is this orange juice? It's 88p.
9 How much is this bag? It's £12.35.

PROJECT

12

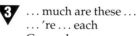

LEARNING DIARY

1 1 Is 2 Are
   is are are are
   'm   're
   's   're

2 1 I'm not sixteen.
2 We aren't from Australia.
3 Terry isn't our neighbour.
4 These apples aren't very good.

3 … much are these …
… 're … each
Can … have
40p
Here
That's … change
Thank

---

4 1 a large watch
2 two black T-shirts
3 three small photos
4 an old car

5 1 this
2 These
3 these
4 This

6 What's your name?
How old are you?
Where are you from?

Unit 3

VICTORIA ROAD

1 1 Have you got a date for the dance?
   Yes, I have.
2 What's he like?
   Wait and see.
3 Oh, come on. What's his name?
   It's a secret.

2 **b**

1 has 2 has 3 have 4 have
5 has 6 have 7 have 8 has
9 has 10 have

c

1 Darren's got short hair.
2 He's got a girlfriend.
3 They've got a new neighbour.
4 I've got an English book.
5 Sue's got a brother.
6 We've got a good teacher.
7 I've got a new telephone number.
8 Terry's got a date for Saturday.
9 Hartfield's got a leisure centre.
10 You've got my pen.

3 **b**

1 Terry hasn't got a sister.
2 I haven't got twenty Bros records.
3 Michael Jackson hasn't got fair hair.
4 Casey hasn't got a new neighbour.
5 We haven't got a new car.
6 Mikhail Gorbachev hasn't got long hair.
7 Vince and Sue haven't got brown eyes.
8 I haven't got your bag.
9 Kamala hasn't got a cat.
10 You haven't got a white T-shirt.

4 Student's own answers

READING

5 **b**

This is Carla's pen.
This is Alan's bag.
This is Casey's record.
This is Ann's watch.
This is Jane's radio.
This is John's badge.
This is Sue's T-shirt.
This is Vince's cassette.
This is Darren's pencil.

6 1 grandfather
2 daughter
3 granddaughter
4 wife
5 son
6 father
7 husband
8 grandmother
9 brother
10 grandparents
11 mother
12 parents

7 Student's own answers

LISTENING

8 **Carla**
short
black hair
brown eyes

Sam
very tall
blond hair
blue eyes

Jane and Joanne
tall
long fair hair
green eyes

John
short
short dark hair
brown eyes

You
Student's own answer

9 1 Sam is very tall. He has got blond hair and blue eyes.
2 Jane and Joanne are tall. They have got long fair hair and green eyes.
3 John is short. He has got short dark hair and brown eyes.
4 (Student's own answer) I am … I have got … hair and … eyes.

10 Student's own answers

11 1 He's a footballer.
2 He's a doctor.
3 She's a teacher.
4 He's a student.
5 She's an engineer.
6 She's a singer.

INTERACTION

b
1 Have you got a car?
2 Have you got a good job?
3 Have you got a computer?
4 Have you got a brother or sister?
5 Have you got a stereo?
6 Have you got a best friend?
7 Have you got a favourite pop group?

c
1 Has she got a car?
2 Has she got a good job?
3 What colour eyes has she got?
4 What colour hair has she got?
5 Has she got a boyfriend?
6 Has she got a favourite pop group?

PROJECT

b
1 I've got Jane's book. It's in the bag.
2 How much are these postcards? They're 10p each.
3 Terry's date's Darren's girlfriend.
4 What's this? It's Kamala's pen.
5 Jane's friend's in this photograph.
6 Where's my bag? I don't know. I haven't got it.

LEARNING DIARY

male	female
	grandmother
	mother
brother	
husband	
	daughter
	granddaughter

2 Hi. My name's Ann. I've got long fair hair and blue eyes. I've got a brother, but I haven't got a sister. My brother is very tall. He hasn't got fair hair. He's got short dark hair. My brother's name is Simon. He hasn't got a job. He's a student.

3
1 What's your name?
2 What colour hair have you got?
3 What colour eyes have you got?
4 Have you got a brother or a sister?
5 What's your brother's name?
6 Has he got fair hair, too?
7 What colour eyes has he got?

Unit 4

VICTORIA ROAD

1 It's over there.
2 But I can't swim!
3 Sorry!
4 I'm sorry. I can't hear.
5 Would you like to dance?
6 Excuse me. I can't see.

LANGUAGE WORK

1 She can't swim.
2 He can play football.
3 She can't play the guitar.
4 They can sing.
5 He can speak Russian.
6 She can't read.
7 They can't ski.
8 She can dance.

b
1 Can you swim?
  No, I can't.
2 Can you play football?
  Yes, I can.
3 Can you play the guitar?
  No, I can't.
4 Can you sing?
  No, we can't.
5 Can you speak Russian?
  Yes, I can.
6 Can you read?
  No, I can't.
7 Can you ski?
  No, we can't.
8 Can you dance?
  Yes, I can.

1 He can play the guitar.
2 He can play tennis.
3 He can play the violin.
4 He can play basketball.
5 He can play rugby.

Student's own answers

READING

1 History
2 French
3 Science
4 Maths (Mathematics)
5 PE (Physical Education)
6 Geography
7 Technology
8 English
9 Music
10 Art

7 Student's own answers

8 Tuesday
Wednesday
Thursday
Friday
Saturday
Sunday

LISTENING

1 ten past five
2 twenty-five to three
3 five to seven
4 quarter past ten
5 half past eight
6 six o'clock.
7 twenty-five past nine
8 ten to two
9 twenty to four
10 five past eleven

What's the time?
It's ten o'clock.

INTERACTION

b
at nine o'clock
on Tuesday
at half past two
at lunchtime
on Sunday
on my birthday
at three thirty

a
to ... party
When
on
house
What
at ... o'clock
address
19 ... Street
Thanks ... you ... Saturday
Can ... your
Bye

13 (Possible answer)
Can you come to my birthday party?
When is it?
It's on Friday.
OK. What time?
It's at half past seven.
What's your address?
54 Victoria Road.
Thanks. See you on Friday.
Yes, bye.

14 Student's own answer

PROJECT

15 These are the correct spellings of the incorrect words:

History	fifty-two
Wednesday	quarter past five
eight	sixteen
Monday	address
daughter	
grandfather	
eyes	
Geography	
English	
appointment	
guitar	

LEARNING DIARY

 1 have ... appointment ... sorry ... on
... Can ... on ... at ... can't ... in ...
Have ... in ... at ... o'clock

 2 1 Can you swim?
No, I can't.
2 Can Vince play the guitar?
Yes, he can.

 3 1 Music
2 Geography
3 Maths
4 History
5 French
6 English

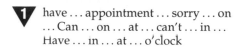 **4** 1 twenty to eleven
2 half past three
3 five past eight
4 twenty-five to four
5 quarter to two

Unit 5

VICTORIA ROAD

1 1 What's the time?
2 ... I must go. ... an appointment
at the doctor's
See you at the party tomorrow.
3 ... And don't be late.
Yes, see you.

2 1 Do not touch.
2 Please put your trays here.
3 Read the instructions carefully.
4 Please close the door.
5 Don't open your eyes.
6 Do not feed the animals.
7 Get out of the way.
8 Come here.

READING

3 b
1 You must be careful.
2 You mustn't smoke.
3 You mustn't take photographs.
4 You mustn't swim.
5 You mustn't talk.
6 You mustn't park.
7 You must wear a seat belt.
8 You mustn't touch.

 4 1 in
2 on ... on
3 on
4 on ... in ... in
5 on
6 in

5 1 You can park here at any time.
2 You mustn't park here from 8 am
to 6 pm.
3 You can park here for 1 hour.
4 You mustn't park here.

LISTENING

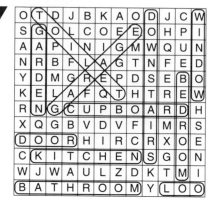 **6**

 7 b
1 There are ... on the desk.
2 There is ... on the disks.
3 There are ... on the desk.
4 There is ... the disk drive.
5 There is ... on the desk.
6 There are ... on the disk drive.
7 There is ... the computer.
8 There is ... on ...
9 There are ... under the desk.
10 There are ... in the large bag.

8 Student's own answers

 9 b
1 Is there ... on the desk?
2 are there under the desk?
3 Is there a drink
4 Are there ... pencils
5 Is there a disk
6 records are there in the

INTERACTION

 10 1 Would you like to go to the
leisure centre?
...
2 Would you like to go shopping?
...
3 Would you like to have a drink?
...
4 Would you like to listen to my
new cassette?
...
5 Would you like to play
badminton?
...
6 Would you like to see our new
car?
...
7 Would you like to look at my
photographs?
...
8 Would you like to read this
book?
...
9 Would you like to come to my
party?
...
10 Would you like to go to the cafe?
...

PROJECT

 11 a
1 the front bedroom
2 the front door
3 the back bedroom
4 the back door

b
1 the kitchen window
2 the kitchen door
3 the toilet (loo) door
4 the toilet (loo) window
5 the bathroom window
6 the bathroom door
7 the bedroom door
8 the bedroom window

LEARNING DIARY

 1 1 back garden
2 dining room
3 kitchen
4 living room
5 garage
6 3 bedrooms upstairs
7 toilet
8 bathroom
9 cupboard

2 Is there
There's ... there isn't ... are there
There are

3 1 mustn't   3 must be
2 must wait   4 mustn't swim

4 1 Don't put drinks on the
computer.
2 Don't open the window.
3 Look at that.
4 Please sit down.

Unit 6

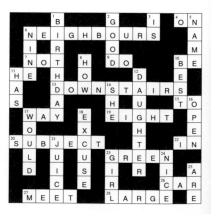

Unit 7

VICTORIA ROAD

b
1 plays
2 play
3 plays
4 plays
5 play
6 plays

c
(Student's answers – verb forms as follows)
1 play …
2 play …
3 plays …

live lives go get comes go talk listen helps goes play plays comes go have meet

READING

b
1 He has his breakfast at quarter to eight.
2 He catches the bus at quarter past eight.
3 He starts school at nine o'clock.
4 He goes home at half past three.
5 He watches television from four to six.
6 He has dinner at half past six.
7 He does his homework at quarter past seven.
8 He finishes his homework at nine o'clock.
9 He practises the guitar from nine to ten.
10 He goes to bed at half past ten.

Student's own answer

1 up … in
2 to … with
3 … at … from … to
4 in … at
5 out … on
6 in … in
7 to … on
8 for … of

LISTENING

b
1 doesn't
2 doesn't
3 don't
4 don't
5 don't
6 don't
7 doesn't
8 doesn't
9 doesn't
10 don't

1 Terry doesn't live in King Edward Avenue. He lives in Victoria Road.
2 Terry doesn't go to school by car. He goes by bus.
3 Terry and his friends don't get the 8.30 bus. They get the 8.15 bus.
4 They don't come home at six o'clock. They come home at half past three.
5 Terry doesn't play football on Wednesdays. He plays table tennis.
6 Terry doesn't come home late on Tuesdays. He comes home late on Wednesdays.
7 Terry's friends don't come home late on Wednesday. They come home at half past three.

Student's own answers

b
1 at
2 in
3 at
4 on
5 in
6 on
7 at
8 at
9 at
10 on
11 in

INTERACTION

b
1 Do
2 Do
3 Does
4 does
5 Does
6 do
7 do
8 Do
9 Does
10 do

1 When do you get up?
2 When do you practise?
3 Where do you practise?
4 Does your mother take you to the rink?
5 Does he watch you?
6 Where does he work?
7 What does he do?
8 Do other skaters practise with you?
9 Do they practise every day, too?
10 When do you go out with your friends?

start – finish
old – new
black – white
early – late
stand – sit
large – small

good – bad
wonderful – terrible
dark – fair
long – short

PROJECT

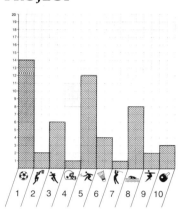

1 football – 14
2 basketball – 2
3 rugby – 6
4 American football – 1
5 tennis – 12
6 badminton – 4
7 golf – 1
8 swimming – 8
9 ice skating – 2
10 table tennis – 3

LEARNING DIARY

works presents plays talks get up drive start starts finishes don't go take meet talk don't choose chooses go doesn't go plays watches goes

1 … do you get up
2 … does your programme start
3 Do you choose
4 … do you do
5 … does the programme finish

1 doesn't work
2 doesn't choose
3 don't take
4 don't play
5 doesn't start

Unit 8

VICTORIA ROAD

b
1 He doesn't want to work in a shop. He wants to be a rock and roll singer.
2 She doesn't want to wash the car. She wants to play football.
3 I don't want to get up. I want to stay in bed.

4 He doesn't want to do his homework. He wants to watch television.
5 He doesn't want to help with the housework. He wants to go to a party.
6 I don't want to catch the bus. I want to drive a fast car.

 Student's own answers

 b
1 you ... me ... I
2 it ... it
3 him
4 her ... she
5 I ... them ... they
6 us ... We

READING

 b
Can you buy clothes there?
No, you can't.

Can you have a meal there?
Yes, you can.

Can you go swimming there?
Yes, you can.

Can you dance there?
Yes, you can.

Can you watch films there?
Yes, you can.

Can you go windsurfing there?
No, you can't.

Can you play table tennis there?
Yes, you can.

Can you go ice-skating there?
No, you can't.

1 They're at the post office.
2 They're at the restaurant.
3 They're at the souvenir shop.
4 They're at the cinema.
5 They're at the tennis court.
6 They're at the museum.
7 They're at the swimming pool.
8 They're at the supermarket.
9 They're at the beach.

LISTENING

animal	building
spider	house
dog	shop
snake	hut
tiger	cinema
cat	church
insect	supermarket
horse	hospital

natural feature
hill
river
beach
sea
island

 b
two beaches
two addresses
two forests
two lions
two watches
two letters
two banks
two huts
two princesses
two churches
two castles
two buses
two photographs
two insects

 b
1 some	5 some
2 any	6 any
3 some	7 any
4 any	8 some

 b
They've got some badges.
They haven't got any videos.
They've got some films.
They haven't got any envelopes.
They've got some cassettes.
They've got some apples.
They haven't got any oranges.
They haven't got any eggs.

c
Have you got any badges?
Yes, we have. How many do you want?

Have you got any videos?
No, I'm sorry. We haven't.

Have you got any films?
Yes, we have. How many do you want?

Have you got any envelopes?
No, I'm sorry. We haven't.

Have you got any cassettes?
Yes, we have. How many do you want?

Have you got any apples?
Yes, we have. How many do you want?

Have you got any oranges?
No, I'm sorry. We haven't.

Have you got any eggs?
No, I'm sorry. We haven't.

INTERACTION

 1 Can you open the door for me, please?
Yes, OK.

2 Can you carry this bag for me, please?
OK. Give it to me.

3 Can you help with the housework?
I'm sorry. I must do my homework.

4 Can you give this book to Carol?
Yes, if I see her.

5 Can you wait for me?
I'm sorry. I'm in a hurry.

6 Can you close the door, please?
Why can't you do it?

 a
to does past we
at ... at you

b
1 Let's go to the football match.
OK. What time does it start?
Two o'clock.
What time must we meet?
One o'clock, I think.
OK. See you at the club at one o'clock.
Fine. See you.

2 Let's go to the pop concert.
OK. What time does it start?
Nine o'clock.
What time must we meet?
Eight o'clock, I think.
OK. See you at the theatre at eight o'clock.
Fine. See you.

PROJECT

castle
girlfriend
school
who
walk
wrong
guitar
cupboard
surprise
what
breakfast
island
program**me**
know
white
heavy
write

14 hill
lion
one
new
week
weekend
end
dance
every
very
you
up
upstairs
stairs
shark
keep
picnic
church

LEARNING DIARY

1
1 them
2 him ... I ... He
3 her ... She
4 you ... us

2
1 any ... any ... some
2 some ... any ... some
3 any

3
1 to ... on   6 in
  at ... at   7 at
2 on   8 in
3 In ... to   9 in
4 in   10 at ... in
5 at   11 at

Unit 9

VICTORIA ROAD

1
1 Wait a minute
  I'm in a hurry
2 Where are you going?
  I've got an appointment ... I'm
  late
3 ... round the corner
  ... at the hospital
4 What's the matter?
  I can't explain ... See you

LANGUAGE WORK

2 b
1 are going
2 are playing
3 am eating
4 are drinking
5 is wearing

c
1 We aren't going to the cinema.
2 Vince and Casey aren't playing
  football.
3 I'm not eating a hamburger.

4 You aren't drinking my
  milkshake.
5 Terry isn't wearing a green
  sweater.

3 b
swimming
doing
waiting
singing
getting
driving
speaking
writing
watching
missing
choosing

4
1 're swimming ... 'm not
  swimming ... 'm swimming
2 are playing ... aren't playing ...
  're playing
3 's taking ... isn't taking ...
  's putting
4 's fishing ... isn't fishing ...
  's fishing
5 're coming ... aren't coming
  ... 're coming
6 'm sitting ... aren't sitting ...
  're sitting

5 b
1 Where's Rebecca going?
2 Are you doing your homework?
3 Are Vince and Casey playing
  football?
4 What's Kamala wearing?
5 Am I sitting in your seat?
6 What's Mrs Moore doing?
7 Are you having a shower?
8 Why are you putting your coat
  on?

READING

6
The labels should read down:
shirt   sweatshirt
tie   belt
jacket   jeans
suit
trousers

scarf   top
dress   skirt
tights   socks
           shoes

7
The girl isn't wearing tights.
The man is wearing a tie.
The woman isn't wearing a skirt.
The girl isn't wearing a dress.
The boy isn't wearing a jacket.
The woman is wearing a scarf.
The man is wearing a shirt.
The girl isn't wearing trousers.
The man isn't wearing jeans.

8 b
1 these   4 These
2 those   5 those
3 Those

LISTENING

9 b
1 do   7 clean
2 's doing   8 listens
3 'm sitting   9 's listening
4 gets up   10 'm wearing
5 go   11 wear
6 's cleaning

10 'm sitting ... 'm waiting.
... 's helping ... does ... 's playing
... 's shopping ... goes ...
's washing ... 'm listening ...
's playing ... 's singing ... 's coming

INTERACTION

11 b
1 this   5 these
  it's   them
2 are these   them
  They're   6 these ... them
3 is this   they're
  It's   7 this ... it
  it   it's
4 this
  it
  it

12
1 help
  much ... these
2 They're ... want ... them on
  please
3 There's ... changing room
  Thank
4 They're ... them
  £22 ... else
5 Can ... have
  altogether
6 you are
  Thank you
7 change
  Thank you

PROJECT

13
1 Casey doesn't play the guitar.
2 I'm wearing my new jeans.
3 She hasn't got the photographs.
4 We don't go to school on
  Saturdays.
5 I can't go to the party.
6 It's ten o'clock.
7 We're going to the disco.
8 I've got a new tie.
9 She's waiting for me.
10 They aren't here.

14 trousers skirt sunglasses
shirt tights shoes socks
sweater dress tracksuit suit
jumper jacket belt shorts
trainers

LEARNING DIARY

1 are you
  're having
2 's practising
3 's sitting

4 are ... doing
  aren't doing
5 's he doing

1 watch
2 'm watching
3 is wearing

4 goes
5 helps
6 isn't helping

1 are these
  They're
  them
2 is this
  It's
  it

3 these
  they're

Unit 10

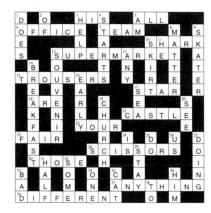

Unit 11

VICTORIA ROAD

 b
1 their ... to
2 on our way back ... school
3 on his way to the station
4 's on his way back from the station
5 're on our way to the beach
6 're on their way back from the beach

LANGUAGE WORK

 b
1 was
2 were ... was
3 were ... were
4 was
5 were
6 was
7 was ... was ... was

c
1 weren't on the bridge.
  They were on the bench.
2 weren't three girls in the boat.
  There were two boys (in it).
3 wasn't under the table. It was on the table.
4 wasn't dark. It was fair.
5 weren't on the grass. We were by the lake.

 b
1 Where were you?
2 Were you alone?
3 Was your boyfriend near the lake, too?
4 Where was your little sister?
5 Were your dogs with her?
6 How many people were there at the cafe?
7 Where was the woman's bag?

Were
was
Was
was
Was
was ... weren't ... was ... weren't
was
were
were
was
was

READING

 b
played ... helped ... moved (or carried) ... carried (or moved) ... tried ... was ... was ... wanted ... waited ... was ... missed ... walked ... were ... started ... arrived ... were ... was ... rained ... stayed ... watched ... listened ... finished

 b
sixteen twenty-five
nineteen ninety-two
eighteen oh seven
fifteen sixteen
seventeen sixty-three
twenty-one ninety

LISTENING

1 a minute
2 half an hour
3 a week

4 an hour
5 a day
6 a year

 b
1 twenty-five minutes ago
2 this house two years ago
3 arrived two days ago
4 grandfather died twenty-one years ago
5 an hour ago

owned ... was
gambled ... needed ... wanted
was ... offered
accepted ... refused ... wanted
lived ... was ... loved
refused ... locked ... cried ... cried
jumped ... died

INTERACTION

 man
king
waiter

father
brother
boyfriend

princess

girl
policewoman

daughter
lady

1 'd better go to the dentist
2 'd better get a taxi
3 'd better hide
4 'd better go
5 'd better get up
6 'd better have a rest
7 'd better call the doctor
8 'd better call the police

PROJECT

 b
They arrived at the bank at ten past eleven and parked their car.
They walked into the bank and locked the door.
They showed their guns and shouted 'Give us the money.'
They grabbed the bags of money and hurried to their car.
The manager picked up the telephone and called the police.
The police chased the men and arrested them.

LEARNING DIARY

lived ... was ... was ... appeared ... was ... was ... stopped ... looked ... opened ... appeared ... were ... were ... jumped ... walked ... wanted ... wasn't ... were ... picked up ... carried ... closed ... disappeared

1 Why were you near the beach?
2 Where was the spaceship?
3 How many men were there?
4 Were they big?
5 What colour were they?

1 wasn't ... was
2 wasn't ... was
3 weren't ... were
4 weren't ... were
5 weren't ... were

Unit 12

VICTORIA ROAD

 1

1 ... something strange ... rat
2 Don't do that!
  Oh dear!
3 There it is!
4 What's going on?
5 You'd better go to the hospital.
  It's all my fault.
6 you'd better

 b

1 left
2 went
3 took
4 missed
5 saw
6 gave
7 ran
8 had
9 helped
10 did
11 stopped
12 came

 Student's own answer

LANGUAGE WORK

 disappeared ... left ... went ... saw
arrived ... came ... said ... got ...
had ... took ... came ... couldn't ...
waited ... called ... found ... gave

 b

1 She didn't leave home at 11 o'clock. She left home at 10 o'clock.
2 She didn't go to the airport. She went to the station.
3 Her brother didn't see her at 10 o'clock. Her neighbour saw her.
4 A taxi didn't arrive at 11 o'clock. It arrived at 10 o'clock.
5 She didn't have two large bags. She had one small bag.
6 Her neighbour didn't call the police. Her husband called them.
7 Her husband didn't come home in the afternoon. He came home in the evening.
8 A man didn't find her bag in London. He found it in Dover.
9 The man didn't throw the bag away. He gave it to the police.

 Student's own answers

READING

1 gave
2 took ... left ... went/ran
3 caught/grabbed/attacked ... grabbed/caught ... put/threw
4 took ... threw/put
5 were ... escaped ... jumped landed
6 attacked ... hit ... swam
7 swam ... climbed ... could ... was
8 flew ... jumped ... grabbed
9 landed ... ran ... was
10 threw
11 flew/went ... gave

LISTENING

 b

1 on
2 in ... in
3 at ... in
4 to
5 in
6 to
7 at ... at ... in ... in
8 to
9 to
10 in ... on

 b

  sixteen million dollars
  twenty thousand pounds
£7m
DM100,000
  fourteen thousand dollars
  five hundred marks
  three million pounds
$400,000
  nine hundred thousand pounds
  sixty million dollars

INTERACTION

 b

How did you travel?
What clothes did you take?
Where did you stay?
Did you see the news?
When did you come home?
What did you do?
How did you get money?
Did someone find you?
Why did you disappear?

1 Where did you go?
2 Who did you go with?
3 Did you fly?
4 Did you stay in a hotel?
5 Did you visit Paris?
6 Did you like Paris?
7 What did you see?
8 Did you buy any souvenirs?
9 Did you get back yesterday?

PROJECT

 a

b

infinitive	past
fly	flew
swim	swam
catch	caught
bring	brought
find	found
wake up	woke up
see	saw
take	took
leave	left
go	went
throw	threw
do	did
make	made
become	became
give	gave
fall	fell
run	ran
come	came
have	had
can	could

1 When Lord Good gave Cindy the cat, she said goodbye and left her old friend.
2 When Doctor Strange's men saw Cindy, they grabbed her and put her into a bag.
3 When Cindy escaped from the bag, she jumped out of the helicopter and landed in the sea.
4 When Cindy swam to a small island, she climbed a tree and saw Doctor Strange's island.
5 When a small plane flew over Cindy, she jumped up and grabbed the wheels.
6 When Cindy arrived in New York, she landed at the United Nations and gave the cat to the President.

LEARNING DIARY

1 escaped ... crashed ... happened ... threw ... found ... said ... stopped/ crashed ... could ... got ... ran ... found ... wasn't ... was ... left ... went/ran ... looked ... couldn't ... came ... saw ... had ... shouted ... brought ... was ... was ... cried ... escaped ... died

2 1 The pilot didn't find Sabina. A stewardess found her.
2 The crash didn't happen in the evening. It happened in the afternoon.
3 Mr Lori didn't stay with his wife. He left her.
4 He didn't see a man with a baby. He saw a woman.

3 1 What time did the crash happen?
2 Where did the plane crash?
3 Did all the people escape?
4 Did you find Sabina?
5 How did you escape?
6 Did you find your wife?

Unit 13

VICTORIA ROAD

1 **a**
1 down   5 off
2 in   6 away
3 on   7 up
4 round   8 out

b
1 up ... round   5 up
2 off   6 down ... out
3 in ... down   7 up
4 on ... out   8 away

LANGUAGE WORK

2 1 fast   4 loudly
2 carefully   5 quietly
3 hard

3 **c**
new ... big ... friendly ... hard ... bravely ... easy ... strong ... weak ... sadly ... regularly ... strong ... fast ... heavy ... easily ... brave ... big ... quickly

4 **b**
thirty-first
sixteenth
twelfth
third
twenty-ninth
sixty-second
fiftieth
eighth

---

5 Mrs Moreland lives on the thirtieth floor.
Mr Freeman lives on the twenty-eighth floor.
Miss Clegg lives on the twenty-third floor.
Prem Singh lives on the twentieth floor.
Frank and Betty Marsden live on the fifteenth floor.
Jane Schofield lives on the twelfth floor.
Mr and Mrs Khan live on the ninth floor.
The Wilberts live on the fifth floor.
Mr and Mrs Taylor live on the second floor.

READING

6 **b**
1 old enough   6 tall enough
2 long enough   7 short enough
3 big enough   8 heavy enough
4 loud enough   9 fast enough
5 good enough

7

```
NOVEMBER    J        M
C           U        A
T    JANUARY  Y      D
O     A   L  U       E
B   AP M  L  N       C
E   P  A  Y  U       E
FEBRUARY     A        R
R   I  R     R        B
    L  C      SEPTEMBER
       H
```

8 **b**
Student's own answers

LISTENING

9 **b**
the first of September
the twentieth of August
the twenty-second of July
the eighth of January
the twenty-fifth of December
the eleventh of March
the sixth of May
the seventeenth of April

10 **b**
1 in   7 in   12 in
2 on   8 on   13 on
e on   9 on   14 in
4 at   10 in   15 at
5 in   11 in   16 at
6 at

11 **a**
Student's own answers
(3 in 1939)
(8 in 1955)

b
Student's own answers

INTERACTION

12 1 What time does it go?
2 What time does it start?
3 What time does it close?
4 What time does it finish?
5 What time does it start?
6 What time does it arrive?

13 What's on?
Who's in it?
Where's it on?
What time does it start?

PROJECT

14 receive   neighbour
quietly   piece
twentieth   eighteen
hurries   interview
eight   movies
friendly   carried
believe   science

15 **b**
Student's own answer

LEARNING DIARY

1 twelfth   sixteenth
second   twenty-second
twenty-sixth third
fourth   eighth
twentieth   fourteenth

2 1 well   4 quickly
2 good   5 nice
3 quietly   6 nicely

3 *January*   July
February   August
March   September
April   October
May   November
June   December

4 the twenty-seventh of June
the second of June
the third of June

5 1 at ... on   4 at ... in
2 in   5 in
3 on

Unit 14

REVISION TEST Unit 6

1 Complete this list of the days of the week.

Sunday, ___, ___, ___, ___, ___, Saturday

1 mark for each day

2 Complete these sentences with 'have' or 'has'.

1 I _____ got two English books.
2 Kamala _____ got black hair.
3 _____ you got my pen?
4 Our house _____ got three bedrooms.
5 My neighbours _____ got a big car.

1 mark for each sentence

3 Complete these sentences with the correct form of the verb 'to be'.

1 How much _____ this computer?
2 Where _____ my books?
3 She _____ a student.
4 It _____ half past eight.
5 I _____ in the living room.
6 We _____ from Australia.
7 Terry and Casey _____ at the leisure centre.
8 What _____ he like?
9 _____ I bossy?
10 You _____ late for your appointment.

1 mark for each sentence

4 Put in 'a' or 'an'.

_____ egg
_____ apple
_____ hamburger
_____ envelope
_____ boy
_____ disk
_____ orange

1 mark for each word

5 Turn these into questions.

1 Darren can play the guitar.
2 You've got blue eyes.
3 There's a toilet upstairs.
4 This is Terry's girlfriend.
5 Jane has got a nice voice.
6 You're from Italy.
7 You can speak English.
8 These are our drinks.
9 There are two disks on the desk.
10 They've got my bag.

1 mark for each sentence.

6 Put in 'this' or 'these'.

1 How much are _____ apples?
2 Is _____ your book?
3 _____ tracksuit is nice.
4 _____ pens are 65p.
5 Can I have _____ badge, please?
6 Put _____ disk in its envelope.
7 _____ is my brother.
8 _____ are my friends.

1 mark for each sentence

7 Make these sentences negative.

1 I'm seventeen.
2 Casey's our neighbour.
3 I've got a new computer.
4 Sit here.
5 The Queen is my grandmother.
6 John's got a good job.
7 There's a cellar in our house.
8 Vince can sing.
9 You must tell Terry about Darren.
10 We're friends with you

1 mark for each sentence

8 Write the questions for these answers.

Vince Scott.
S-C-O-double T.
I'm from Hartfield in England.
18 Victoria Road, Hartfield.
I'm fifteen.
Blue.
Fair.
Yes, I've got a sister.
Sue.
She's fifteen, too.

2 marks for each question
1 for correct form
1 for correct spelling

9 Write these numbers in full.

2	12
18	6
33	11
50	95
9	13

1 mark for each number

10 Rewrite these sentences with the adjective in brackets.

1 I've got hair. (dark)
2 That's our car. (new)
3 How much is this T-shirt? (red)
4 This is a house. (big)
5 I've got a job. (boring)

1 mark for each apostrophe

11 Put in the apostrophes.

1 Shes got two brothers.
2 This is my sisters computer.
3 Whats the time?
4 Its five oclock.

1 mark for each apostrophe

12 Write the correct preposition.

1 ___ Tuesday
2 ___ ten o'clock
3 ___ Saturday
4 ___ quarter past three
5 ___ the afternoon

1 mark for each preposition

TOTAL 100

REVISION TEST Unit 10

1 Complete the sentences. Use the verbs in brackets in the present simple tense.

1 Casey _____ in Victoria Road. (live)
2 Sue _____ television at six o'clock. (watch)
3 I _____ at seven o'clock.(get up)
4 Terry _____ his breakfast at eight o'clock. (have)
5 We _____ tennis after school. (play)
6 Kamala _____ to the leisure centre on Fridays. (go)
7 Vince _____ his homework in the evening. (do)
8 They _____ in an office. (work)
9 I _____ swimming on Saturdays. (go)
10 Kamala often _____ the bus. (miss)

> 1 mark for each sentence

2 Make these sentences negative.

1 I like windsurfing.
2 Vince plays table tennis.
3 Sue does her homework at lunchtime.
4 Terry's mother works in London.
5 We go to school at seven o'clock.
6 The manager chooses the team on Fridays.
7 I practise in the afternoons.
8 We have lunch on the beach.
9 I buy new clothes every week.
10 Casey knows Darren.

> 1 mark for each sentence

3 Turn these statements into questions.

1 You live in New York.
2 She works in a bank.
3 They go to school at eight o'clock.
4 He likes Tina Turner.
5 Bobby Best plays for Liverpool.
6 Selina goes to school.
7 You like Paradise Island.
8 They go to the beach every day.
9 Casey plays the guitar.
10 Kamala watches television after school.

> 1 mark for each sentence

4 Complete these sentences. Use the verbs in brackets in the present continuous tense to describe what is happening at the moment.

1 Casey _____ basketball. (play)
2 He _____ the bus. (get on)
3 Three boys _____ for Terry. (wait)
4 I _____ my new coat. (wear)
5 We _____ our dinner. (have)
6 Kamala _____ Sue's bags. (carry)
7 Terry _____. (hide)
8 I _____ this photograph. (cut out)
9 Sue and Vince _____ to a party. (go)
10 She _____ in the sea. (swim)

> 2 marks for each sentence
> 1 for the correct part of 'to be'
> 1 for correct spelling

5 Make these sentences negative.

1 Terry's eating a hamburger.
2 I'm buying a T-shirt.
3 We're going to the cinema.
4 She's wearing a blue dress.
5 They're waiting for Casey.

> 1 mark for each sentence

6 Turn these statements into questions.

1 Jane's wearing a coat.
2 You're going to the beach.
3 He's waiting for Sue.
4 Kamala's helping in the shop.
5 You're buying a video.

> 1 mark for each sentence

7 Complete these sentences. Put the verbs in brackets into the present simple or the present continuous tense.

1 Casey _____ his homework at the moment. (do)
2 The players _____ the team doctor now. (see)
3 I _____ with my friends every Saturday. (go out)
4 Jane _____ a green tracksuit today. (wear)
5 Karen _____ to bed at seven o'clock every evening. (go)
6 We _____ the bus to school every day. (catch)
7 Sue _____ a letter at the moment.(write)
8 Bobby Best's girlfriend _____ in bank. (work)

> 2 marks for each sentence
> 1 for correct tense
> 1 for correct form/spelling

8 Complete the sentences with the correct word from the brackets.

1 Please wait for _____. (I/me/my)
2 Look. There's Vince. Can you see_____? (him/her/he)
3 _____'re going to the shops.(them/we/us)
4 Do you want to come with _____? (them/we/us)
5 Are Jane and Darren here? I can't see _____. (they/them/their)

1 mark for each word

9 Complete the sentences with 'some' or'any'.

1 Have you got _____ change?
2 We need _____ new shoes.
3 Vince has got _____ Madonna records.
4 I haven't got _____ friends.
5 There aren't _____ disks for the computer.
6 Are there _____ shops near here?

1 mark for each sentence

10 Complete these sentences with the correct preposition.

1 I go _____ the leisure centre _____ eight o'clock _____ Fridays.
2 Let's meet _____ the restaurant _____ the evening.

1 mark for each preposition

11 Complete these sentences with 'this', 'these', 'it's' or 'they're'.

1 Do you like _____ jeans?
    Yes, _____ very nice.
2 How much is _____ shirt?
    _____ £18.
3 I like _____ dress, but _____ very expensive.
4 How much are _____ trousers?
    _____ £32.

1 mark for each word

TOTAL 100

REVISION TEST Unit 14

1 Complete these with 'was' or 'were'.

1 Sue and Kamala _____ at a party on Friday.
2 _____ Darren at the party, too?
3 Where _____ you on Friday?
4 I _____ at home.
5 Sue's coat _____ in the water.
6 We _____ at the Vanilla Ice concert on Saturday.
7 It _____ great.
8 Where _____ the concert?
9 It _____ in London.
10 Casey and Vince _____ with us.

> **1 mark for each sentence**

2 Complete these sentences with the past tense of the verbs in brackets.

1 I _____ some new trousers. (buy)
2 We _____ the 2.30 bus. (catch)
3 She _____ in America for two years. (live)
4 Lucy Loxley _____ a long time ago. (die)
5 The aeroplane _____ into the sea. (crash)
6 It _____ very quickly. (sink)
7 I _____ my arm on holiday. (break)
8 Sue _____ to the cinema. (go)
9 The bus _____. (stop)
10 Kamala _____ Sue's coat home. (carry)
11 Darren and his friends _____ the coat. (grab)
12 They _____ it into the lake. (throw)
13 We _____ the party at twelve o'clock. (leave)
14 I _____ some money in the street. (find)
15 I _____ it to the police. (give)
16 Sue _____ for the hamburgers. (pay)
17 Ruth Less _____ a big car. (have)
18 Someone _____ my bag. (take)
19 I _____ home at six o'clock. (come)
20 We _____ it was a good film. (think)

> **1 mark for each sentence.**

3 Make these sentences negative.

1 We went to the match.
2 Terry kicked Darren.
3 It was Terry's fault.
4 The policewoman arrested Kamala.
5 She asked a lot of questions.
6 There were a lot of people in the park.
7 James Dean made six films.
8 Lucy Loxley married Lord Griston.
9 I saw the Loch Ness monster.
10 We were at the leisure centre on Friday.

> **2 marks for each sentence**
> 1 for the correct construction
> 1 for correct form/spelling

4 Turn these statements into questions.

1 You met Terry on holiday.
2 He was with his friends.
3 Vince and Casey chased Terry.
4 James Dean played the clarinet.
5 You locked the door.
6 Darren ran away.
7 Terry's friends were angry.
8 The shirt was £20.
9 Kamala missed the bus.
10 Lucy cried.

> **2 marks for each sentence**
> 1 for the correct construction
> 1 for correct form/spelling

5 Complete these sentences with the correct word from the brackets.

1 Terry didn't fight _____. (brave/bravely)
2 Vince plays the guitar _____. (good/well)
3 Kamala is a _____ tennis player. (brilliant/brilliantly)
4 Harrison Ford is a _____ actor. (good/well)
5 We are travelling very _____. (slow/slowly)
6 English is an _____ language. (easy/easily)
7 You must speak _____ in a library. (quiet/quietly)
8 Don't do this test _____ . (quick/quickly)
9 Sue was _____ with Terry. (angry/angrily)
10 A Porsche is a _____ car. (fast/fastly)

> **1 mark for each sentence**

6 Complete this list of the months.

January, _____, _____, _____
_____, _____, _____, _____
_____, _____, _____, December

> **1 mark for each month**

7 Write these out as ordinal numbers.

| 3 | 19 | 9 | 24 | 12 |
| 32 | 1 | 8 | 20 | 5 |

> **1 mark for each number**

> **TOTAL 100**

▼ Monday, Tuesday, Wednesday
Thursday, Friday

▼
1 have   4 has
2 has   5 have
3 Have

▼
1 is   6 are ('re)
2 are   7 are
3 is ('s)   8 is ('s)
4 is ('s)   9 Am
5 am ('m)   10 are ('re)

▼
an egg   an envelope   an orange
an apple   a boy
a hamburger   a disk

▼5
1 Can Darren play the guitar?
2 Have you got blue eyes?
3 Is there a toilet upstairs?
4 Is this Terry's girlfriend?
5 Has Jane got a nice voice?
6 Are you from Italy?
7 Can you speak English?
8 Are these our drinks?
9 Are there two disks on the desk?
10 Have they got my bag?

▼6
1 these   5 this
2 this   6 this
3 This   7 This
4 These   8 These

▼
1 I'm not seventeen.
2 Casey isn't our neighbour.
3 I haven't got a new computer.
4 Don't sit here.
5 The Queen isn't my grandmother.
6 John hasn't got a good job.
7 There isn't a cellar in our house.
8 Vince can't sing.
9 You mustn't tell Terry about Darren.
10 We aren't friends with you.

▼8
What's your name?
How do you spell Scott?
Where are you from?
What's your address?
How old are you?
What colour eyes have you got?
What colour hair have you got?
Have you got a brother or sister?
What's her name?
How old is she?

▼9
two   twelve
eighteen   six
thirty-three   eleven
fifty   ninety-five
nine   thirteen

▼10
1 I've got dark hair.
2 That's our new car.
3 How much is this red T-shirt?
4 This is a big house.
5 I've got a boring job.

▼11
1 She's got two brothers.
2 This is my sister's computer.
3 What's the time?
4 It's five o'clock.

▼12 1 on 2 at 3 on 4 at 5 in

▼1
1 lives   6 goes
2 watches   7 does
3 get up   8 work
3 has   9 go
5 play   10 misses

▼2
1 I don't like windsurfing.
2 Vince doesn't play table tennis.
3 Sue doesn't do her homework at
4 Terry's mother doesn't work in London.
5 We don't go to school at seven o'clock.
6 The manager doesn't choose the team
   on Fridays.
7 I don't practise in the afternoons.
8 We don't have lunch on the beach.
9 I don't buy new clothes every week.
10 Casey doesn't know Darren.

▼3
1 Do you live in New York?
2 Does she work in a bank?
3 Do they go to school at eight o'clock?
4 Does he like Tina Turner?
5 Does Bobby Best play for Liverpool?
6 Does Selina go to school?
7 Do you like Paradise Island?
8 Do they go to the beach every day?
9 Does Casey play the guitar?
10 Does Kamala watch television after school?

▼4
1 's (is) playing   6 's (is) carrying
2 's (is) getting on   7 's (is) hiding
3 are waiting   8 's (is) cutting out
4 'm (am) wearing   9 are going
5 're (are) having   10 's (is) swimming

5
1 Terry isn't eating a hamburger.
2 I'm not buying a T-shirt.
3 We aren't going to the cinema.
4 She isn't wearing a blue dress.
5 They aren't waiting for Casey.

6
1 Is Jane wearing a coat?
2 Are you going to the beach?
3 Is he waiting for Sue?
4 Is Kamala helping in the shop?
5 Are you buying a video?

7
1 's (is) doing   5 goes
2 are seeing   6 catch
3 go out   7 's (is) writing
4 's (is) wearing   8 works

8
1 me   3 We   5 them
2 him   4 us

9
1 any   2 some   3 some
4 any   5 any   6 any

10
1 to...at...on   2 at...in

11
1 these...they're
2 this...It's
3 this...it's
4 these...They're

TEST ANSWERS Unit 14

1
1 were   6 were
2 Was   7 was
3 were   8 was
4 was   9 was
5 was   10 were

2
1 bought   11 grabbed
2 caught   12 threw
3 lived   13 left
4 died   14 found
5 crashed   15 gave
6 sank   16 paid
7 broke   17 had
8 went   18 took
9 stopped   19 came
10 carried   20 thought

3
1 We didn't go to the match.
2 Terry didn't kick Darren.
3 It wasn't Terry's fault.
4 The policewoman didn't arrest Kamala.
5 She didn't ask a lot of questions.
6 There weren't a lot of people in the park.
7 James Dean didn't make six films.
8 Lucy Loxley didn't marry Lord Griston.
9 I didn't see the Loch Ness monster.
10 We weren't at the leisure centre on Friday.

4
1 Did you meet Terry on holiday?
2 Was he with his friends?
3 Did Vince and Casey chase Terry?
4 Did James Dean play the clarinet?
5 Did you lock the door?
6 Did Darren run away?
7 Were Terry's friends angry?
8 Was the shirt £20?
9 Did Kamala miss the bus?
10 Did Lucy cry?

5
1 bravely   6 easy
2 well   7 quietly
3 brilliant   8 quickly
4 good   9 angry
5 slowly   10 fast

6
February   July
March   August
April   September
May   October
June   November

7
third   twenty-fourth
thirty-second   twentieth
nineteenth   twelfth
first   fifth
ninth
eighth